Tastes in PLAID

Alamance County Entertains

Published by
Alamance County Historical Museum, Inc.
Route 1, Box 71
Burlington, North Carolina
27215

1990

Published by
Alamance County Historical Museum, Inc.
Route 1, Box 71
Burlington, North Carolina
27215

First Printing
1990

ISBN: 0-9626558-2-1
Library of Congress Catalog Card Number:
90-84104

Printed in the USA by
WIMMER BROTHERS
A Wimmer Company
Memphis • Dallas

COOKBOOK COMMITTEE

Co-chairmen

Peggy Carter Lackey
Nora Lee Cook Tate

Steering Committee

Frances Trax Bennett
Patricia Allebach Donnell
Elinor Samons Euliss
Frances Lee Gillespie
Martha Curtis Hudgins
Dale Harris Leahy
Gilberta Jeffries Mitchell
Patsy Hand Mobley
Cleo Rumbley Smith
Grace Anderson Thompson

Cover Art

Jean Simons

Illustrators

Lillian Arnold
Bob Arthur
Bob DeVoe
Patricia Donnell
James Fell
Vic Gillespie
Kathy Gwinnett
Larry Johnson
Anna Sims
Marianne Wells

Historian

William Murray Vincent, Ph.D.
Executive Director
Alamance County Historical Museum, Inc.

It has been our attempt throughout this cookbook to be as specific as possible. Where generalities exist, measurements are left to the cook's taste and good judgment.

The recipes included herein have been collected from citizens of our community. Neither the Alamance County Historical Museum, Inc., nor the contributors, printer or seller of this cookbook are responsible for errors or omissions.

To order copies of TASTES IN PLAID, send a check for $16.95 plus $3.05 for postage and handling per book to:

ALAMANCE COUNTY HISTORICAL MUSEUM, INC.
Route 1, Box 71
Burlington, North Carolina 27215
919-226-8254
(North Carolina residents please add $0.85 sales tax)

TABLE OF CONTENTS

LIST OF ILLUSTRATIONS

FOREWORD

Tastes In Plaid celebrates the traditional cooking of the Carolina Piedmont and its evolution in contemporary culture. The title of our book reflects not only the heritage of good foods characteristic of Alamance County, but it also refers to the history of our community as the birthplace of the Southern textile industry, the origins of which lie in the creation of cotton fabrics known as "Alamance Plaids." The history of these plaids—recorded in the pages which follow—reflects the changing dimensions of the textile industry, and the evolving tastes of the consumer, in a way that is reminiscent of the evolution of cooking and the ritual of eating in the rural South.

The ritual of setting a good table has been a veritable religion in the South since the earliest days. It is not surprising then that some of the first publications in the South were cookbooks. The earliest of these appears to be *The Complete Housewife, or Accomplished Gentlewoman's Companion,* printed in Williamsburg, Virginia, in 1742. This volume was followed shortly thereafter by Hannah Glasse's *The Art of Cooking Made Plain and Simple* (1747).

Within the Piedmont region of North Carolina, one of the first collections of recipes for medicinal cures and diet drinks was recorded about 1790 by Rachel Allen, an early settler in what is now Alamance County. During the early 1800s, copies of Mary Randolph's *Virginia Housewife* (1824) were widely circulated in North Carolina, and the cookbook is known to have been used in many households in Orange, Caswell and present-day Alamance County.

Cookbooks have thus been guides to southern ways of eating since the colonial period. They have reinforced southern traditions and the belief that the food eaten, and the manner in which it is partaken, have social and cultural significance. In antebellum times, the great distances between homes meant that any social gathering was a real occasion, and food became a central component of the event. Descriptions of "dinings" and elegant dinners at "Melrose", a nineteenth century plantation located in nearby Caswell County, reinforce this image:

> *It is around Melrose that many of my fondest rememberances of early boyhood are associated. In those days, "dinings" were a big part of the social life of Caswell, and it was my privilege to participate in the family feasts that went the annual rounds... To me, Melrose transcended in hospitality and table bounteousness. I have never seen such abundance in the storerooms; (the) cellar was stocked with preserves, pickles and provender of all sorts. There were outside kilns of turnips and sweet potatoes, and the smokehouse was filled with hickory-cured hog meat with occasionally a hind or two of dried beef.*
> *(Tom Henderson, "Recollections of Melrose", c. 1930)*

Dinners were extravagant and elegant affairs, and the table, set with silver castors and fresh flowers, groaned under the weight of the food:

> *A mammoth two-year-old ham rested in a two-foot earthen dish at the head of the table, while a platter of ready-cut baked hens, or guineas, or, sometimes a large uncut baked turkey was placed at the foot... Scattered over the table were large dishes and bowls with steaming vegetables of all kinds... Hot browned biscuits were brought in from the kitchen, along with pones of bread made of meal, milk and salt and no yellow of eggs, thank you! There was honey from the home hives, and homemade preserves and pickles... The dessert was really in three courses, the main item of which was a dried cherry roll, about the size of a lamb's leg, seasoned with hard butter sauce. The next goody on the list was sweet potato custard, cooked in brandy. The final part of the dessert was a giant dominique cake with filling and icing of rich butterscotch or caramel. Afterwards, we cracked walnuts and hickory nuts, or ate watermelon and mushmelons, whichever were in season. (Ibid.)*

Such hospitality and abundance was not uncommon in affluent homes of the period. One young visitor to the Holt plantation in the Spring of 1872 was similarly impressed with the quantity of foods served by the Holts and the quality of the food's preparation.

Food preparation, and the kinds of foods utilized, reflected the origins and traditions of the people themselves. Within the Piedmont area, and Alamance County in particular, the dominant influence of English and Scots-Irish cooking was ultimately tempered by Indian and African influences. Native American foods, such as maize, sweet potatoes, squash, beans and nuts, came to be intermingled with typically African foodstuffs such as field peas, eggplant, yams and tomatoes. These items complemented the traditional southern diet, which placed emphasis on the use of salt meat, corn meal and molasses.

In the period of Reconstruction through the early 1920s, the emphasis on the use of cookbooks declined in the South, as it did elsewhere in the United States. During this period most recipes—called receipts—were not written down or formally compiled in book form. Instead, they were carried around in the cook's head, or, at best, recorded on slips of paper which were filed at the cook's disposal.

An exception to this rule is a cookbook entitled *Choice Recipes,* published in 1907 by the First Christian Church of Burlington, North Carolina. Many of the recipes contained therein are embellished with few directions, and were likely written down from memory by good cooks who took for granted that their readers were possessed of a modicum of cooking ability. As a tribute to these traditional Alamance County cooks we include excerpts from that early cookbook in our retrospective section entitled, "Reflections in Plaid."

The accelerated growth of the Piedmont during the last twenty-five years has resulted in an evolution and growing cosmopolitanism in southern cooking. As Burlington, N.C. native Marion Brown noted in the preface to the 1968 edition of her now-famous *Marion Brown's Southern Cook Book*, "the line as to whether a recipe is distinctly "Southern" has been broadened...because our population now embraces so many residents who are not Southern, but who belong to us anyway."

These good cooks have blended new ideas, tastes and cooking talents with the traditional recipes of the area's past to create an ever-expanding and lively repertoire of good foods. Just as the warp and weft of the textile industry was built upon the blending and evolution of diverse raw materials and the use of innovative technology, the recipes included in *Tastes in Plaid* reflect a transition in southern cooking from homogeneity to diversity. In this book we have therefore attempted to present to you some of the best in cooking from both the old and the new South.

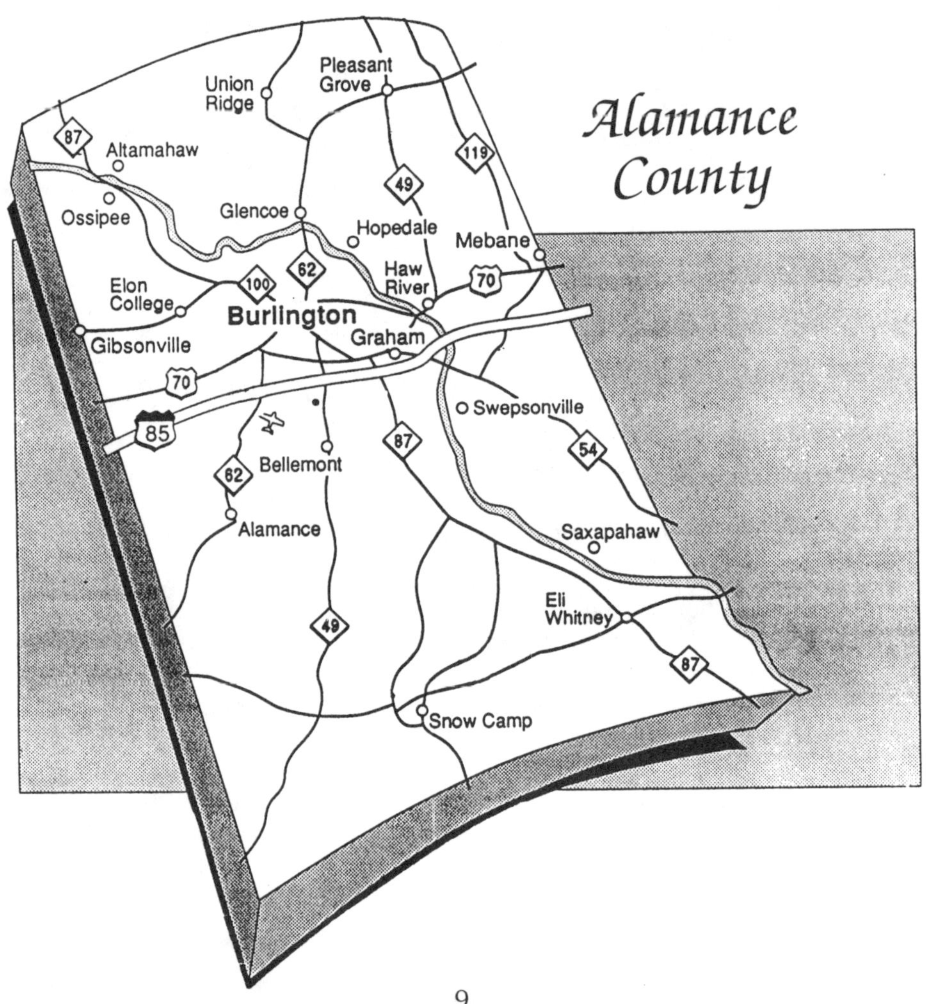

ALAMANCE COUNTY HISTORICAL MUSEUM
Alamance Battleground Rd.

The Alamance County Historical Museum is the birthplace of Edwin Michael Holt, a pioneer in the southern textile industry. In the 1870s the house became home to Holt's sixth son, Lynn Banks Holt, and his wife, the former Mary Catherine (Cattie) Mebane.

Miss Cattie was noted for her hospitality, and the Holt house was a social center of its day. Speaking of a visit to the Holt home in the Spring of 1872, one young guest wrote, "At the Holt's…there was plenty of everything. Here there was fried chicken almost everyday, peach preserves and Miss Cattie's specialty, Mammoth jelly cakes—with 4 layers…I loved to follow Miss Cattie with her big string of keys as she made the rounds of her storehouses and to see the great cans of lard, big home-cured hams, boxes of raisins and the other goods in which those shelves abounded." (from *High Time To Tell It* by Mary Alves Long)

ALAMANCE COUNTY HISTORICAL MUSEUM

Listed in the National Register of Historic Places, the Alamance County Historical Museum was the birthplace of Edwin Michael Holt, a pioneer in the southern textile industry. The oldest section of the house, constructed in 1790, consisted of a two-room structure identified in the vernacular of its time as a "dog-trot." In 1800, this modest early home was overbuilt to create a two story hall-and-parlor house typical of many nineteenth century Piedmont farm houses.

The house acquired its present appearance in 1875, when Holt's sixth son, Lynn Banks Holt, made extensive additions to the family dwelling and remodeled the exterior to conform with prevailing tastes of the mid-Victorian period. The Italianate Revival character of the house, with its extensive use of bracketing and sawn ornamentation, can be traced to the 1875 remodeling, as can be the exterior color scheme of tan and gray.

During its period of Holt occupancy the house was the focus of an extensive plantation operation: in addition to farming, the Holts operated a blacksmith shop, a distillery, a woodworking shop and a grist mill. In 1837, the family grist mill was modified by E. M. Holt to create the Alamance Cotton Factory, one of the first textile mills to be located south of the Potomac River.

Burlington, N. C.
Old Almanace Mill, and its founder, Edwin M. Holt. The first Colored Cotton Fabric manufactured in the South was woven in this Mill, built 1837 on Alamance River. Burned and re-built 1871.

ALAMANCE COTTON FACTORY

The success of Holt's mill resulted, in 1853, in the production of what came to be known throughout the country as "Alamance Plaids"; these Alamance Plaids bear the distinction of being the first commercially produced plaids manufactured in the southern United States. By 1900, more than twenty textile mills in the local area were owned and operated by descendants of Edwin Michael Holt.

E.M. Holt House ca. 1790

The Alamance County Historical Museum contains period room settings typical of the late nineteenth century, as well as exhibits dealing with local county history. Guided tours of the house museum are available on a daily basis. Additionally, the Museum hosts many special events throughout the year, including the Fiddlers' Picnic, held on the second weekend in June, and the Annual Christmas Tour of Homes and Candlelight Tea, held on the first Sunday in December. These events, with foods ranging from "down-home" barbecue to elegant party and reception fare, showcase the talents of area cooks and foster a continuing tradition of hospitality that is synonymous with Alamance County.

Alamance Plaids bear the distinction of being the first factory dyed cotton materials made south of the Potomac River. Their history begins in 1837, when Edwin Michael Holt constructed a cotton factory on the banks of Alamance Creek, due south of the present town of Burlington, N.C.

THE GRIFFIS-PATTON HOUSE

Bason Road

The Griffis-Patton House, located on Bason Road north of Mebane, is a fine example of transitional Federal/Greek Revival architecture. The house may have been constructed as early as 1835, and was built by William Griffis and his wife, Sarah Horn Griffis. The house was subsequently owned by Griffis' son, Dr. Thomas Griffis, a prominent local physician. In 1913 the Griffis-Patton House was purchased by Lonnie and Mary Bason Patton.

Recently the house was restored to its original appearance by the present owners, Mr. and Mrs. Eric Hinshaw. The removal of late-Victorian additions to the house reveals the home's impressive fenestration and hand-made brick, supposedly made by slave labor on the nearby Bason Plantation.

SARA'S SUPER SEAFOOD SUPPER

*Crab Pie

*Boiled Shrimp with Cocktail Sauce

*Grilled Mackerel with Bar-B-Que Sauce

*Broiled Scallops

*Oyster Fritters

Corn on the Cob

*Marinated Cole Slaw

*Marinated Cucumbers

Cornbread

This is a menu I serve often to family and guests at the beach. It beats fighting traffic and eating out! My children gave it this name.

CRAB PIE

1 pound crab meat
1 teaspoon prepared mustard
1 teaspoon salt
1 teaspoon pepper
1 tablespoon Worcestershire sauce
Dash of TABASCO pepper sauce
2 hard-boiled eggs, chopped
4 tablespoons mayonnaise
Round buttery cracker crumbs
Butter or margarine, melted

Pick crab meat, breaking into pieces. Mix with mustard, salt, pepper, Worcestershire sauce, TABASCO pepper sauce, chopped eggs and mayonnaise. Spoon into greased pie plate. Sprinkle with cracker crumbs and pour melted butter over. Bake at 400° for 20 minutes. Do not let get too brown.

BOILED SHRIMP

3 pounds fresh shrimp
2 tablespoons shrimp and crab boil

Bring water to a boil in a 6-quart pan adding crab boil. Let boil for 5 minutes. Put in shrimp and cook until they turn pink—don't overcook. Drain and rinse under cold running water until cool. Refrigerate until ready to peel and eat.

Cocktail Sauce:
1 bottle chili-sauce
½ to 1 cup ketchup
2 tablespoons horseradish or to taste
2 tablespoons Worcestershire sauce
Juice of ½ lemon
Dash of TABASCO pepper sauce

Mix ingredients together and refrigerate.

This was made up by my father, Dr. Robert L. McMillan of Winston-Salem. He was an avid fisherman and great seafood cook.

GRILLED MACKEREL

Mackerel or any firm-fleshed fish
Melted butter or margarine
1 cup ketchup
¼ cup brown sugar
1 teaspoon prepared mustard
1 teaspoon Worcestershire sauce
Minced onion to taste

Cut Mackerel into 1-inch thick steaks. Spread with melted margarine. Mix remaining ingredients together and heat until sugar dissolves. Add some water if too thick. Using outdoor grill, which has been reduced to low heat, place steaks on grill. Baste with sauce and cook until done. Fish will become flaky and may stick to grill. Try to turn over only once.

This recipe was introduced to us by our son, Mike Brown, who catches his own fish to grill.

BROILED SCALLOPS

1 pound scallops
½ stick of butter
Garlic salt or minced garlic
Fresh chives, chopped
Paprika

Rinse scallops and pat dry. Melt butter in a 9x9-inch baking dish. Stir scallops in butter to coat and arrange in single layer. Sprinkle with small amount of garlic and chives. Broil 2 minutes, turn and broil 2 additional minutes or until done. Oysters may be used in place of scallops.

OYSTER FRITTERS

1 cup whole oysters
1 cup plain flour
1 teaspoon baking powder
¼ teaspoon pepper
1 teaspoon salt
1 egg
Dash of TABASCO pepper sauce
Dash of Worcestershire sauce
Milk

Mix all ingredients adding just enough milk to thicken. Drop by tablespoon full into iron skillet in half deep hot bacon drippings or corn oil. Cook until brown.

This recipe was used by Mrs. R. S. Dingle at the Tip Top Inn on Pawley's Island, S.C. Our family spent many summers there enjoying delicious Southern meals.

MARINATED COLE SLAW

½ cup salad oil
½ cup vinegar
⅞ cup sugar
1 teaspoon mustard
1 teaspoon salt
2 medium heads of cabbage, shredded
1 small onion, minced

Using a whisk, combine first 5 ingredients in a saucepan and bring to a boil. Stir until sugar is melted. Combine cabbage and onion. Pour marinade over and mix well. Refrigerate for 24 hours.

Yield: 24 servings

MARINATED CUCUMBERS

3 cucumbers
1 small onion, Vidalia
1 cup vinegar
2 teaspoons cooking oil
3 tablespoons sugar
1 teaspoon black pepper
Fresh Dill

Peel and slice cucumbers in a bowl. Add thinly sliced onion. Mix together remaining ingredients and pour over cucumbers and onions. Sprinkle with cut up fresh dill. Cover with plastic wrap and refrigerate for 6 hours.

Sara's husband, "Buster", is a great, great grandson of Edwin Michael Holt.

Complete menu by Sara McMillan Brown
Burlington

FRIENDS OF THE MUSEUM LUNCHEON

*Chicken Salad in Pastry Shells

*Shrimp Salad

*Frozen Fruit Salad

*Tomato Cucumber Stack Sandwiches

*Sour Cream Muffins

*Pumpkin Muffins

*Iced Banana Berry Salad

Tea

Coffee

CHICKEN SALAD

1 (3-4 pound) chicken, cooked
3 eggs, boiled and diced
1 (4-ounce) can sliced water chestnuts
½ cup sweet salad cubes
½ cup sliced stuffed olives
Salt to taste
Pepper to taste
Mayonnaise
Purple onions to garnish

Cool, bone and chop chicken. Mix all ingredients except mayonnaise. Adjust seasonings. Add enough mayonnaise to moisten and place in shells.

Pastry:
½ cup shortening
¼ cup boiling water
1½ cups cake flour
½ teaspoon baking powder
½ teaspoon salt

Place shortening in bowl and pour in water. Beat ingredients until cold and creamy. Chill. Add dry ingredients and mix until they form a smooth ball. Cover and chill. Roll between waxed paper. Cut with biscuit cutter and place in muffin cups. Bake at 350° until brown.

Yield: 6 to 8 servings

SHRIMP SALAD

½ pound small shell macaroni
1 pound medium or large shrimp
1 (16-ounce) carton sour cream
½ cup canned milk
¼ teaspoon paprika
1 teaspoon dill weed
1 tablespoon chopped chives, fresh or dried
¼ to ½ cup chopped green olives
Salt to taste
Pepper to taste
Fresh parsley

Cook macaroni and shrimp; set aside. Combine remaining ingredients well and add to macaroni and shrimp. Marinate overnight for flavor blending. This may need extra milk for more moisture. Adjust. Garnish with parsley.

FROZEN FRUIT SALAD

1 cup peaches, chopped and drained
1 cup apricots, chopped and drained
½ cup strawberries, sliced
1 banana, sliced and soaked in lemon juice
½ cup coconut, grated
½ cup pineapple juice
3 ounces orange juice concentrate, thawed
½ cup sugar

Mix all ingredients well; place in paper lined muffin tins and freeze.

TOMATO CUCUMBER STACK SANDWICHES

20 (2-inch) rounds wheat bread
10 (2-inch) rounds white bread
10 (2-inch) rounds tomato slices
10 (2-inch) rounds cucumber slices, if possible
Mayonnaise
10 whole pimento stuffed olives
10 long food picks

Set up assembly line. Begin with wheat bread on bottom and alternate slices of bread, and vegetables, spreading with mayonnaise to hold rounds together. End with wheat bread on top. Garnish with olive and secure with pick.

Yield: 10 sandwiches

SOUR CREAM MUFFINS

1 stick margarine or butter, softened
1 cup sour cream
2 cups buttermilk baking mix

Mix first two ingredients then add dry mix. Blend well. Drop into greased muffin cups. Bake at 400° for 10 to 15 minutes.

Yield: 8 to 10 servings

PUMPKIN MUFFINS

⅓ cup oil
1 cup pumpkin
3 eggs
2⅓ cups buttermilk baking mix
1¼ cups sugar
2 teaspoons ground cinnamon
½ teaspoon ground cloves
½ teaspoon ginger
½ cup raisins

Mix all ingredients except raisins, just until blended. Stir in raisins. Fill paper lined muffin tins ⅔ full. Bake 350° 20 to 25 minutes.

Yield: 8 to 10 servings

ICED BANANA BERRY SALAD

¾ cup sugar
1 cup sour cream
2 cups non-dairy whipped topping
1 tablespoon grated lemon rind
2 tablespoons lemon juice
1 cup bananas, sliced
1 cup blueberries
1 cup strawberries or raspberries
Mint leaves

Mix together first five ingredients and set aside. Gently fold fruits into cream mixture. Spoon into plastic wrap lined loaf pan and freeze. Remove from freezer about 5 minutes before slicing. Garnish with mint leaves and strawberry fans.

Yield: 10 servings

Complete menu by Peggy Carter Lackey (Mrs. Mack E.)
Burlington

HOLIDAY DINNER

Turkey

Baked Ham

*Dressing

Rice and Gravy

*Asparagus Casserole

Fresh Green Beans

*Candied Sweet Potatoes

*Squash Casserole

*Cranberry Salad

Rolls and Butter

*Coconut Cake

*Tipsy Pudding

*Pecan Pie

DRESSING

1 (16-ounce) package herb stuffing mix
1 (8-ounce) package cornbread stuffing mix
2 onions, chopped
2 cups celery, chopped
1 cup pecans, chopped
2 eggs, slightly beaten
1 cup broth from turkey
Sage, to taste
1 stick margarine, melted
Milk
Water

Mix all dry ingredients together. Add broth and equal amounts of milk and water to moisten, being careful to toss as little as possible so dressing won't be sticky. Put into 4 (8x8x2-inch) greased pans. Bake at 450° for 10 to 15 minutes. This keeps until ready to bake and reheats well.

ASPARAGUS CASSEROLE

1 can asparagus spears
Slivered almonds
1 (10¾-ounce) can mushroom soup
Sharp cheese, grated

Place asparagus spears in a large greased pie plate. Sprinkle almonds over asparagus and cover with mushroom soup. Sprinkle cheese over all. Bake at 350° for 20 to 25 minutes or until cheese bubbles.

CANDIED SWEET POTATOES

6 sweet potatoes
Brown sugar
Butter or margarine

Bake sweet potatoes at 350° until soft. Peel, slice and layer in casserole dish putting brown sugar and butter over each layer. Bake at 350° until sugar and butter are melted. Once or twice during baking, spoon syrup that has melted over potatoes.

SQUASH CASSEROLE

1 stick butter or margarine
1 (8-ounce) package seasoned stuffing mix
3 cups yellow squash, cooked and drained
1 (10¾-ounce) can cream of mushroom or cream of chicken soup
2 medium onions, chopped
1 cup sour cream
Dash of pepper

Melt margarine and stir into stuffing mix. Line casserole dish with half of stuffing mixture. Combine other ingredients and spoon on top. Cover with remaining stuffing mix and bake at 350° for 1 hour.

CRANBERRY SALAD

2 small packages lemon flavored gelatin
1 large can whole cranberries
1 (15-ounce) can crushed pineapple, drained
1 cup celery, chopped
1 cup nuts, chopped

Dissolve gelatin according to package directions. Chill until partially set. Add the other ingredients and return to refrigerator. Chill until set.

COCONUT CAKE

1 cup butter or margarine, softened
2 cups sugar
4 eggs
3 cups plain flour
3 scant teaspoons baking powder
½ teaspoon salt
½ cup buttermilk
½ cup water
1 teaspoon vanilla extract

Cream butter and sugar. Add eggs, one at a time, beating after each addition. Sift dry ingredients together and add alternately with buttermilk and water. Add vanilla and mix well. Pour into 3 11½x7½x1½-inch greased pans. Bake at 375° for 20 minutes. Do not overbake. Let stand in pans a few minutes to cool. When completely cool, divide layers, making 2 cakes.

Icing:
1 coconut
Sugar to taste
½ pint cream, whipped

Prepare coconut and drain milk. Grate coconut, adding milk and sugar to taste. Refrigerate several hours. Add vanilla and sugar to taste to cream. Spread cream on first layer and sprinkle with coconut. Repeat. For two cakes, double icing recipe.

TIPSY PUDDING

1 angel food cake
Slivered almonds (use any amount you want)
Sherry (to taste)
¼ cup sugar
1 tablespoon cornstarch
1 egg, slightly beaten
2 cups milk
1 teaspoon vanilla

In a glass bowl or casserole, break angel food cake into pieces and cover bottom. Sprinkle sherry over and add almonds. Continue layers for amount desired. Mix together sugar and cornstarch in the top of double boiler. Add egg and mix well. Gradually stir in milk, keeping smooth. Cook, stirring constantly until thickened. Stir in vanilla. Pour custard sauce over all, being sure to cover completely. Refrigerate several hours prior to serving.

PECAN PIE

3 eggs
1 cup sugar
½ cup light corn syrup
¼ cup butter or margarine, melted
1½ ounces bourbon
1 cup pecans
1 (9-inch) unbaked pie shell

Beat eggs slightly. Stir in sugar, corn syrup and melted butter. Add bourbon and pecans. Pour into pie shell. Bake at 375° for 35 to 40 minutes or until filling is slightly firm.

Complete menu by Anne Sapp Morrison, Alene Stonestreet Sapp Ventura, Peggé Sapp Haywood
Burlington

EASY EASTER BRUNCH

*Broccoli Quiche

*Iced Five Layer Sandwich

*Pasta Salad

*Stuffed Cherry Tomatoes

*Glazed Orange Juice Muffins

Fresh Strawberries with Cream

Coffee, Tea and Juice

BROCCOLI QUICHE

1 (10-ounce) package frozen broccoli, thawed and drained
4 ounces Monterey Jack cheese, shredded
½ cup chopped onion
1½ cups milk
3 eggs
¾ cup buttermilk baking mix
1 teaspoon garlic salt
¼ teaspoon pepper

Preheat oven to 400°. Grease a 10½x2-inch deep quiche or pie pan. Mix broccoli, cheese and onion in plate. Beat remaining ingredients until smooth. Pour into plate and bake 40 to 50 minutes or until knife inserted in center comes out clean. Cool 5 to 10 minutes before cutting.

Yield: 6 servings

ICED FIVE LAYER SANDWICH

1 loaf wheat bread, unsliced
Ham salad spread
Egg salad spread
2 (8-ounce) packages cream cheese, softened
Mayonnaise to moisten

Slice bread lengthwise into three equal slices. Spread one slice with ham salad, the second with egg salad so that the finished sandwich has bread on top and bottom. Ice bread with cheese that has been moistened with enough mayonnaise to spreadable consistency. Cover and refrigerate. Slice vertically for serving.

Yield: 6 to 8 servings

PASTA SALAD

1 pound assorted color twist macaroni, cooked and drained
1 cup stuffed olives, sliced
½ pound fresh mushrooms, sliced
1 cup thinly sliced pepperoni, cut into fourths
½ large purple onion, sliced
1 cup Cheddar cheese, cubed
1 cup garbanzo beans, optional

Dressing:
2 small bottles Italian dressing
1 tablespoon oregano
1 tablespoon sesame seeds
1 tablespoon garlic salt
½ teaspoon black pepper

Marinate all ingredients overnight in dressing.

Yield: 6 to 8 servings

STUFFED CHERRY TOMATOES

12 to 18 cherry tomatoes
1 (8-ounce) package cream cheese, softened
1 small package buttermilk dressing mix, dry
Parsley

Wash, cut tops from tomatoes, scoop out center and drain well. Mix cheese and dressing until well blended. Stuff tomatoes with cheese and garnish with parsley.

Yield: 6 to 8 servings

GLAZED ORANGE JUICE MUFFINS

1 egg, beaten
2 cups buttermilk baking mix
⅔ cup orange juice
2 tablespoons sugar
2 tablespoons vegetable oil
1 tablespoon orange rind

Glaze:
¾ cup powdered sugar
3 to 4 tablespoons orange juice

To beaten egg add remaining muffin ingredients. Stir just until blended. Pour into 12 paper lined muffin cups. Bake 400° for 15 minutes. Spread with glaze while warm.

Yield: 6 to 12 servings

Complete menu by Peggy Carter Lackey (Mrs. Mack E.)
Burlington

NEW YEAR'S EVE DINNER BUFFET

*Savory Pork Roast

Stuffed Mushrooms

*Kraut Relish

*Broccoli Salad

Black Eyed Peas

*Potato Casserole

Sarah's Rolls

*Chocolate Mousse

PORK ROAST

1 boned (4 pound) loin of pork
2 tablespoons butter
Salt and pepper
1 carrot, diced
1 stalk celery, diced
1 onion, diced
1 tablespoon rosemary
1 tablespoon parsley, chopped
½ teaspoon thyme
1 bay leaf

Ask the butcher to bone and tie the loin. Also, ask for bones and trimmings. Place roast on the bones in roasting pan. Sprinkle with salt, pepper and butter. Place in 350° preheated oven. Cook 30 to 35 minutes per pound. Thirty minutes before the end of roasting time, add onion, celery, carrot, parsley, bay leaf and rosemary. Continue cooking. Transfer roast to platter (keep warm). Use pan drippings for gravy.

Yield: 4 to 6 servings

KRAUT RELISH

2 (16-ounce) cans sauerkraut, drained
2 medium bell peppers, chopped
2 onions, chopped
2 small jars pimento, drained
1 teaspoon celery seed
2 cups sugar
¾ cup vinegar

Drain juices. Boil sugar and vinegar. Pour over vegetables. Marinate overnight. Drain well before serving. This relish has a long life refrigerated.

BROCCOLI SALAD

3 bunches broccoli
3 hard boiled eggs, grated
6 green onions, chopped
¾ cup mayonnaise
Fresh grated Parmesan cheese
6 slices cooked bacon, crumbled
Salt and pepper to taste

Wash and chop broccoli into bite size pieces. Add onion, eggs, mayonnaise, salt and pepper, Parmesan cheese and crumbled bacon. Cover and refrigerate overnight.

POTATO CASSEROLE AU GRATIN

3 pounds potatoes
1 medium onion, chopped
6 tablespoons butter
6 tablespoons flour
1 teaspoon salt
¼ teaspoon pepper
3 cups milk
½ cup chopped parsley

Pare potatoes, slice thinly. Cook in small amount of boiling water for 5 minutes. Drain. Sauté onion in butter until tender. Stir in flour, salt and pepper until smooth. Gradually stir in milk until hot and thickened. Add chopped parsley. Place potatoes into a 2-quart buttered baking dish. Pour sauce over potatoes. Bake at 350° for 15 minutes. Add cheese topping. Bake an additional 15 minutes or until top is brown and casserole is bubbly.

Cheese Topping:
2 tablespoons melted butter
¼ cup breadcrumbs
½ cup of shredded Cheddar cheese

Yield: 6 to 8 servings

CHOCOLATE MOUSSE

12 ounces chocolate chips
¼ cup water
5 egg yolks, beaten
7 egg whites

Melt chocolate chips in hot water. When melted, beat until smooth. Add eggs and beat again over low heat, about 5 minutes. Cool for about 10 minutes. Beat egg whites until almost dry. Add to cooled chocolate mixture, folding in whites gently. Refrigerate for several hours.

Elizabeth Stewart (Mrs. B. L.)
Burlington

COOKOUT FOLLOWING AN AFTERNOON OF GOLF

*Grilled Chicken Breasts

*Creamy Roquefort Coleslaw

Corn on the Cob

Baked Beans with Honey Mustard

*Hot Herb Bread

*Lemon Tarts

Iced Tea

LANE'S GRILLED CHICKEN

8 chicken breasts

1 large bottle Italian salad dressing

Pierce chicken breasts with meat fork. Marinate overnight in Italian dressing. (You may wish to remove skin before marinating.) Grill to well done.

Yield: 8 servings

CREAMY ROQUEFORT COLESLAW

1 cup mayonnaise
¼ cup light cream or half and half
¼ cup Roquefort cheese, finely crumbled
1 tablespoon tarragon vinegar
1 teaspoon sugar
Salt and freshly-ground pepper, to taste
1 large cabbage, coarsely shredded

Blend the dressing ingredients thoroughly; toss with shredded cabbage. Cover and chill at least two hours before serving.

Yield: 8 cups

HOT HERB BREAD

1 loaf Italian bread
¼ pound butter or margarine, softened
1 teaspoon parsley flakes
¼ teaspoon oregano
¼ teaspoon dill weed
1 clove garlic, minced
1 teaspoon lemon juice
Grated Parmesan cheese

Cut bread diagonally into 1-inch slices. Blend butter, parsley, oregano, dill, garlic and lemon juice. Put bread slices together with butter mixture. Shape foil around loaf, boat-fashion, twisting ends and leaving top open. Sprinkle top liberally with cheese and additional parsley. Heat at 400° for 10 minutes.

LEMON TARTS

1 package lemon flavored gelatin
1 cup boiling water
1 can sweetened condensed milk, chilled
Juice of 1 lemon
⅔ cup sugar
12 graham cracker tart shells
Whipped topping
Zest of lemon

Dissolve gelatin in boiling water. Refrigerate to cool. Whip chilled condensed milk. Add lemon juice, sugar and gelatin. Pour into tart shells and chill until set. Top each with a dollop of whipped topping and a sprinkle of lemon zest.

Yield: 12 Tarts

Becky's husband, Shamrock Golf pro, is the originator of the popular Alamance Parent-Child Golf Tournament.

Rebecca Moore Walker (Mrs. Steve)
Burlington

A FAVORITE BRUNCH AT ELON COLLEGE

*Cheese Soufflé

*Hot Crab and Cheese

*Baked Fresh Asparagus

*Fruit Skewers with Poppy Seed Dressing

*Individual Cheesecakes

These recipes were popular among guests at Centennial events on the Elon College campus.

CHEESE SOUFFLÉ

½ cup butter
⅓ cup flour
4 cups hot milk
10 eggs, separated
1 pound Cheddar cheese, grated
¼ teaspoon salt
¼ teaspoon paprika
¼ teaspoon dry mustard
⅛ teaspoon cream of tartar
⅛ teaspoon salt

Melt butter. Blend in flour and cook over low heat for 10 minutes. Add milk and cook until thick and smooth. Beat egg yolks until thick. Stir into cream sauce. Add cheese and seasoning and mix well—keep warm until needed. Beat egg whites with salt and cream of tartar until stiff. Fold by hand into hot sauce. Mix until thoroughly combined. Pour into greased 8x11-inch pan. Place pan on tray with ¼-inch water and bake at 350° until browned and set, 60 to 75 minutes. Serve immediately.

Yield: 10 servings

HOT CRAB AND CHEESE

1 (8-ounce) package cream cheese
1 (4-ounce) jar Old English cheese
1 (8-ounce) can crab meat
1 small onion, grated
Salt
Worcestershire sauce, to taste
Milk, to thin, if necessary

Slowly melt cheese—add remaining ingredients. Serve warm in chafing dish with shredded whole wheat wafers.

BAKED FRESH ASPARAGUS

2 pounds fresh asparagus
3 tablespoons minced fresh parsley
2 tablespoons olive oil
2 tablespoons melted butter, no substitute
Salt and pepper, to taste

Wash, dry and break off tough white ends of asparagus spears. Arrange in one layer in baking pan if possible. Sprinkle with parsley. Combine the oil and melted butter and drizzle over the asparagus, then add salt and pepper. Cover baking dish with aluminum foil and bake at 400° for 15 minutes—unless you must arrange asparagus in two layers. In that case, increase time to 25 minutes.

Yield: 6 servings

FRUIT SKEWERS WITH POPPY SEED DRESSING

1 cantaloupe, cut into ½-inch cubes
1 pineapple, cut into ½-inch cubes
10 to 12 strawberries
2 to 3 kiwi, cut into ¼-inch slices
10 to 12 bamboo skewers

On 6-inch bamboo skewers thread: 1 cantaloupe cube, 1 kiwi slice, 1 pineapple cube, 1 strawberry, 1 pineapple cube, 1 kiwi slice, 1 cantaloupe cube. Repeat with remaining fruit and skewers. Lightly ladle dressing on top.

Yield: 10 to 12 servings

Poppy Seed Dressing:
⅓ cup sugar
2 tablespoons vinegar
1 tablespoon lemon juice
½ teaspoon salt
½ teaspoon dry mustard
½ cup vegetable oil
1 tablespoon poppy seed

Combine sugar, vinegar, lemon juice, salt and mustard in quart bowl. Gradually add oil, beating with electric mixer until thick and smooth—stir in poppy seed. Cover and refrigerate 2 hours.

INDIVIDUAL CHEESECAKES

4 (3-ounce) packages cream cheese
⅔ cup sugar
2 eggs
1 teaspoon vanilla extract
1 teaspoon lemon extract
15 vanilla wafers
15 cupcake papers

Beat together cream cheese, sugar, eggs, vanilla and lemon flavoring. Place vanilla wafers in bottom of cupcake paper in muffin pan. Fill almost full with cream cheese mixture. Bake at 350° for 10 minutes or a little longer. Cool.

Topping:
¾ cup sour cream
¼ cup sugar

Mix together sour cream and sugar and spread on top of cheesecakes. Garnish, if desired, with blueberries, cherries, or strawberries. Can be frozen. If frozen, remove 5 minutes before serving.

Yield: 12 to 15 servings

Complete menu by Bill Butler, Director of ARA Food Services, Elon College
Elon College

DINNER AT EIGHT

*Roast Leg of Lamb

*Rice Supreme

*Cauliflower Casserole

Green Beans

*Pineapple Crunch

*Hot Biscuits with Mint Jelly

*Meringues with Boiled Custard

ROAST LEG OF LAMB

Select the finest leg you can find; wash and place in roasting pan in about an inch of water, into which you have chopped a large onion. Rub the top of the leg with this paste:

2 tablespoons flour
2 tablespoons apple cider vinegar
1 teaspoon mustard, regular or spicy

Bake covered at 400° for 1 hour, then turn down to 350° for remainder of cooking (approximately 3 hours in all). The roast is done when the meat leaves the bone. If meat is not brown enough, then turn to broil for desired color.

This method of cooking lamb was handed down to me from Rachel Wilson, long-time companion of my mother and cook "par excellence."

RICE SUPREME

1 cup rice
1 (10½-ounce) beef bouillon
1 (10½-ounce) can onion soup
½ stick butter, melted
1 can mushrooms and liquid

Mix rice, soups and butter together and place in casserole. Bake covered at 350° for 1 hour. Add mushrooms and liquid 15 minutes before done.

CAULIFLOWER CASSEROLE

1 cup mushroom soup
1½ cups sharp cheese, grated
⅓ cup mayonnaise
½ teaspoon curry powder
1 large cauliflower, broken, cooked, salted and drained
Breadcrumbs from 3 pieces of bread
2 tablespoons margarine or butter, melted
½ cup sharp cheese, grated

In medium bowl, stir soup, cheese, mayonnaise and curry powder until well blended. Place cauliflower in flat 8x12-inch dish. Pour sauce over. Mix breadcrumbs and butter and spread on top. Sprinkle ½ cup sharp cheese on top. Bake uncovered at 350° for 30 minutes.

PINEAPPLE CASSEROLE

1 (20-ounce) can pineapple chunks, drained
3 tablespoons flour
½ cup sugar
½ to 1 cup sharp cheese, grated
Round buttery cracker crumbs to bountifully cover casserole
½ stick butter or margarine

Place pineapple chunks in flat casserole or large quiche pan. Combine flour and sugar mixture. Cover with cracker crumbs. Pour melted butter over all this. Cook at 350° until browned and bubbly.

BISCUITS

1 cup plain flour
1 stick butter
1 (8-ounce) package cream cheese

Mix ingredients in food processor. Roll thin, using as little extra flour as possible. Cut in desired size. Bake at 400° until brown.

MERINGUES

4 egg whites
2 cups sugar
1 teaspoon vanilla extract

Beat egg whites until stiff. Gradually add ⅔ of sugar and continue beating. Add flavoring and fold in remaining sugar. Shape with spoon on cookie sheet covered with brown paper making small cups. Bake at 250° for 50 minutes. May be stored in tin cans.

BOILED CUSTARD

1 quart milk (whole milk or part half and half and part milk if you desire an extra rich sauce)
½ cup sugar
6 egg yolks
2 tablespoons flour
1 to 1½ teaspoons vanilla extract

This is a strange name for this marvelous sauce because one thing you do not do is boil it. I prefer to cook this in a double boiler, but a regular pan may be used if you watch it closely. Heat milk, but never bring it to a boil. Mix eggs, sugar, and flour with a little of the hot milk. Then add this mixture slowly to the heated milk, stirring constantly. Cook, always stirring, to the desired thickness. Set aside to cool. Pour through strainer and add vanilla. Refrigerate until cold before using. In case of curdling while cooking, add a pinch of baking soda to smooth sauce. If it thickens too much while chilling, just add a little milk to thin. To serve, place each meringue in crystal dessert bowl. Scoop small amount of vanilla ice cream in meringue. Pour boiled custard bountifully over this. Then add fresh strawberries. A dollop of whipped cream may be added for final touch.

Lemon curd may be placed in meringue with custard over it. My aunt's favorite dessert was a serving of lemon gelatin in dessert bowl with custard poured over and pecans crumbled on top. You can be creative with the meringues and custard. Chocolate and caramel sauces are good. Boiled custard is a wonderful thing to take to someone who is sick. The old saying is "boiled custard and chicken soup will cure anything."

Complete menu by Catherine Holt McCormick
Burlington

COMPANY DINNER

*Pork Loin with Snow Peas

Rice

Chinese Noodles

*Mustard Glazed Carrots

*Watercress, Avocado, Orange Salad with Curry Dressing

*Hot Gingerbread with Lemon Sauce
Coffee and Tea

PORK LOIN

2 to 3 pounds whole pork tenderloin, cut into bite-sized pieces

Marinade:
1 tablespoon sherry
½ tablespoon ginger root, minced
2 tablespoons soy sauce
¼ teaspoon sugar
1 teaspoon cornstarch
2 tablespoons oil
½ teaspoon baking soda

Add pork loin to the marinade which has been mixed. Let stand 30 minutes. Drain. Heat vegetable oil and sauté meat quickly.

Snow Peas:
½ pound snow peas
2 cups boiling water
2 cups cold water
¼ teaspoon salt
1 clove garlic, crushed

Blanch snow peas for 10 seconds in boiling water. Plunge into cold water and drain. Sauté 1 clove garlic in reserved oil. Add snow peas and reduce heat. Add seasoning sauce and pork.

Seasoning Sauce:
¼ cup chicken broth
½ teaspoon cornstarch
2 tablespoons water
1 tablespoon soy sauce
¼ teaspoon sugar
¼ teaspoon salt
1 teaspoon sesame oil

Mix all ingredients and add to peas and pork and stir until thick. Serve over rice and Chinese noodles.

Yield: 4 to 6 servings

MUSTARD GLAZED CARROTS

2 pounds carrots, sliced
3 tablespoons butter
3 tablespoons mustard
¼ cup brown sugar
¼ cup parsley

Cook carrots until crisp tender. Mix butter, mustard and brown sugar and cook for 3 minutes until syrupy. Pour over carrots and simmer for 5 minutes. Sprinkle parsley on top.

Yield: 4 to 6 servings

WATERCRESS, AVOCADO, ORANGE SALAD

4 bunches watercress, washed and chilled in damp towel
2 oranges, peeled, segmented and chilled
1 avocado, peeled and sliced at last minute
1 teaspoon shallots, chopped

Curry Dressing:
6-8 tablespoons olive oil
2 tablespoons wine vinegar
1 tablespoon lemon juice
1 tablespoon curry
Salt and pepper, to taste

Arrange greens, oranges, and avocados on plate. Pour dressing over and sprinkle chopped shallots on top.

Yield: 4 to 6 servings

GINGERBREAD

1 cup plus 2 tablespoons flour, sifted
1¼ teaspoons baking powder
¼ teaspoon baking soda
1 teaspoon ginger
¼ teaspoon nutmeg
¾ teaspoon cinnamon
⅛ teaspoon salt
⅓ cup butter
½ cup boiling water or coffee
⅓ cup brown sugar
½ cup molasses
1 egg, beaten

Sift together dry ingredients. Mix butter with boiling water (or coffee) until melted. Add to brown sugar and molasses and combine with dry ingredients. Add egg and beat until smooth. Pour into buttered, floured 9-inch square pan. Bake at 350° for 30 minutes.

Lemon Sauce:
½ cup sugar
1 tablespoon cornstarch
¼ teaspoon salt
¼ cup cold water
¾ cup boiling water
3 tablespoons lemon juice
1 teaspoon grated lemon rind
½ teaspoon vanilla extract
2 tablespoons butter

Combine sugar, cornstarch and salt. Gradually stir in cold water. Add to boiling water and cook for 3 minutes. Add lemon juice, lemon rind, vanilla and butter. Serve over gingerbread.

Yield: 6 to 8 servings

Complete menu by Sandra Elder Harper
Burlington

BOAT OR RIVER PICNIC

*Tabouli

*Orzo Salad

*Thai Beef Salad

These foods are made ahead of time, kept cold and served on lettuce leaves. The lettuce leaf may also be used as a spoon—in the Asian manner. These foods do not spoil readily and are good on hot summer days when foods may set out for a while.

TABOULI

¾ cup bulgur
¼ cup cooked garbanzo beans, coarsely chopped
1 cup finely chopped green onions
1 large tomato, peeled and chopped
½ cup chopped parsley
¼ to ½ cup fresh mint leaves, chopped
¼ cup olive oil or safflower oil
¼ cup lemon or lime juice
½ cup plain yogurt
Salt to taste

Rinse bulgur several times. Soak in cold water for 2 hours. Press out all water. Mix bulgur with all other ingredients. Chill. Serve on lettuce leaves.

Yield: 6 servings

ORZO SALAD

8 cups cooked orzo
Salt to taste
Pepper to taste
¼ cup olive oil
1¼ cups mild wine vinegar
1 tablespoon lemon juice
1 sweet red pepper, cut in cubes
1 green pepper, cut in cubes
6 scallions, finely sliced
½ cup currants, softened in vinegar and drained
½ cup sliced black olives
½ cup sliced raw carrots
¼ cup chopped Italian parsley
1 small purple onion, peeled and sliced

Cook orzo al dente—no more. While warm, season with salt and pepper, olive oil, vinegar and lemon juice. Toss with all other ingredients and chill for 4 hours. Serve on lettuce leaves.

Yield: 6 to 8 servings

THAI BEEF SALAD

1 pound prime beef tenderloin
2 garlic cloves
2 fresh coriander leaves
½ teaspoon sugar
2 teaspoons light soy sauce
2 teaspoons fresh lime juice
Salt to taste
Freshly ground pepper
2 bulbs spring onions
6 small red chillies, very hot (optional)
2 small green chillies, seeded and sliced very thinly
1 teaspoon fresh parsley, chopped

Cook beef to medium rare. Cut into small, thin slices and put in wooden bowl. Make a marinade for the beef as follows: crush the garlic, finely chop coriander leaves and pound together with sugar, soy sauce, lime juice, salt and pepper. Cut onions and chillies into very thin slices (use gloves) and add to above marinade. Add all to sliced beef and stir thoroughly. Can serve immediately or allow to marinate for several hours. Do not let stand overnight as lime juice becomes bitter. Serve on lettuce leaves. Garnish with thinly sliced carrots, cucumbers and tomato wedges.

Yield: 4 servings

Complete menu by Helen Moseley Gant (Mrs. Cecil, Jr.)
Burlington

CHILDREN'S BIRTHDAY PARTY

*Cake in a Cup

*Peppermint Snowballs

*Jell Blox

Cheese cubes

Mini Pretzels

Lemonade

CAKE IN A CUP

1 package ice cream cone cups
1 box favorite cake mix, prepared as directed
Frosting

Preheat oven to 400°. Fill cone cups ¾ full with cake mix. Place on a baking sheet. Bake for 30 to 35 minutes. Cool and frost as desired.

Yield: 24 servings

PEPPERMINT SNOWBALLS

1 quart vanilla or chocolate ice cream
2 cups peppermint candies, crushed
Chocolate sauce
Baking cups

Line muffin tin with baking cups. Place scooped ice cream in baking cups. Sprinkle with crushed peppermint candy. Top with chocolate sauce. These may be done ahead of time and placed in freezer until ready to serve.

JELL BLOX

4 envelopes plain gelatin
3 envelopes flavored gelatin, child's favorite
4 cups hot water

Mix gelatins together. Add hot water and stir until dissolved. Pour into a 9x13-inch dish. Refrigerate. Cut in squares or with cookie cutters when set.

A CHILDREN'S CHRISTMAS PARTY

*Homemade Playdough

Cookie Cutters

*Peanutty Nuggets

*Chocolate Squares

Sugar Cookies

*Punch

For a small group of your children's friends, ready your kitchen table for a pretend "cookie-making party" with playdough and cookie cutters. After the party, the children can take their playdough and cookie cutters home as a party favor.

PLAYDOUGH

½ cup salt
1 cup flour
2 tablespoons cream of tartar
2 tablespoons oil
Food coloring

Mix together salt, flour and cream of tartar. Add oil and 1 cup food colored water. Cook over low heat until it is dry and not sticky. Double this recipe for a good batch.

PEANUTTY NUGGETS

⅓ cup peanut butter
½ cup margarine
3 cups miniature marshmallows
4 cups toasted oat cereal, whole pieces

Combine peanut butter and margarine in a 4 quart glass bowl. Cook in microwave at high about 1 minute and mix well. Add marshmallows and mix well. Cook at high about 1 minute and 30 seconds and mix well. Fold in cereal and spread onto greased cookie sheet. Chill until firm. Break into nuggets. Store in tightly covered container in refrigerator.

Yield: 8 servings

Variation: Spoon ½ cup coated cereal mixture into muffin cups lined with paper baking cups.

CHOCOLATE SQUARES

2 cups crushed graham crackers
2 cups powdered sugar
1 cup melted butter or margarine
12 ounces smooth peanut butter
12 ounces chocolate chips

Mix first 4 ingredients and press into a 9x13-inch pan. Melt the chocolate chips and spread over the peanut mixture. Place in refrigerator until the chocolate hardens enough to cut smoothly into 1-inch squares. May be frozen.

FRUIT PUNCH

1 (16-ounce) bottle fruit punch concentrate
2½ quarts cold water
2 (46-ounce) cans pineapple juice, chilled
3 quarts orange juice, chilled
3 (28-ounce) bottles lemon-lime soda, chilled
Ice or ice ring

Add all ingredients to punch bowl.

Yield: 26 servings

Childrens' Parties by Cynthia DeArmon Tate (Mrs. Denny C.)
Burlington

TEA PARTY FOR ASHLEY

Favorite Juice

*Coffee Cake Fruit Squares

*Orange Blossoms

*Fruit Kabobs

*Summer Tea (for Mommies)

Invite favorite girl friends to a Tea Party to celebrate honoree's birthday. If possible, gather together small tables and chairs. Set tables with lucite tea cups and dessert plates. Cups can be personalized for guests to take home. A small paper doilie may be used to dress up each plate.

COFFEE CAKE FRUIT SQUARES

½ pound butter or margarine, softened
1½ cups sugar
2 eggs
1 pint dairy sour cream
2 teaspoons baking soda
2 teaspoons baking powder
3⅓ cups plain flour
2 teaspoons vanilla extract
1 (21-ounce) can pie filling—blueberry, cherry or apple

Cinnamon Nut Topping:
½ cup brown sugar, firmly packed
2 tablespoons plain flour
1 tablespoon cinnamon
2 tablespoons butter, softened
½ cup chopped nuts

Preheat oven to 350°. Grease a 9x13-inch baking dish and set aside. Prepare Cinnamon Nut Topping: in a bowl, mix ingredients together until crumbly. Set aside. In a large bowl, cream butter or margarine and sugar. Add eggs, one at a time. Beat after each addition. Mix in sour cream. Add baking soda, baking powder, flour and vanilla. Mix until blended. Spread half the batter in prepared baking dish. Spread pie filling over batter in baking dish. Carefully spread remaining batter over pie filling. Sprinkle topping over batter. Bake 60 to 70 minutes or until wooden pick inserted comes out clean. Cool and cut into 2 to 3 inch squares. May be frozen.

Yield: 15 servings

ORANGE BLOSSOMS

1 box yellow cake mix with pudding
2 oranges
2 lemons
1½ pounds powdered sugar, sifted

In a large bowl, mix cake according to directions on box. Grate the rinds of the oranges and lemons. Add to the batter. In a small bowl squeeze the juice from the oranges and lemons and mix with the sifted powdered sugar. Set aside. Pour cake batter in well greased and floured mini muffin tins. Fill ⅔ full. Cook until slightly brown and spongy to the touch. Dip in juice-sugar mixture while hot and place on waxed paper to cool.

Yield: 36 servings

FRUIT KABOBS

½ cup sugar
¼ cup water
¼ cup lemon juice
¼ cup orange juice
2 apples, unpeeled
2 pears, unpeeled
1 (8¼-ounce) can pineapple chunks, drained
1 (11-ounce) can mandarin orange segments, drained
14-16 (6-inch) wooden skewers

Mix liquids and sugar in a large bowl. Core apples and pears and cut into 1½-inch pieces. Add to marinade. Toss to coat. Add pineapple and orange segments, cover and refrigerate several hours or overnight. To serve, drain fruit and thread on wood skewers.

Variation: berries, peaches or melons may be substituted if in season. If using berries, do not marinate.

Yield: 14 to 16 servings

SUMMER TEA

1 quart hot water
6 regular tea bags or 3 family size bags
1 cup sugar
½ cup lemon juice
½ cup white grape juice
1 quart cold water

Heat 1 quart water with tea bags in microwave for 5 to 6 minutes. Add remaining ingredients and cold water. Dissolve well and chill.

Yield: 9 servings

Susan Strong Holt (Mrs. Ralph M., III)
Burlington

From 1837 until 1853 Edwin Holt's Alamance Cotton Mill produced yarns and coarse undyed sheeting and Osnaburgs. In the fall of 1851, however, Holt's eldest son, Thomas Michael Holt, returned from Pennsylvania, where his employment in a Philadelphia dry goods store had exposed him to a rich array of colored fabrics, including imported Scotch plaids. This exposure led the younger Holt to propose to his father the production of similar materials, which came to be known as "Alamance Plaids."

"ELMHURST" Graham, N.C.

Constructed in 1878, "Elmhurst" was the residence of Captain James N. Williamson and his wife, Mary Elizabeth Holt. The house was built on land acquired by Williamson in 1868 from his father-in-law, Edwin Michael Holt. Like Holt, James Williamson was active in the local textile industry, and operated mills at Carolina, Hopedale (Big Falls) and Ossipee.

The Williamson home is considered the finest example of Second Empire Victorian architecture in Alamance County. The house is listed in the National Register of Historic Places.

ASPARAGUS ROLLS

20 to 25 slices white bread, trimmed
1 (8-ounce) package cream cheese, softened
1 egg
1 package buttermilk-style dressing, dry
1 large can asparagus spears
½ pound butter, melted

Roll bread until very flat and set aside. Blend cheese, egg and dry dressing mix until well blended. Spread mixture on bread and place asparagus spear in center. Roll up. Cut each roll into 4 sections and secure each with a toothpick. Dip each roll into butter until coated. Freeze. Bake at 400°, frozen, for 15 minutes or until brown.

Yield: 80 to 100 rolls

Aaron Lance Minehart
Burlington

VEGETABLE SPREAD

1 envelope gelatin
1 cucumber, peeled and finely diced
1 tomato, peeled and finely diced
1 green pepper, finely diced
1 cup diced celery
1 small onion, grated
1 pint mayonnaise

Soak gelatin in 3 tablespoons cold water. Dissolve over hot water. Sprinkle 1 teaspoon salt over diced vegetables. Place in colander in sink and let drain. Add gelatin to mayonnaise and mix well. Add vegetables to gelatin mixture. Place in tight fitting container in refrigerator. Will keep for 2 to 3 weeks. Good with rye crackers, wheat wafers or as a sandwich.

Yield: 1 quart

Peggy Joyner Sibley (Mrs. S. Dan)
Burlington

VIDALIA ONION RELISH

½ jar Vidalia onion relish, drained (or pickled Vidalia onions)
1 (8-ounce) package cream cheese
¾ cup chopped pecans
Mayonnaise

Mix all ingredients together, except mayonnaise. Add mayonnaise until spreading consistency. To serve, spread on crackers or melba toast.

Yield: 2 cups

Patricia Wallace Sibley (Mrs. Scott)
Burlington

MAMA NEWLIN'S RAISIN SANDWICH SPREAD

1 box (15-16-ounce) raisins
2 cups salted, dry roasted peanuts
⅔ cup mayonnaise
Juice of 1½ lemons

Put raisins in processor. Pulse 3 or 4 times. Add remaining ingredients and process until finely ground. Spread on whole wheat bread. Keeps for weeks in refrigerator.

Yield: 1 quart, approximately

Jeanette Zimmerman Newlin (Mrs. Thomas)
Haw River

TOASTY ONION STICKS

1 envelope dry onion soup mix
½ pound margarine, softened
15 slices of bread

Blend soup mix with margarine. Trim crusts from bread and spread onion butter on bread slices. Cut each slice into 5 strips. Place strips on ungreased baking sheet. Bake at 375° for 10 minutes or until golden brown.

Yield: 75 appetizers

Joy Kristen Smith
Delray Beach, Florida

GARLIC-TOMATO BREAD

¼ cup olive oil
⅛ teaspoon salt
3 to 4 garlic cloves, crushed
1 loaf Italian bread, day old

Topping: (mix to taste)
6 tomatoes, chopped
Garlic, to taste
⅓ tablespoon oregano
6 tablespoons cilantro, fresh

Heat olive oil, salt and garlic for 5 minutes. Cut bread into 1-inch slices. Brush with oil. Grill over charcoal on both sides. Serve with mixture of tomatoes, garlic, oregano, and cilantro. Eat as you would an open-faced sandwich with your fingers.

Yield: 15 to 20 servings

When my husband and I lived in Italy, this was the appetizer served at our favorite Naples restaurant. The Italian word is Bruschetta.

Sandra Elder Harper
Burlington

TEX-MEX DIP

1 cup sour cream
¼ cup mayonnaise
1 package taco seasoning mix
2 (10½-ounce) cans jalapeño bean dip
1 (8-ounce) package sharp Cheddar cheese, shredded
1 large bunch green onions with tops, sliced
2 (3½-ounce) cans pitted ripe olives, drained and chopped
Round corn chips

Combine sour cream, mayonnaise and taco seasoning. To assemble: spread bean dip on a large shallow serving platter. Spread the sour cream mixture over the bean dip. Sprinkle with chopped onions and olives. Cover with shredded cheese. Serve chilled or at room temperature with round corn chips as dippers.

Yield: 15 to 20 servings

Martha Young Clark (Mrs. T. N.)
Burlington

MEXICAN PIE PLATE DIP

2 cans refried beans
1 package taco seasoning
1 (16-ounce) carton sour cream
2 cups grated sharp Cheddar cheese

Mix 2 cans refried beans with the taco seasoning. Spread in an 8 or 9-inch pie plate. Spread with the sour cream. Cover that with grated cheese. Bake at 400° for 30 minutes.

Yield: 4 cups

Anne Hyde Fortner (Mrs. C. H.)
Burlington

CRABMEAT DIP OR SPREAD

1 (7-ounce) can crabmeat or ½ pound fresh crab
1 (8-ounce) package cream cheese, room temperature
2 tablespoons ketchup
2 tablespoons cream
2 tablespoons onions, finely diced
½ teaspoon salt
¼ teaspoon Worcestershire sauce
2 tablespoons mayonnaise

Mix all ingredients, with exception of the crabmeat, using an electric mixer. When evenly blended, fold in the crab. Be sure to allow cream cheese to reach room temperature for easier mixing.

Yield: 2 cups

Beulah Pritchard Wilson (Mrs. John J.)
Burlington

SHRIMP DIP

1 (8-ounce) package cream cheese, room temperature
½ cup mayonnaise
¼ cup ketchup
1 small onion, grated
1 cup chopped shrimp
2 tablespoons mild horseradish
1 tablespoon lemon juice

Blend cream cheese with mayonnaise. Fold in remaining ingredients. Chill. Serve with buttery sesame crackers.

Frances Anderson Johnson (Mrs. Eldridge J.)
Greensboro, North Carolina

SHRIMP SALAD OR DIP

3 pounds shrimp, cooked and chopped
3 (8-ounce) packages cream cheese
1 cup mayonnaise
1 pint sour cream
2 tablespoons chopped green pepper
1½ cups chopped celery
2 tablespoons chopped onion
3 hard-boiled eggs, chopped
Juice of 2 lemons
1 tablespoon Worcestershire sauce
Salt to taste
Dash of TABASCO pepper sauce

Soften cream cheese. Add all other ingredients and mix well. Better if prepared the day before serving.

Yield: 40 servings

Edith Brown
Burlington

HOT CRAB SPREAD

1 (8-ounce) package cream cheese
1 tablespoon milk
1 (6½-ounce) can flaked crab, picked of shell
2 tablespoons finely chopped onion
½ teaspoon horseradish, cream style
¼ teaspoon salt
Dash of pepper
⅓ cup or more sliced almonds

Blend softened cream cheese and the milk. Add crab, salt and pepper. Blend well, or blend in blender, and spoon into oven proof dish. Sprinkle with the sliced almonds and bake at 375° for 15 minutes. Serve hot with crackers or party rye bread. This may be made a day ahead and heated before serving.

Yield: 14 servings

Peggy Joyner Sibley (Mrs. S. Dan)
Burlington

CRAB STUFFED MUSHROOMS

18 medium mushrooms
2 tablespoons oil
1 egg
1 (6-ounce) frozen crabmeat, thawed
2 tablespoons mayonnaise
2 tablespoons chopped onion
1 teaspoon lemon juice
½ cup breadcrumbs
2 tablespoons butter, melted

Rinse and dry mushrooms; remove stems. Dip caps in oil. Set in baking dish. Combine crab, egg, mayonnaise, onion, lemon juice, ¼ cup breadcrumbs and stuff the mushroom caps. Combine remaining ¼ cup breadcrumbs with melted butter. Sprinkle over mushrooms. Bake at 375° for 15 minutes.

Yield: 18 appetizers

Linda Collins Abplanalp (Mrs. Bill)
Burlington

MARCIA'S CRAB MUFFINS

1 can crabmeat
1 stick butter
1 jar Old English cheese
½ teaspoon seasoning salt
½ teaspoon garlic salt
2 tablespoons mayonnaise
6 English muffins (split)

Melt butter and cheese and combine with remaining ingredients. Spread on muffins. Bake at 350° for 15 minutes. Serve hot. May cut muffins in quarters for appetizers.

Yield: 12 large or 48 small servings

Madge O'Kelly Brannock
Elon College

CRABGRASS

1 (10-ounce) package frozen spinach
1 onion, finely chopped
¼ cup butter, melted
1 (6-ounce) can crabmeat, drained
¾ cup Parmesan cheese, grated

Cook spinach according to package directions; drain well and set aside. Sauté onion in the butter until transparent. Snip spinach finely with shears. Combine all ingredients. Heat gently, stirring until cheese is melted. Serve on shredded whole wheat wafers.

Yield: 25 to 30 servings

Former Living Editor of the Burlington TIMES-NEWS, originator of the paper's food section and weekly Recipe Swap.

Essie Cofield Norwood (Mrs. Ralph)
Burlington

CAVIAR APPETIZER

1 stick butter or margarine
1 (3-ounce) package Neufchatel cheese with herbs
1 small jar red or black caviar
1 can buttermilk biscuits

In a pie pan melt butter with cheese. Mix well. Sprinkle caviar over the cheese mixture. Cut biscuits into quarters. Put points down in the mixture. Bake at 350° 12 minutes or until golden brown. Serve by picking up biscuits and dipping in mixture.

Yield: 15 to 20 servings

Martha Young Clark (Mrs. T. N.)
Burlington

BEER CHEESE BALL

½ pound sharp Cheddar cheese, grated
½ pound cream cheese
¼ cup beer
2 tablespoons Worcestershire sauce
1 teaspoon garlic salt
2 tablespoons dry tarragon vinegar
Paprika

Soften cream cheese and mix with grated Cheddar cheese. Add half of beer and remaining ingredients that have been mixed together. Add remaining beer. Mix and form into a ball. Chill. Roll in paprika until coated.

Yield: 8 to 12 servings

Sara Shaw Young
Burlington

BRANDIED BLUE CHEESE BALL

1 (8-ounce) package blue cheese, crumbled
1 (6-ounce) package cream cheese
1 (8-ounce) package Cheddar cheese, finely grated
2 tablespoons mayonnaise
2 tablespoons brandy
1 teaspoon caraway seeds
½ teaspoon garlic salt

Bring cheeses to room temperature. Combine all ingredients and mix well. Roll into ball and cover with caraway seeds.

Yield: 1 appetizer ball

Carolyn Neely Eckert (Mrs. Edward F.)
Gibsonville

CHIPPED BEEF CHEESE BALL

1 (3-ounce) jar snipped dried beef
1 (8-ounce) package cream cheese, softened
¼ cup Parmesan cheese
¼ cup chopped pimento olives
2 teaspoons horseradish
2 cups crushed potato chips or corn chips

Mix all ingredients but chips into ball. Pat on crushed potato or corn chips. Chill for 1 hour. Serve with crackers.

Yield: 8 to 10 servings

Linda Collins Abplanalp (Mrs. Bill)
Burlington

BAKED BRIE

1 (8-ounce) wheel Brie cheese
2 tablespoons butter or margarine, room temperature
¼ cup sliced almonds, optional
French bread or crackers, sliced apples or pears

Preheat oven at 350°. Set Brie in ovenproof serving dish. Spread butter over top. Arrange sliced almonds on butter. Bake until softened and heated through, about 12 to 15 minutes. Serve with warm bread or crackers and fruit.

Yield: 6 to 8 servings

Accent Editor of the Burlington TIMES-NEWS.

Patricia Wallace Sibley (Mrs. Scott)
Burlington

CHEESE STRAWS

½ pound margarine
½ pound extra sharp Cheddar cheese, grated
¼ teaspoon cayenne pepper
½ teaspoon salt
2 cups plain flour, sifted

Cream margarine well and add cheese in small amounts beating well after each addition. Add dry ingredients which have been sifted together. Make into rings, wheels or straws. Bake at 375° for 12 minutes. Watch closely as they burn easily.

Yield: 5 to 6 dozen

This recipe belonged to Mrs. Thad Eure, whose husband was North Carolina Secretary of State from 1936 to 1988!

Eunice Evans Carden
Mebane

OYSTER CRACKER TIDBITS

6 cups oyster crackers
1 envelope buttermilk dressing with herbs (dry)
½ teaspoon dill weed
¼ teaspoon lemon pepper
¼ teaspoon garlic salt
¼ cup cooking oil

Mix dry ingredients together. Stir in crackers. Pour oil over cracker mixture and stir from the bottom. Seal in airtight container. These stay fresh for several weeks.

Yield: 6 cups

Carolyn Neely Eckert (Mrs. Edward F.)
Gibsonville

CHEESE POPS

¼ pound grated sharp cheese
¼ pound softened butter
½ cup flour
¼ teaspoon salt
½ teaspoon paprika
24 small stuffed olives

Blend butter and cheese. Stir in flour, salt and paprika. Place 1 teaspoon dough in your hand and wrap around olive. Bake at 400° for 10 to 15 minutes. Can be frozen after baking.

Yield: 24 appetizers

Linda Collins Abplanalp (Mrs. Bill)
Burlington

HOT SAUSAGE APPETIZERS

1 (8-ounce) package refrigerated butterflake rolls
½ pound hot sausage, crumbled
4 eggs, lightly beaten
2 cups cottage cheese
2 tablespoons chives
Dash of pepper
½ cup grated Parmesan cheese

Generously grease miniature muffin tins. Separate rolls into eight sections. Press each piece between ⅓ and ¼-inch thick and fit into muffin tins. Brown sausage in skillet; drain if needed. Spoon equally into dough cups. Mix eggs, cottage cheese, chives and pepper; stir in cheese. Spoon over sausage and bake at 350° for about 20 minutes until filling is lightly browned.

Yield: 36 to 48 appetizers

Peggy Joyner Sibley (Mrs. S. Dan)
Burlington

KIELBASA DIP

1 (8-ounce) package cream cheese
⅓ cup sour cream
⅓ cup milk
1 tablespoon mayonnaise
1 teaspoon Worcestershire sauce
8 ounces Kielbasa, finely chopped
½ cup sliced green onions
¼ cup grated Parmesan cheese
Vegetables, crackers or party rye can be used for dippers

Soften cream cheese; add milk, sour cream, mayonnaise and Worcestershire sauce. Add Kielbasa, onion and Parmesan. Stir well. Cook in microwave on high 2 minutes. May be served hot or cold.

Yield: 2½ cups

Marian O'Connor Hirsch (Mrs. Raymond K.)
Burlington

COCKTAIL CHICKEN DRUMETTES

12 chicken drumettes

Marinade:
2 tablespoons soy sauce
1 teaspoon brown sugar
1 teaspoon dry sherry

Split skin at bottom of drumettes. Push up until leg bone has no skin or meat on it. Marinate overnight. Drain, flour and fry.

Yield: 12 appetizers

Well worth the effort!

Martha Curtis Hudgins (Mrs. Ed)
Burlington

BRANDIED CHICKEN LIVER PATÉ

½ cup butter
1 pound chicken livers
½ cup sliced onion
1 small bay leaf
½ teaspoon dry mustard
¼ teaspoon curry powder
1 teaspoon salt
¼ cup excellent brandy

Melt butter in skillet. Add chicken livers, onion, bay leaf, mustard, curry and salt. Cover and cook 8 to 10 minutes. Remove bay leaf and add brandy. Cool for 5 minutes. Whirl smooth in food processor or blender. Pack into a buttered crock. Cover and chill several hours or store in freezer. Serve with crackers or toast points.

Yield: 1½ cups

Martha Curtis Hudgins (Mrs. Ed)
Burlington

BACON PINEAPPLE ROLL-UPS

1 (20-ounce) can pineapple tidbits, drained and juice reserved
½ cup brown sugar
1 pound bacon

Mix sugar and juice from pineapple and marinate pineapple 4 to 5 hours. Drain pineapple, reserving juice mixture. Cook bacon until limp and then wrap each tidbit with ½ slice of bacon and secure with a toothpick. Broil until bacon is crisp, turning once. Baste with marinade.

Yield: 40 appetizers

Cindy Browning Kearns (Mrs. Paul)
Burlington

SAUSAGE BACON ROLL-UPS

12 slices lean bacon, halved crosswise
½ pound bulk pork sausage
1 (8-ounce) package cream cheese
12 slices white bread

Cook bacon until transparent. Drain well on paper towels and set aside. Cook sausage over medium heat until browned, stirring to crumble and drain. Combine sausage and cream cheese, stir well and set aside. Trim crust from bread and cut slices in half. Spread cream cheese mixture over bread. Starting with narrow end, roll up each slice of bread, jellyroll fashion. Wrap each with bacon and secure with a toothpick. Place roll-ups on an ungreased baking sheet. Bake at 350° for 15 minutes. Roll-ups may be frozen before adding bacon. Remove from freezer (do not thaw), wrap with bacon and secure with toothpicks. Bake as directed.

Yield: 24 appetizers

Eda Contiguglia Holt (Mrs. Ralph M., Jr.)
Burlington

BACON ROLL-UPS

¼ cup butter or margarine
½ cup water
1½ cups packaged herb-seasoned stuffing
1 egg, slightly beaten
¼ pound hot or mild, bulk pork sausage
½ to ⅔ pound sliced bacon

Melt butter in water in saucepan. Remove from heat; stir into stuffing, then add egg and sausage. Blend thoroughly. Chill for about an hour for easier handling, then shape into small oblongs about the size of pecans. Cut bacon strips into thirds, crosswise; wrap one piece around dressing mixture and secure with wooden pick. Place on rack in shallow pan and bake at 375° for 35 minutes, or until brown and crisp, turning at half-way point in cooking. Drain on paper towels and serve hot. May be made the day before baking; also freezes well before baking.

Yield: 36 appetizers

Peggy Jones McCuiston (Mrs. John)
Burlington

"GOOD MORNING" MUG OF COFFEE

1 rounded teaspoon of American instant coffee
1 level teaspoon of French style instant coffee
Sugar to taste
Milk, if desired
Boiling water

Mix the coffees and sugar in a mug. Pour in boiling water to almost full. Add milk to fill and stir. Serve immediately.

Yield: 1 (8-ounce) mug

This is my favorite "Good Morning" hot beverage; it is also good as an iced brunch or lunch drink. A combination of American and French brands give the exotic flavor in just one brand.

Marion Lea Brown
Burlington

HOT APPLE CINNAMON TEA

½ gallon apple cider
¼ cup unsweetened instant tea mix
2 tablespoons honey
1 teaspoon ground cinnamon

Mix all ingredients. Heat and serve hot.

Yield: 2 quarts

Holly Jill Smith
Delray Beach, Florida

RUSSIAN TEA MIX

1 cup instant orange flavored drink mix
1 large package dry lemonade mix
1½ cups sugar
¾ cup instant tea
½ teaspoon ground cloves
1 teaspoon ground cinnamon

Mix all ingredients well. Use 2 to 3 heaping teaspoons of mix to 1 cup of hot water.

Yield: 3½ cups

Elinor Samons Euliss (Mrs. Wade)
Burlington

SOUTHERN MINT TEA

1 quart boiling water
7 regular size tea bags
2 cups sugar
2 cups fresh mint
1 (6-ounce) frozen orange juice concentrate
1 (7½-ounce) frozen lemon juice

Pour boiling water over tea bags, sugar and fresh mint. Steep 20 minutes. Strain. Add orange juice concentrate, lemon juice and enough water to make 1 gallon. Chill. Pour over crushed ice. Decorate with additional mint.

Yield: 1 gallon

Martha Curtis Hudgins (Mrs. Ed)
Burlington

CHAMPAGNE PUNCH

2 (1 fifth) bottles champagne
2 (48-ounce) bottles of apple cider
2 (12-14 ounce) bottles of white grape juice
2 quarts ginger ale

Chill all ingredients before mixing together. After mixing serve immediately.

Yield: 40 to 60 servings

Patsy Hand Mobley (Mrs. Wayne)
Burlington

GOLDEN PUNCH

2 (46-ounce) cans pineapple juice
1 (46-ounce) can sweetened orange juice
1 (46-ounce) can unsweetened orange juice
1 (6-ounce) can fresh or frozen lemon juice
1 quart water
3 bananas, sliced
2 quarts ginger ale
1 pint lime or pineapple sherbet

Mix juices and water. Chill. When ready to serve, add bananas, ginger ale and sherbet.

Yield: 40 servings

Virginia McPherson Hamby (Mrs. Clayton)
Mebane

CRANBERRY PUNCH

2 quarts cranberry juice
1 (46-ounce) can pineapple juice
2½ cups sugar
2 quarts ginger ale

Bring all ingredients to a boil except ginger ale to dissolve sugar. Cool. Pour into gallon containers and freeze. Partially thaw and add 2 quarts ginger ale.

Yield: 40 to 50 servings

Violet Wagoner Brame
Burlington

FRUIT PUNCH

2 (3-ounce) packages strawberry gelatin
2 cups boiling water
1 cup sugar
6 cups water
2 small cans orange juice
1 small can lemonade
1 (46-ounce) can unsweetened pineapple juice
2 quarts ginger ale

Dissolve gelatin in 2 cups water. Add sugar, 6 cups water and juices. Freeze before adding ginger ale if a slushy punch is preferred; otherwise add ginger ale after mixing.

Yield: 30 servings

Virginia Harvey Sharpe (Mrs. Edwin F.)
Burlington

COFFEE MARSHMALLOW FLOAT

1 cup double strength coffee
1 pound marshmallows, cut in eighths
1 pint heavy cream, chilled
Fresh coffee

Pour 1 cup of hot double strength coffee over marshmallows. Stir until dissolved. Whip cream until stiff and fold into marshmallow mixture. Chill thoroughly or freeze until firm, stirring once. Fill glasses half full—with regular strength, freshly made coffee. Top with marshmallow mixture.

Yield: 10 servings

Marion Lea Brown
Burlington

HOT APPLE-APRICOT CIDER

4 quarts apple juice or cider
1 (46-ounce) can apricot nectar
4 cinnamon sticks
2½ teaspoons whole cloves
2 teaspoons whole allspice
¼ cup brown sugar
1 orange, sliced

Mix juice and nectar. Put spices in cheese cloth bag and add with sugar and orange. Cover and bring to a boil. Reduce heat. Simmer 15 minutes.

Yield: 40 to 50 servings

Edith Ruth Brannock
Elon College

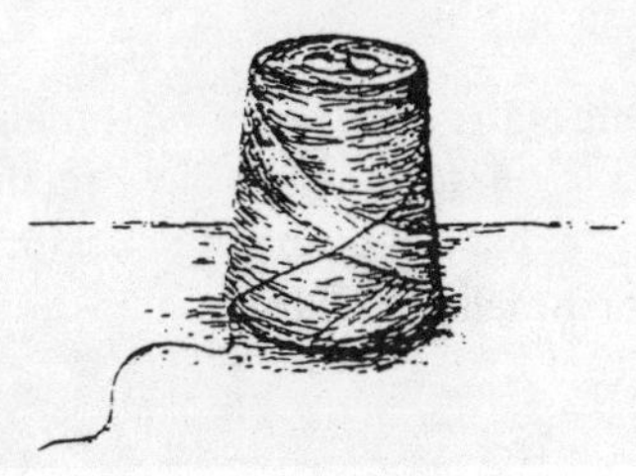

Writing in the 1890s, Thomas Holt described the development of the Alamance Plaids with the following words: "In 1853 there came to our place of business on Alamance Creek a Frenchman, who was a dyer, and who was 'hard-up' and out of money, without friends. He proposed to teach me how to color cotton yarns if I would pay him the sum of one hundred dollars and give him his board. I persuaded my father to allow me to accept the proposition, and immediately went to work."

CONFEDERATE MONUMENT

Graham, N.C.

The Confederate Monument, located on the north side of Courthouse Square, Graham, was erected in May of 1914. It stands on the site of the old Town Scales.

The imposing memorial is 29 feet in height and was carved from Italian marble. The inscription reads: "To commemorate with grateful love, the patriotism, valor and devotion to duty of the brave soldiers of Alamance County, this monument is erected through the efforts of the Graham Chapter of the United Daughters of the Confederacy."

PROCESSOR PITA BREAD

Cook's Secret: Climate affects the consistency of the flour. If dough is heavy to the touch, add a small amount of water (approximately 1 tablespoon). The dough should feel soft and light to the touch.

1 envelope active dry yeast (check date on package)
¾ cup lukewarm water (115°)
1 teaspoon sugar
2 cups all purpose flour *(not sifted)*
½ teaspoon salt

Add sugar to ¾ cup lukewarm water, stir, sprinkle yeast over sugar and water mixture and stir. Set aside until you prepare the flour. Put 2 cups flour and salt in the processor bowl. Start machine and add liquid and beat until it forms a ball. Turn on for 30 seconds more to knead. With flour on hands, take dough out and divide into 7 pieces quickly. Form into smooth balls. On a lightly floured surface, roll each ball into a 5-inch circle. Place on a towel and cover with a towel. Let them rest for 30 minutes to 1 hour or until it almost doubles in size. Place an empty cookie sheet into oven about 7½ inches from broiler. Turn broiler on and heat pan until it is very hot. Transfer dough from towel to hot cookie sheet, making sure opposite side is up. Broil on one side until it is puffed and lightly browned. Turn bread over and brown on other side. Remove from oven. Cool and pack in plastic bags. Freeze bread if keeping more than one day. Heated from freezer to microwave oven takes about 10 to 15 seconds. This recipe may be done by hand.

Yield: 7 pitas

These are good split in half as a minipizza using pizza sauce, Mozzarella cheese and your favorite topping.

Marie Koury (Mrs. Ernest A.)
Elon College

HONEY-BRAN BRAIDS

3 to 4 cups plain white flour
2 cups whole wheat flour
1 cup bran cereal
2 cups milk
2 eggs
2 packets dry yeast
⅓ cup honey
⅓ cup shortening
1 teaspoon salt
1 beaten egg white
2 tablespoons poppy seeds

Preheat oven to 375°. In large mixing bowl, combine 2 cups white flour, yeast, salt. In saucepan, heat milk to 105°. Add shortening, honey, bran cereal. Cool. Add liquid mixture to flour mixture. Mix at low speed until thoroughly combined. Add eggs. Beat at medium speed until smooth. Using dough hooks or by hand, thoroughly mix in whole wheat flour. Add enough white flour to make dough elastic but not sticky. Knead 5 to 6 minutes. Form into ball and grease lightly. Cover and let rise to double. Punch down dough. Divide into 2 equal pieces. Let rest for 5 minutes. Divide each piece into 3 equal portions. On lightly floured surface, roll each portion into 12-inch ropes; braid loosely and transfer to greased cookie sheet. Repeat. Cover and let rise to double. Brush with egg white. Sprinkle with poppy seeds. Bake for 25 to 30 minutes or until golden brown. Cool thoroughly on cooling racks.

Yield: 2 large loaves

Bill Weckerly
Graham

ICE BOX ROLLS I

1 package yeast
1 cup water
1 egg
1 tablespoon salt
¼ cup sugar
⅓ cup shortening
1 cup milk
5 cups flour

Dissolve yeast in water, set aside. Beat egg. Add salt, sugar, melted shortening and milk. Then add yeast and flour. Put in greased bowl. Cover and place in refrigerator. When ready to use, add a little more flour and knead as used. Form into small balls and place in well greased pan. Bake 350° until browned.

Yield: 50 to 60 rolls

Mary Robertson Vaughn (Mrs. Homer)
Graham

ICE BOX ROLLS II

1 cup boiling water
1 cup vegetable shortening
½ cup sugar
1½ teaspoons salt
2 packages yeast
¾ cup warm water
6 cups plain flour, sifted
2 eggs, beaten

Pour boiling water over vegetable shortening, sugar and salt, cool to lukewarm. Dissolve yeast in warm water. Sift flour in a large bowl. Add eggs and all other ingredients and beat well. This will be a thick batter. Place in refrigerator overnight to rise. Add flour and knead well. Roll and cut into desired shapes, brush with melted margarine, let rise until doubled in size. Bake at 400° until golden brown.

Yield: 2 dozen rolls

Nancy Elizabeth (Bettie) Wilson
Burlington

PARMESAN ROLLS

1 package dry yeast
¼ cup warm water
1 cup margarine
3 cups bread flour
2 eggs, slightly beaten
1 cup luke-warm scalded milk
¼ cup sugar
1 teaspoon salt
1½ to 2 cups flour
⅓ cup margarine
3 tablespoons grated Parmesan cheese

Soften yeast in warm water. Cut margarine into flour until particles are size of large peas. Add slightly beaten eggs, scalded milk, sugar and salt. Mix well. Add additional flour to form a stiff dough. Mix well after each addition. Cover and chill 2 to 3 hours. Melt ⅓ cup margarine. Divide dough into 5 parts. Roll out one part on floured surface to a 9 inch circle. Brush with melted margarine; sprinkle with Parmesan cheese. Cut into 8 wedges with pizza cutter. Roll wedge, starting with wide end and rolling to point. Place point-side down on greased baking sheet. Repeat process with remaining parts (or make pinwheel rolls or fan tans). Let rise in warm place 85° until light, about 1 hour. Bake at 375° for 15 to 18 minutes. Dough may be stored in refrigerator up to 4 days and baked as needed.

Yield: 18 to 20 rolls

Donna Thompson Bonds (Mrs. John E.)
Kernersville, North Carolina

REFRIGERATOR BRAN ROLLS

1 cup shortening
¾ cup sugar
1½ teaspoons salt
1 cup wheat bran cereal
2 packages yeast
1 teaspoon sugar
2 eggs well beaten
6 cups flour
2 cups water

Combine in large mixing bowl: 1 cup shortening, ¾ cup sugar and salt. Pour 1 cup boiling water over these, then add cereal. In a separate bowl dissolve yeast in 1 cup luke-warm water and 1 teaspoon sugar. When first mixture is luke-warm add eggs and yeast mix. Add 3 cups flour, beat well, add remaining flour and mix well. Place in large bowl, grease dough with oil, let stand over night. Roll out dough to ¼″ to ½″ thickness. Cut with biscuit cutter, fold in half, dip in butter, place in pan, cover with cloth. Let rise 2 to 3 hours. Bake at 425° for 12 to 15 minutes or until light brown.

Yield: 18 to 20 rolls

Peggy Howe Helms (Mrs. Steve T.)
Burlington

CHEESE-PIMENTO ROLLS

⅓ cup milk
1 package dry yeast
¼ cup warm water
2¼ cups flour, sifted
1 stick softened margarine
1 tablespoon sugar
½ teaspoon salt
1 egg
¼ cup sharp Cheddar cheese, grated
2 tablespoons green pepper, chopped
1 tablespoon pimento, chopped

Scald milk; cool to luke-warm. Sprinkle into warm water in mixer bowl. Stir to dissolve. Add milk, 1¼ cups flour, margarine, sugar, salt and egg, blend at low speed; beat 1 minute at medium speed. Dough will be very soft. Add 1 cup flour, grated cheese, green pepper and pimento, beat 1 minute. Spoon into 12 large greased muffin cups, cover; let rise in warm place away from draft, until double in size, about 1 hour. Bake at 400° for 20 minutes or until golden brown.

Yield: 12 large rolls

Donna Thompson Bonds (Mrs. John E.)
Kernersville, North Carolina

REBECCA ALEXANDER'S OVERNIGHT ROLLS

1 cup margarine, melted
1 cup boiling water
1 cup cold water
½ cup sugar
2 teaspoons salt
2 packages yeast
¼ cup warm water
3 eggs, beaten
6 cups flour

Mix all ingredients except 3 cups of the flour and beat with mixer until well blended. Add remaining flour and stir in with spoon. Place in a covered bowl and refrigerate overnight. When ready to use, roll out on floured board. Cut with biscuit cutter. Place on greased baking pan to rise. Melt extra margarine and brush tops of rolls. Let rise again. Bake at 400° until brown.

Yield: 3 to 4 dozen

Mildred Spoon Alexander (Mrs. Carl B.)
Burlington

CHUNK O'CHEESE BREAD

1¾ cups water
½ cup corn meal
2 teaspoons salt
½ cup molasses
2 tablespoons shortening
1 package yeast
½ cup warm water
4-5 cups plain flour
1 pound Cheddar cheese (cut into ¼″-½″ cubes)

Combine 1¾ cups water, corn meal and salt in 2-quart saucepan. Bring to boil stirring constantly: Cook until slightly thickened. Remove from heat. Add molasses and shortening. Cool to lukewarm. Soften yeast in ½ cup warm water in a large mixing bowl. Add corn meal mixture; blend thoroughly. Add flour gradually to form a stiff dough. Knead on well floured surface until smooth and satiny, about 5 minutes. Place in greased bowl and cover. Let rise in warm place (85°) until double in size 1 to 1½ hours. Line two 8 or 9-inch round pans with 12-inch square of aluminum foil, edges extending over sides; grease well. Place dough on surface, sprinkle with corn meal, work cheese into dough ¼ at a time until cubes are evenly distributed. Divide into two parts. Shape into round loaves, covering cheese cubes. Let rise in warm place until doubled in size, about 1 hour. Bake at 350° for 45 to 55 minutes.

Yield: 10 to 12 servings

Helen Flynn Walton (Mrs. Clarence R.)
Burlington

GINNY'S FAMOUS HOMEMADE BREAD

¾ cup sugar
2 teaspoons salt
⅔ cup vegetable shortening
1 cup cooked potatoes, mashed
2 eggs, beaten
1 package yeast, dissolved in ½ cup warm water
1 cup scalded milk, cooled
5 cups sifted flour (6 if not thick enough)

Mix sugar, salt, shortening with hot mashed potatoes until shortening is melted. Add a little at a time and mix well the eggs, yeast, milk and 1 cup flour, alternately with the liquids until well blended. Add remaining flour. Cover with waxed paper and place in refrigerator, let rise about 2 hours. Take out and divide dough into 4 parts, place in baking pans 8½x4½x2½-inch size, greased and floured. Let these rise 1½ to 2 hours. Bake at 350° for 45 minutes.

Yield: 4 loaves

Peggy Jones McCuiston (Mrs. John)
Burlington

HOT ROLLS OR BUNS

1 cup shortening
4 tablespoons sugar
1 cup water
2 teaspoons salt
2 packages dry yeast
¼ cup warm water
2 eggs, beaten
1 cup milk
5 cups flour
⅓ cup extra flour
1 cup margarine, melted

Heat shortening, sugar, water and salt in a saucepan. Stir until sugar dissolves and shortening melts. Cool. Soften yeast in ¼ cup warm water in large bowl. Add cooled shortening, then eggs and milk. Using mixer, gradually add flour. After four cups, you will have to use a spoon. Turn out and knead adding extra flour. Put in greased bowl, turning once to grease all sides. Cover and let rise 2 hours, until doubled in size. Then turn out on a floured board. Divide into 3 equal parts. Cover and let rise 5 minutes. Form into small balls and place in well greased pans. Cover and let rise 1 hour. Place some melted margarine over each roll when rising and when baked. Bake at 375° 20 to 25 minutes.

Yield: 60 to 80 rolls

Lucy Clapp Wagoner (Mrs. John)
Burlington

CRANBERRY FRUIT AND NUT BREAD

¾ cup butter or margarine, softened
1½ cups sugar
3 eggs
2½ cups all purpose flour
1½ teaspoons baking powder
1½ teaspoons baking soda
1 teaspoon salt
¼ teaspoon nutmeg
1½ cups sour cream
1 teaspoon vanilla extract
¾ cup chopped cranberries
½ cup chopped pecans
½ cup golden raisins
⅓ cup chopped dried apricots
Pecan halves
Whole cranberries
1 cup sifted powdered sugar
1½ to 2 tablespoons milk

Cream butter and gradually add sugar, beating well. Add eggs, one at a time. Beat well after each addition. Combine flour, baking powder, soda, salt and nutmeg. Add to creamed mixture alternately with sour cream. Begin and end with flour mixture. Stir in vanilla. Fold in cranberries, pecans, raisins, and apricots. Pour into 2 greased and floured 8½x4½x3-inch loaf pans. Bake at 350° for 55 to 60 minutes. Cool in pans for about 10 minutes. Remove and cool completely. Use pecan halves and whole cranberries to arrange on top. Combine powdered sugar and milk and drizzle over loaves.

Yield: 2 loaves

Peggy Joyner Sibley (Mrs. S. Dan)
Burlington

POPPY SEED BREAD

½ cup shortening
2 eggs, beaten
1 cup milk
3 cups biscuit mix
2 cups grated Cheddar cheese
2 tablespoons poppy seeds
2 tablespoons dried minced onion

Mix all ingredients together. Grease pan, pour in batter. Bake at 375° for 25 minutes.

Yield: 8 to 10 servings

Cynthia Kuepferle Lindley (Mrs. Tom, Jr.)
Burlington

DATE NUT BREAD

1 cup chopped dates
1½ teaspoons baking soda
½ teaspoon salt
¼ cup shortening
¾ cup boiling water
½ teaspoon vanilla extract
2 eggs
1½ cups plain flour
1 cup sugar
¾ cup chopped nuts

Combine dates, soda, salt in mixing bowl. Add shortening to boiling water. Let stand 15 minutes. Stir to blend. Add vanilla and beaten eggs. Sift flour and sugar together and add to above mixture. Stir in nuts. Bake at 350° for 1 hour in greased 9x5x3-inch loaf pan.

Yield: 1 loaf

Elsie Pentecost Clapp (Mrs. W. Keith)
Saxapahaw

PUMPKIN BREAD

1 cup softened margarine
3 cups sugar
3 eggs
3 cups flour
1 teaspoon baking powder
1 teaspoon baking soda
1 teaspoon salt
1 teaspoon cinnamon
1 teaspoon ground cloves
½ teaspoon ground nutmeg
1 (16-ounce) can pumpkin
1 teaspoon vanilla extract
1 cup raisins
1 cup chopped pecans

Cream margarine; gradually add sugar, beating well. Add eggs, beating after each addition. Combine next 7 ingredients and add to creamed mixture alternately with pumpkin. Stir in vanilla, raisins and pecans. Spoon into 2 greased 9x5-inch loaf pans. Bake at 350° for 1 hour. Cool in pans 10 minutes before removing.

Yield: 2 loaves

David Robert Whitesell
Burlington

SWEET POTATO BREAD

1 teaspoon nutmeg
1 teaspoon cinnamon
1½ teaspoons salt
1 cup vegetable oil
4 eggs
1 cup cooked sweet potato
3 cups self-rising flour
⅔ cup water
2 teaspoons baking soda

Beat together nutmeg, cinnamon, salt, sugar, vegetable oil, and eggs. Add cooked sweet potato, water, soda and flour. Mix well. Fill 3 loaf pans half full or 3 (1-pound) coffee cans, well greased and floured. Bake at 350° for 1 hour. Persimmon or pumpkin may be used instead of sweet potatoes.

Yield: 3 loaves

Clara Smith May (Mrs. Roy E.)
Burlington

ZUCCHINI BREAD

3 eggs
2 cups sugar
1 cup vegetable oil
2 cups grated, peeled, raw zucchini
3 teaspoons vanilla extract
3 cups all purpose flour
¼ teaspoon baking powder
1 teaspoon baking soda
3 teaspoons cinnamon
1 cup chopped nuts

Beat eggs until light and foamy. Add sugar, oil, zucchini and vanilla. Mix lightly but well. Combine flour, salt, soda, baking powder and cinnamon. Add to egg-zucchini mixture. Stir until well blended. Add nuts, pour into 2 loaf pans well greased and floured. Bake at 350° for 1 hour. This freezes very well.

Yield: 2 loaves

Mary Jane McKibbin Lindley (Mrs. W. Clarke)
Burlington

APRICOT-BANANA NUT BREAD

2 cups flour
1½ teaspoons baking powder
½ teaspoon baking soda
¼ teaspoon salt
½ cup raisins
½ cup dried apricots
1 cup mashed banana
2 eggs, beaten
1 cup sugar
½ cup melted margarine
1 teaspoon lemon juice
1½ tablespoons buttermilk
½ cup chopped pecans

Sift dry ingredients. Rinse raisins and apricots and put through a medium blade food chopper. In a mixing bowl, combine bananas, eggs, sugar, butter, lemon juice and buttermilk and beat until smooth. Stir in flour mixture, raisins, apricots and pecans. Pour batter into greased and floured bundt pan. Bake at 350° for 1 hour. Cool. Unmold and sprinkle with a little powdered sugar.

Yield: 12 to 16 servings

Dorothy Ruffin Scott (Mrs. Don E., Jr.)
Burlington

CHERRY BREAD

¼ cup melted shortening
1 cup white sugar
2 eggs
1½ teaspoons baking powder
1½ cups flour
¾ cup chopped nuts
5 ounces maraschino cherries, chopped and undrained

Combine shortening and sugar. Add eggs one at a time and blend. Sift flour and baking powder together; add to mixture. Fold in nuts, cherries and juice. Bake in a greased or waxed paper lined loaf pan at 350° for 40 minutes. Watch: Avoid burning the edges.

Yield: 1 loaf

Catherine Nagel Gilbertson (Mrs. George)
Burlington

VERY SPECIAL CORNBREAD

1 cup plain flour
1 cup self-rising cornmeal
4 teaspoons baking powder
1 teaspoon salt
½ teaspoon garlic powder
2 eggs, beaten
1 cup sweet milk
¼ cup oil
1 cup finely chopped onion
1 small can cream style corn
1 tablespoon hot pepper, finely chopped
2 tablespoons sugar
¼ cup grated cheese

Mix all ingredients together in a mixing bowl, except the cheese. Pour into a greased 13x9x2-inch pan. Sprinkle cheese on top. Bake at 350° about 40 minutes until brown. Cut into squares.

Yield: 8 to 12 servings

Helen Robertson Stewart (Mrs. Buck)
Burlington

SHARON'S CHEDDAR BREAD

3¾ cups plain flour
2½ teaspoons baking powder
½ teaspoon salt
⅓ cup margarine
2½ cups (10-ounces) sharp Cheddar cheese, shredded
1½ cups milk
2 eggs, slightly beaten

Combine flour, baking powder and salt. Cut in margarine until mixture resembles coarse crumbs; stir in cheese. Combine eggs and milk, add to cheese mixture just enough to moisten. Spoon into greased and floured 9x5-inch loaf pan. Bake at 350° for 1 hour. Remove from pan immediately, cool on rack.

Yield: 4 to 6 servings

Edith Ruth Brannock
Elon College

BROCCOLI CORNBREAD

4 eggs, beaten
6 ounces cottage cheese
1 small onion, chopped
1 (8½-ounce) quick cornbread mix
1 (10-ounce) package frozen, chopped broccoli, thawed
1 stick margarine, melted

Combine eggs, cheese and onion, mixing well. Add cornbread mix, but do not over mix. Stir in broccoli and margarine. Pour into a deep dish pie plate or 8x8-inch pan. Bake at 350° for 30 to 40 minutes or until done.

Yield: 6 to 8 servings

Amelia Humphries Muelenaer
Smyrna, Delaware

CRUSTY CORNBREAD

1 cup cornmeal
½ cup plain flour
1 tablespoon baking powder
½ teaspoon soda
½ teaspoon salt
1 egg, beaten
1 cup buttermilk
¼ cup shortening

Combine first 6 ingredients; mix well. Add egg and buttermilk; stir until smooth. Put shortening in an 8-inch cast iron skillet; heat at 425° for 5 minutes. Remove from oven, pour hot shortening into batter; mix well. Quickly pour into skillet. Bake at 425° for 25 minutes or until golden brown.

Yield: 6 servings

Hazel Swanson Roney (Mrs. James A.)
Mebane

CORNBREAD

1 small box corn muffin mix
1 regular size can cream corn
½ pint sour cream
½ cup corn oil
1 teaspoon salt
3 eggs, beaten slightly

Mix all together. Pour into large rectangular greased baking dish (or pan). Bake 375° to 400° for 35 to 45 minutes (depends on oven).

Yield: 12 to 14 servings

Nancy Kernodle Sain (Mrs. Tom)
Burlington

MEXICAN CORNBREAD

1 cup self-rising cornmeal
2 eggs, beaten
1 cup cream style corn
½ cup oil
1 cup sour cream
2 teaspoons crushed red peppers

Combine all ingredients. Mix well. Bake in a greased 9-inch cake pan or a cast iron frying pan at 375° for 1 hour.

Yield: 6 to 8 servings

Norma Robertson Smith (Mrs. Banks)
Burlington

KENTUCKY SPOON BREAD

1½ cups milk
¼ cup cornmeal
1 teaspoon salt
1½ teaspoons baking powder
1½ teaspoons sugar
2 eggs, well beaten

Scald milk. Stir in cornmeal gradually and stir over low heat until thickened. Add salt, baking powder, sugar. Mix well and add gradually to beaten eggs. Pour into greased 1-quart casserole dish. Bake at 375° for 25-30 minutes or until firm.

Yield: 4 servings

Anne Patterson Miller (Mrs. Jesse)
Burlington

SPOON BREAD

¾ cup boiling water
1 cup cornmeal
1 teaspoon salt
1 tablespoon sugar
1 egg beaten
½ teaspoon soda
1 cup buttermilk
1½ tablespoons shortening

Pour boiling water over cornmeal in a bowl; stir, cover and let cool. Mix in salt, sugar and egg. Dissolve soda in buttermilk; beat into the mixture along with shortening. Pour into a greased 11¼x7½-inch baking dish. Bake at 400° for 30 minutes. To serve, "spoon" the bread from the baking pan or bake 5 minutes longer and cut into squares.

Yield: 8 servings

Elizabeth Salmons King
Burlington

SOUTHERN BATTER BREAD

2 cups boiling water
1 cup cornmeal
1 tablespoon butter
1 teaspoon salt
2 cups milk
2 eggs, well beaten
2 teaspoons baking powder

Pour boiling water over cornmeal. Boil 5 minutes, stirring constantly. Remove from heat. Add butter, salt and milk. Mix thoroughly. Add beaten eggs, sift in baking powder. Mix and pour into greased 1-quart size baking dish. Bake at 350° for 30 minutes. Serve from dish in which it is baked.

Yield: 4 to 6 servings

Ann Cates Moore (Mrs. Richard J.)
Burlington

CORNMEAL MUFFINS

¾ cup yellow cornmeal
¾ cup white cornmeal
½ cup all purpose flour
1 teaspoon soda
½ teaspoon baking powder
2 eggs, slightly beaten
2 tablespoons oil
1½ to 1¾ cups buttermilk

Sift first five ingredients together. Stir eggs and oil into mixture. Then add enough buttermilk to make a soft batter. Beat with a big spoon until there are no lumps. Grease a 12-cup size muffin pan. Place pan in hot oven to heat before adding batter. Pour ⅓ cup into each muffin cup. Bake at 475° for 30 minutes or until brown.

Yield: 12 muffins

Virginia May Corbett (Mrs. Clyde E.)
Burlington

APPLE MUFFINS

1½ cups brown sugar, firmly packed
⅔ cup oil
1 egg
1 cup buttermilk
1 teaspoon salt
1 teaspoon soda
1 teaspoon vanilla
2 cups plain flour
1½ cups chopped tart apples
½ cup chopped nuts

Mix sugar, oil and egg. Set aside. Mix buttermilk, salt, soda and vanilla. Stir and mix thoroughly into sugar, egg, oil mixture. Add flour all at once, mixing until there are no dry spots. Fold in apples and nuts. Bake in greased muffin cups at 350° for 30 minutes.

Yield: 18 muffins

Essie Cofield Norwood (Mrs. Ralph)
Burlington

BUTTER PECAN MUFFINS

1½ cups self-rising flour
1 cup chopped pecans
½ cup firmly packed brown sugar
1 egg
¾ cup milk
¼ cup margarine, melted
½ teaspoon vanilla

Combine flour, pecans and brown sugar in mixing bowl. Set aside. In another bowl, beat egg; stir in milk, margarine and vanilla. Add liquid ingredients all at once to flour mixture. Stir only until flour is moistened. Fill greased muffin cups ⅔ full. Bake at 400° about 15 minutes or until golden brown.

Yield: 10 to 12 muffins

Kathleen Johnston Miles
Burlington

ORANGE-CORN MUFFINS

1 cup cornmeal
1 cup sugar
2 cups flour
1 teaspoon soda
½ teaspoon salt
½ cup vegetable oil
2 eggs, beaten
2 tablespoons grated orange rind

Mix all ingredients in a large bowl. Fill greased muffin pans ⅔ full; bake at 375° for 12 minutes. While muffins are still hot, place 1 tablespoon of the following sauce on each muffin:

Sauce:
Juice of 2 oranges
1 cup powdered sugar
Grated rind of 1 orange

Add orange juice gradually to powdered sugar, blending well. Combine with orange rind.

Yield: 10 to 12 muffins

This contributor's recipe was a state winner in the 4-H Club competition.

Linda Rumbley Daniels (Mrs. Eddie, III)
Burlington

ORANGE MUFFINS

1 cup sugar
½ cup margarine
2 eggs
1 teaspoon soda
1 cup buttermilk
2 cups flour
¼ teaspoon salt
1 cup raisins
Rind and juice of 1 orange

Preheat oven to 400°. Cream sugar and margarine. Add eggs and beat until fluffy. Add soda to buttermilk. Sift flour and salt together. Add to the sugar and butter mixture, alternately with buttermilk. Stir until well blended. In a food processor, grind the raisins with the whole orange, after seeds have been removed; add to batter. Fill greased muffin cups ⅔ full. Bake about 12 minutes or until brown. Sprinkle lightly with granulated sugar while warm.

Yield: 1 dozen muffins

Ann Spoon Cooper (Mrs. Collins)
Windsor, North Carolina

OAT BRAN MUFFINS

2 cups oat bran cereal
¼ cup firmly packed brown sugar
2 teaspoons baking powder
½ teaspoon salt, optional
1 cup skim milk
2 egg whites, slightly beaten
¼ cup honey or molasses
2 tablespoons vegetable oil

Combine dry ingredients, add milk, egg whites, honey and oil; mix until dry ingredients are moistened. Fill prepared muffin pan almost full. Bake at 425° 15 to 17 minutes or until golden brown.

Variations: Add raisins, nuts, bananas, blueberries or apples and cinnamon.

Yield: 1 dozen

Elizabeth Hoffman Pleasant (Mrs. Thomas)
Burlington

OAT BRAN MUFFINS

1¼ cups Lindley Mills Oatbran
¼ cup graham flour
2 teaspoons baking powder
¼ cup toasted oats
½ cup toasted sunflower seeds

Options:
½ cup chopped pecans or ½ cup chopped apple with peel
1 teaspoon brown diet sugar substitute
2 teaspoons cinnamon
1 teaspoon nutmeg
1 teaspoon mace
¼ teaspoon salt
2 egg whites beaten, or 1 egg white and 1 egg substitute, beaten with hand beater
1 cup unsweetened applesauce
2 tablespoons vegetable oil
1 teaspoon vanilla extract

Combine all dry ingredients and mix well with a fork. Combine all other ingredients, adding them all at once to dry ingredients, mix just enough to moisten. Set aside while spraying muffin tins with non-stick vegetable spray. Fill tins ⅔ full. Bake at 400° for 20 minutes until muffins leave sides of tins. Do not overcook or these will become too dry. These muffins are best served warm. Reheat before eating.

Yield: 2 dozen muffins

Helen Moseley Gant (Mrs. Cecil, Jr.)
Burlington

PEACHY BRAN MUFFINS

1½ cups peach lowfat yogurt
2 cups whole bran cereal
½ cup raisins
⅓ cup shredded carrots
1 tablespoon brown sugar
¼ cup corn oil
2 egg whites
1 cup self-rising flour
½ teaspoon cinnamon

Combine yogurt and cereal; mix lightly. Add raisins, carrots, sugar, oil and egg whites. Mix well. Combine dry ingredients and add to cereal mixture; stir just until moistened. Spoon into paper lined muffin cups, filling each almost full. Bake at 400° for 18 to 20 minutes or until golden brown.

Yield: 1 dozen

Cleo Rumbley Smith (Mrs. Richard H.)
Burlington

LEMON MUFFINS

1 (18-ounce) box lemon supreme cake mix
1 small package lemon pudding mix, instant
½ cup vegetable oil
4 eggs
1 cup buttermilk

Mix all ingredients in the order given. Pour into greased miniature muffin tins. Bake at 350° for 10 minutes. Dip warm muffins into glaze. Place on rack to drain.

Glaze:
3 tablespoons lemon juice
6 tablespoons orange juice
1½ teaspoons vanilla
3⅓ to 3½ cups powdered sugar, sifted

Mix first three ingredients, add sugar, mix well.

Yield: 80 to 90 muffins

Marilyn Crouse Lanier (Mrs. Thomas)
Burlington

CHEESY MUFFINS

2 cups quick biscuit mix
1 cup sour cream
½ cup melted margarine
½ cup sharp Cheddar cheese (grated)

Mix all ingredients well. Pour into miniature muffin cups sprayed with cooking spray. Bake at 400° for 10 to 15 minutes.

Yield: 3 dozen muffins

Marilyn Crouse Lanier (Mrs. Thomas)
Burlington

MARGARET'S PANCAKE RECIPE

1 cup flour
2 tablespoons sugar
2 tablespoons baking powder
1 cup milk
2 tablespoons vegetable oil
1 egg

Mix dry ingredients together. Mix the liquid ingredients together. Combine. Set aside about five minutes or until baking powder begins "acting." Cook on greased pan or griddle.

Yield: 4 to 6 servings.

Eda Contiguglia Holt (Mrs. Ralph M., Jr.)
Burlington

HAND BISCUITS

3 tablespoons shortening
2 cups self-rising flour
¾ cup buttermilk, approximately

Cut shortening into flour. Add buttermilk slowly, stirring until dough is soft and moist. Knead lightly. Pinch off ball of dough. Pat and flatten in palm of your hand. (May be rolled and cut). Bake at 475° 12 to 15 minutes.

Yield: 6 to 8 servings

Margaret Sharpe Elkins
Burlington

CHEESE BISCUITS

1 cup self-rising flour
3 tablespoons vegetable shortening
½ cup buttermilk
¼ cup grated sharp Cheddar cheese
1 tablespoon sesame seeds

Mix flour and shortening until crumbly. Add buttermilk and cheese. Stir with fork until well mixed. Turn onto floured surface and knead about 10 times. Pat dough ½-inch thick. Cut with biscuit cutter. Top with sesame seeds. Bake at 450° for 10 minutes.

Yield: 6 servings

Vera Whitesell Howard (Mrs. Wade)
Burlington

CLOUD BISCUITS

2 cups unbleached all purpose flour
1 tablespoon sugar
4 teaspoons baking powder
½ cup vegetable shortening
2 egg whites, beaten
⅔ cup (½%) low fat milk

Mix dry ingredients. Cut in shortening until mixture resembles coarse crumbs. Combine egg whites and milk; add to flour mixture, stir until dough follows fork around bowl. Turn out on lightly floured surface. Knead gently with heel of hand, about 20 strokes. Roll dough ½ inch thickness. Cut with 2-inch biscuit cutter that has been dipped in flour. Bake on ungreased baking sheet at 450° for 10 to 14 minutes.

Yield: 8 to 10 servings

(Low Sodium–low cholesterol). This recipe has been used for 25 years.

Margaret Long Beatty (Mrs. Hayden)
Burlington

MY BISCUITS

2 cups self-rising flour
½ cup butter (no substitute)
½-¾ cup buttermilk

Combine flour and butter with a pastry blender. The mixture should be pebbly in appearance. Moisten with buttermilk. Turn out on floured surface and knead until dough can be cut without sticking. Add flour as needed. Roll and cut biscuits. Bake on well greased cookie sheet at 425° for 8 to 10 minutes or until golden brown.

Yield: 8 to 10 servings

My father-in-law, Dr. T. E. Powell, Jr., always enjoyed these, and they were tops with my daddy, too!

Jacqueline Garrison Powell (Mrs. William C.)
Burlington

BAKED GRITS

4 cups water
1 cup grits
2 teaspoons salt
4 eggs
1 cup milk
¼ cup margarine
1 tablespoon Worcestershire sauce
½ cup grated cheese (reserve ¼ cup for topping)

Mix water, grits and salt in a saucepan and cook until thick. Add the remaining ingredients, stirring until margarine is melted. Pour into large 9x13-inch baking dish. Sprinkle remaining cheese on top. Bake at 350° for 45 minutes.

Yield: 6 to 8 servings

Helen Rumley Cleek (Mrs. Robert A.)
Elon College

GRITS BREAD

1 quart milk
1 teaspoon salt
1 cup grits, regular cooking
½ stick butter
4 eggs, well beaten

Bring milk and salt almost to a boil. Add grits and cook 20 minutes or until thick. Remove from heat and add butter. Beat occasionally until cool. Add eggs to cooled grits and pour into a buttered baking dish. Bake at 350° for 40 to 50 minutes. This recipe is easily halved.

Yield: 4 to 6 servings

Wilma Howell Suddath
Burlington

BAKED OATMEAL

2 cups milk
1 tablespoon butter
1 cup oatmeal
½ cup chopped apples
3 tablespoons brown sugar
¼ teaspoon salt
¼ teaspoon cinnamon, optional

Scald milk, add butter and stir to melt. Add other ingredients and mix well. Pour into a greased 1½-quart casserole and bake at 350° for 20 minutes.

Yield: 4 to 6 servings

A good, nourishing winter breakfast.

Wilma Howell Suddath
Burlington

The initial equipment used by the Holts to dye the early Alamance Plaids was relatively primitive. Thomas Holt stated: "We used such appliances as we could scrape up. These were an eighty-gallon copper boiler which my grandfather used for killing hogs and a large cast iron washpot which happened to be in my father's store at the time. With these implements I learned my A, B, C's in dyeing."

CROSS ROADS PRESBYTERIAN CHURCH

Highway 119 North

Organized in 1783, Cross Roads Presbyterian Church is linked to the early history of Presbyterianism in North Carolina. The church is known as the birthplace of "The Great Awakening", an evangelical movement which swept North Carolina in the early 1800s. Located on a portion of the old Murray Plantation, the church and its surrounding community received national attention in 1975 through its association with Alex Haley's *Roots* saga.

The present church was constructed in 1876, and is listed in the National Register of Historic Places. The church and its parishioners continue the tradition of "Homecomings" and "dinners on the grounds" where superb regional cooking can still be sampled.

HEARTY BEEF VEGETABLE SOUP

1 pound ground beef, cooked, drained and crumbled
3 (13¾-ounce) cans beef broth
1 (14½-ounce) can stewed tomatoes, chopped
1 (10-ounce) package frozen peas and carrots
1 cup uncooked medium egg noodles or other pasta
1 (3-ounce) can sliced mushrooms
½ cup chopped onions
3 tablespoons steak sauce
¼ teaspoon oregano
Salt to taste
Pepper to taste

In large saucepan, combine all ingredients. Bring to boil then reduce heat. Cover and simmer 15 minutes or until noodles and vegetables are tender. Skim fat, if desired. Serve with French bread.

Yield: 10 servings

Frances Lee Gillespie (Mrs. James W.)
Burlington

SENATE BEAN SOUP

2 pounds small Navy beans, washed clean
4 quarts hot water
1½ pounds smoked ham hocks
1 onion, chopped
Butter
Salt
Pepper

In large saucepan combine water, beans, ham hocks and boil slowly for approximately 3 hours. Sauté onion in butter and when light brown, add to soup. Season with pepper, then serve. Do not add salt until ready to serve.

Yield: 8 servings

"In the 1950's I visited my brother Kerr Scott, in Washington, D.C. where he was in the United States Senate. He took his wife, Mary, and me to the Senate Dining Room for lunch, where I had Senate Bean Soup. It was so good that I've made it often since then."

Elizabeth Scott Carrington
Burlington

CREAMED BROCCOLI SOUP

4 (10-ounce) packages frozen broccoli
2 stalks celery, sliced thin
1 large onion, sliced
4 cups boiling chicken stock
Pinch of ground cloves
Salt to taste
Pepper to taste
Lemon juice to taste
TABASCO pepper sauce
1½ to 2 cups half and half

Combine broccoli, celery, onion, and chicken stock in a saucepan. Simmer 15 minutes. Purée in blender. Add next 5 ingredients. Thin soup with half and half to desired consistency. Reheat gently. Do not allow to boil.

Yield: 6 to 8 servings

For a tasty but extra rich soup, add 1½ cups ale (strong beer), opened in advance in order to go flat; 1 cup grated Cheddar cheese.

Sandra Elder Harper
Burlington

ZUCCHINI SOUP

1 pound zucchini
2 tablespoons finely chopped onion
1 garlic clove, minced
2 tablespoons butter or margarine
½ cup half and half or canned milk
1¾ cups chicken broth (1 can)
1 teaspoon curry
½ teaspoon salt

Clean and slice zucchini. Sauté zucchini, onion and garlic in butter. Cover and simmer lightly—approximately 10 minutes. Purée in blender, then combine with liquids and seasonings. Serve hot or chilled.

Yield: 2 to 3 servings

Ella Anthony George
Chapel Hill, North Carolina

MULLIGATAWNY SOUP

4-5 pound roasting chicken
1/3 cup flour
1/3 cup butter
1½ cups chopped onion
2 cups chopped carrots
2 cups chopped celery
1½ cups peeled tart apples, chopped
1½ tablespoons curry powder
4 teaspoons salt
¾ teaspoon mace
½ teaspoon pepper
¼ teaspoon chili powder
¾ cup frozen coconut
1 cup apple juice
1 cup cream

Roll chicken in flour and brown in hot butter. Remove chicken and set aside. Add onion, carrots, celery, apples and any remaining flour to kettle. Cook while stirring for 5 minutes. Add curry, salt, mace, pepper, chili powder, coconut, chicken and 6 cups of cold water. Bring to boil. Reduce heat and simmer covered for 2 hours. Remove from heat. Skim top. Remove skin and bones from chicken. Cut chicken into large pieces. Return to pot. Add apple juice and cream. Reheat. Serve over rice.

Yield: 10 servings

Nancy Norton Holt
Burlington

APPLE SOUP

6 tablespoons unsalted butter
3 large Red Delicious apples, peeled, cored, sliced
3 large Granny Smith apples, peeled, cored, sliced
1 cup chopped onions
1 tablespoon minced garlic
5 cups chicken broth
1½ cups whipping cream
Salt to taste
Pepper to taste

Melt butter and add apples, onion and garlic and cook 5 minutes, stirring occasionally. Add broth and simmer until apples are tender or about 25 minutes. Purée mixture, small amounts at a time, in processor. Return to pan, add cream, salt and pepper. Bring to simmer. Top each serving with unpeeled 2 red and green apple slices.

Yield: 6 servings

Courtesy of Lords Proprietors' Inn
Edenton, North Carolina

CARROT/GINGER SOUP

6 tablespoons butter
1 onion, chopped
⅓ cup fresh ginger root, chopped
4 cloves garlic, minced
7 cups chicken stock
1 cup white wine
1½ lbs. carrots (about 4 bunches) peeled and cut in ½″ pieces
2 tablespoons fresh lemon juice
Pinch curry powder

Melt butter, add onion, ginger and garlic. Cook 15 to 20 minutes over low heat until tender. Add chicken stock, wine, carrots, lemon juice and curry powder. Simmer 45 minutes. Purée in food processor. Serve hot or cold. (Freezes well.)

Yield: 8 servings

Pamela Anne Morrison
New York, New York

CHEESE SOUP

3 tablespoons butter
1¾ cups shredded carrots
1 cup chopped celery
¼ cup sliced onion
2 (10¾-ounce) cream of potato soup
1 (14½-ounce) can chicken broth
2 tablespoons parsley flakes
2 cups grated Cheddar cheese
1 (13-ounce) can evaporated milk
3 tablespoons sherry, optional

Melt butter in large saucepan, then sauté celery, carrots and onion until tender. Add cream of potato soup, chicken broth and parsley. Cook and stir until boiling. Reduce heat. Cover and simmer 25 minutes, stirring occasionally. Stir in cheese, milk. Add sherry, if desired. Heat thoroughly and serve.

Yield: 6 servings

Excellent for freezing. Pita bread sandwiches are a great compliment if serving a big crowd.

Mary Jane McKibbin Lindley (Mrs. W. Clarke)
Burlington

CRAB SOUP

2 cups chicken broth
1½ cups crab meat
½ cup soft breadcrumbs
1 tablespoon diced onion
Parsley to taste
2 cups half and half
Salt
Pepper
Nutmeg
2 tablespoons butter
2 tablespoons flour
3 tablespoons sherry

To the chicken broth add crab meat, crumbs, onion and parsley. Simmer 20 minutes. Stir in half and half. Simmer 15 minutes. Purée and season to taste. Make a paste of butter and flour and stir into broth to make thick, then stir in sherry.

Yield: 4 to 6 servings

Elizabeth Hampton Lasley (Mrs. Jim)
Burlington

SPEEDY CLAM CHOWDER

4 slices bacon
¼ cup chopped onion
1 (10¾-ounce) can condensed cream of potato soup
1 (7½-ounce) can minced clams
½ cup milk
Paprika

In a saucepan cook 4 slices bacon until crisp. Drain, reserving 2 tablespoons drippings. Crumble bacon and set aside. Cook chopped onion in reserved drippings until tender. Stir in soup, clams and milk. Simmer, uncovered 5 minutes; stir occasionally. Stir in bacon and sprinkle with paprika.

Yield: 3 servings

Norma Campbell Moore (Mrs. Vernon)
Burlington

POTATO ASPARAGUS SOUP

1 (10½-ounce) can cut asparagus spears
⅓ cup chopped onion
1 tablespoon margarine
1 cup water
1 chicken-flavored bouillon cube
¾ cup mashed potato flakes
1 cup half and half or evaporated milk
1 teaspoon chopped fresh dill or
¼ teaspoon dill weed
Dash pepper

Drain asparagus, reserving liquid. In medium saucepan, sauté onion in margarine until tender. Stir in reserved asparagus liquid, water and bouillon cube. Bring to a boil. Reduce heat; simmer uncovered 5 minutes. Remove from heat and stir in potato flakes until blended. Add half and half, dill and pepper. Return to heat. Heat gently, stirring frequently; do not boil. Garnish with additional fresh dill, if desired.

Yield: 3 servings

Grace Anderson Thompson (Mrs. A. G., Jr.)
Burlington

HAMBURGER SOUP

2 pounds ground beef
1 onion, chopped
1 (28-ounce) can tomatoes or
2 (15-ounce) cans tomatoes or
1 (15-ounce) can tomato sauce
1 (16-ounce) can cut green beans
1 (16-ounce) can shoe peg corn
1 (16-ounce) can small green butter beans
1 (16-ounce) can diced carrots
1 (16-ounce) can small green peas
1 envelope beef stew seasoning mix

Cook ground beef and onion slowly until beef is done. Drain all fat. Put in large soup pot. Pour all the vegetables and their juices into the soup pot. Stir in the envelope of seasoning mix. Bring to a boil, then turn down and simmer about 2 hours. Do not add any salt to this recipe. Freezes well.

Yield: 5 quarts

Virginia Harvey Sharpe (Mrs. Edwin F.)
Burlington

GAZPACHO

1 (10¾-ounce) can tomato soup, undiluted
1½ cups vegetable cocktail juice or tomato juice
1¼ cups water
½ to 1 cup chopped cucumber
½ to 1 cup chopped tomatoes
½ cup chopped green pepper
½ cup chopped purple onion
2 tablespoons olive oil
2 tablespoons wine vinegar
1 tablespoon commercial Italian dressing
1 tablespoon lemon or lime juice
1 clove garlic, minced
¼ teaspoon salt
¼ teaspoon pepper
¼ teaspoon TABASCO pepper sauce
⅛ teaspoon garlic salt
Dash of Worcestershire sauce
Cucumber slices, optional

Combine all ingredients except cucumber slices in a large bowl; chill at least 6 hours. Mix well before serving. Garnish each serving with cucumber slices, if desired. This is wonderful to serve before a grilled dinner on a hot summer evening.

Yield: 6 servings

Patricia Wallace Sibley (Mrs. Scott)
Burlington

SOUP BOWL SUPPER

2 tablespoons chopped onion
1 tablespoon margarine
1 (10½-ounce) can condensed chicken soup
½ soup can of milk
½ soup can of water
1 cup cubed cooked chicken
½ cup cooked whole kernel corn

Cook onion in margarine until tender. Add remaining ingredients. Heat, stirring often.

Yield: 3 to 4 servings

Holly Jill Smith
Delray Beach, Florida

CHICKEN OKRA SOUP

1 chicken broiler or pieces
2 quarts water
1 teaspoon salt
½ teaspoon pepper
½ teaspoon basil
1 cup chopped celery
½ cup chopped onion
1 (20-ounce) package frozen okra

Place chicken in large 6-quart container. Add water, salt, pepper and basil. Boil slowly until chicken is tender and can be removed from bone. Cut chicken into bite-sized pieces. Cool broth and skim off fat. Add celery and onion to broth and simmer 30 minutes. Add chicken and okra and simmer an additional 15 minutes. Serve immediately.

Yield: 12 servings

Maxine Haith O'Kelley (Mrs. Jack)
Burlington

JARLSBERG VEGETABLE BISQUE

3 tablespoons butter
3 tablespoons flour
4 cups chicken broth
2 cups broccoli, coarsely chopped
¾ cup carrots, chopped
½ cup celery, chopped
1 small onion, chopped
1 small clove garlic, minced
¼ teaspoon thyme, crushed
½ teaspoon salt
⅛ teaspoon pepper
1 cup heavy cream
1 egg yolk
1½ cups Jarlsberg cheese, shredded

In large heavy saucepan, melt butter. Add flour and cook several minutes, stirring well. Remove from heat. Gradually blend in broth. Bring to a boil, stirring well. Add vegetables and seasonings. Cover and simmer 8 minutes until vegetables are tender. Blend cream and egg and gradually blend in several tablespoons soup. Return to soup and cook while stirring, until thickened. Blend in cheese.

Yield: 6 to 8 servings

Rena Lowe Murchison (Mrs. Lynn)
Burlington

HELEN'S BUTTERNUT SQUASH AND APPLE SOUP

1 small butternut squash, peeled and seeded
3 tart green apples, peeled and chopped
1 medium onion, coarsely chopped
¼ teaspoon marjoram
3 (14½-ounce) cans chicken broth
2 cans water
2 slices white bread, cubed
Salt to taste
Pepper to taste
¼ cup heavy cream
2 tablespoons chopped fresh parsley

Combine all ingredients in a large, heavy saucepan. Bring to a boil, then simmer uncovered 45 minutes. Purée mixture in blender ¼ full several times until all is finished. Return mixture to pan, bring to a boil then reduce heat. Before serving, add heavy cream. Sprinkle with parsley on top. Serve hot.

Yield: 6 servings

Madge O'Kelly Brannock
Elon College

PICNIC NOODLE SALAD

1 tablespoon salt
3 quarts boiling water
1 (8-ounce) package medium egg noodles
1½ cups mayonnaise
1 teaspoon caraway seeds
⅛ teaspoon pepper
1 (16-ounce) canned ham, cubed
8 ounces Swiss cheese
½ cup pimento stuffed olives, sliced
½ cup celery, chopped

Add salt to boiling water. Add noodles gradually so that water continues to boil. Cook until tender. Drain. Rinse with cold water and drain again. Combine the remaining ingredients in a large bowl and toss well. Chill.

Yield: 6 to 8 servings

Linda O'Briant Dodson (Mrs. Don)
Gibsonville, North Carolina

MACARONI SALAD

1 pound shell macaroni
1 large green pepper, chopped
1 large onion, chopped
4 carrots, shredded
1 can sweetened, condensed milk
1 cup vinegar
2 cups mayonnaise

Mix all ingredients and refrigerate overnight. If desired, any kind of meat can be added.

Yield: 8 to 10 servings

Lucy Clapp Wagoner (Mrs. John)
Burlington

SHELL MACARONI SALAD

1 small package shell macaroni; cooked and drained
½ cup diced celery
½ green pepper, diced
3 eggs, boiled and diced (optional)
3 tablespoons salad cubes, sweet or sour
1 small can shrimp, drained
½ cup mayonnaise
1 teaspoon prepared mustard
1 teaspoon commercial herb seasoning mix

Mix first 6 ingredients and toss with mayonnaise, mustard and herbs. Refrigerate. More mayonnaise may be added to allow a more moist salad.

Yield: 4 to 6 servings

Francine Holt Swaim (Mrs. D. Cletus)
Liberty, North Carolina

MACARONI SALAD

1 (7-ounce) box macaroni
1 (4-ounce) can diced pimento
1 small green pepper, diced
4 cooked eggs, diced
1 medium onion, diced
½ cup celery, diced
5 tablespoons mayonnaise

Cook macaroni by package directions. Add other ingredients and mix lightly. Serve warm or chilled.

Yield: 6 servings

NOTE: Cubed ham, chicken, turkey or tuna may be added, if desired.

Linda O'Briant Dodson (Mrs. Don)
Gibsonville, North Carolina

BAKED SEAFOOD SALAD

1 cup cooked, cleaned shrimp, split lenghwise
1 cup fresh crabmeat
½ cup green pepper, chopped or 1 small mild banana pepper, chopped
¼ cup white onion, minced
1 cup celery, sliced
1 cup mayonnaise
1 teaspoon Worcestershire sauce
½ teaspoon salt
¼ teaspoon pepper
½ cup fresh breadcrumbs
¼ cup melted butter

Preheat oven to 350°. Mix shrimp and crabmeat. Add remaining ingredients except breadcrumbs and butter. Mix well and spread into a 10x6x2-inch casserole. Toss breadcrumbs with butter and sprinkle over salad. Bake 30 minutes or until brown. Serve with parsley and lemon quarters. Can be made ahead and refrigerated. Also, this recipe can be doubled and by adding bay scallops or lobster makes an elegant dish.

Yield: 4 servings

Betsy Liles Gant (Mrs. Edmund R.)
Burlington

ORANGE CHICKEN SALAD IN THE SHELL

8 large oranges
2 cups cooked, diced chicken
1 cup diced celery
2 tablespoons chopped green pepper
1 tablespoon chopped pimento
¾ cup mayonnaise
Dash salt
Dash seasoned pepper

Slice tops from oranges and carefully remove orange meat leaving shells intact (scallop edges if desired). Cut orange meat into bite-sized pieces. Combine 2 cups orange pieces with chicken, celery, green pepper and pimento. Add mayonnaise; toss. Season with salt and pepper. Spoon into orange shells.

Yield: 8 servings

Nancy Matthews Slott (Mrs. Steven D.)
Burlington

MAIN DISH SALAD

2 cups broccoli
1 cup cauliflower
½ cup celery, chopped
½ cup green pepper, chopped
2 cups chicken, cooked and chopped
Low Cal Italian dressing
Optional:
Sweet or green onions
Tomatoes
Cucumbers
2 cups crabmeat

Coarsely chop any combination of the ingredients and toss with your favorite dressing. Combining mayonnaise and dressing is a nice difference! Nice as a vegetable salad omitting the meat.

Yield: 6 servings

Lorene Turner Lyon (Mrs. James W.)
Burlington

ASPARAGUS SALAD

2 packages plain gelatin
½ cup cold water
1 cup cold water
½ cup white vinegar
¾ cup sugar
½ teaspoon salt
1 small can asparagus
1 small jar pimentos, chopped
½ cup pecans, chopped
1 cup chopped celery

Dissolve gelatin in ½ cup water. Add 1 cup water, vinegar, sugar, salt. Heat to boiling. Cool until partially set. Add remaining ingredients. Pour into 5-cup mold. Chill until set.

Yield: 6 to 8 servings

June Moore Bulla (Mrs. Ben F.)
Saxapahaw

ARTICHOKE ALMOND SALAD

1 can artichoke hearts
3 scallions, chopped
4 cups salad greens
½ cup chopped, salted almonds

Quarter artichoke hearts. Use some green tops of scallions. Mix salad ingredients and toss with dressing at last minute before serving.

Dressing:
½ cup salad oil
¼ teaspoon dry mustard
⅛ teaspoon pepper
¼ cup red wine vinegar
¼ teaspoon salt
Pinch sugar

Mix all ingredients together and blend until dissolved.

Yield: 6 servings

Nancy Norton Holt
Burlington

BEAN AND PEA SALAD

1 (16-ounce) can French style green beans, drained
1 (16-ounce) can Kidney beans, drained and rinsed
1 (16-ounce) can green peas, drained
1 small jar red pimentos
1 onion, sliced and separated into rings
1 cup chopped celery
½ cup vegetable oil
½ cup sugar
1 cup white vinegar

Place all vegetables in medium sized bowl. Dissolve sugar and vinegar over low heat in small pan. Pour vinegar mixture and oil onto vegetables. Refrigerate 24 hours.

Yield: 8 to 10 servings

Ruth Roarick Love (Mrs. James)
Burlington

MOTHER'S MARINATED SLAW

1 large head cabbage, coarsely chopped
1 onion, chopped
1 green pepper, chopped
¾ cup sugar
Cracked pepper
½ cup oil
1 cup white vinegar
1 teaspoon dry mustard
1 teaspoon celery seeds
1 teaspoon salt, optional

Place cabbage, onion and pepper in a large bowl. Mix well. Sprinkle sugar over top. Do not stir. Add lots of cracked pepper on top. Set aside. Bring to boil remaining ingredients. Pour over cabbage mixture. DO NOT STIR! Refrigerate 6 hours or overnight.

Yield: 8 to 10 servings

Great for tailgate picnics, chicken and hamburgers—brings back fun family memories.

Mary McKibbin Lindley (Mrs. W. Clarke)
Burlington

CAULIFLOWER SALAD

1 head cauliflower, sliced thinly
1 head lettuce, torn
1 cup onion, sliced thinly
1 pound bacon, fried crisp and broken
1 (10-ounce) package frozen English peas, cooked
5 ounce can grated Parmesan cheese

Layer ingredients in order and refrigerate overnight. When ready to serve, toss with creamy Italian dressing.

Yield: 12 to 14 servings

Daisie Holt Schwartz
Paris, Texas

EMERALD SALAD

¾ cup boiling water
1 small package lime gelatin
¾ cup cucumber, cubed
2 teaspoons grated onion
1 cup cottage cheese
1 cup mayonnaise
⅓ cup almonds

Dissolve gelatin in boiling water. Cool. Add remaining ingredients. Pour into 5 or 6-cup mold. Chill until set.

Yield: 4 to 6 servings

Virginia Harvey Sharpe (Mrs. Edwin F.)
Burlington

SANDY'S CUCUMBER SALAD

3-4 cucumbers
½ cup sour cream
2 tablespoons lemon juice
½ teaspoon salt
½ teaspoon sugar
Dash cayenne pepper

Peel cucumbers and cut into paper thin slices. Combine other ingredients then fold in cucumbers and refrigerate several hours or overnight.

Yield: 4 to 6 servings

Ann Birmingham Flagg (Mrs. Raymond)
Burlington

DILL PICKLE SALAD

1½ tablespoons plain gelatin
1 cup cold water
1 cup sugar
¼ cup lemon juice
¼ cup dill juice
¼ cup pineapple juice
¼ cup pimento juice
½ cup pimentos, chopped
2 dill pickles, cubed
¼ cup dill juice
1 cup pecans

Dissolve gelatin in water. Bring sugar and juice to boil. Pour over gelatin. Cool and add remaining ingredients. Chill.

Yield: 8 servings

Foy Elder Lane (Mrs. V. Wilton)
Burlington

SPINACH SALAD

2 quarts spinach, washed and broken into pieces
4 slices bacon, fried crisp and crumbled, reserve grease
2 eggs, boiled and chopped
2 teaspoons vinegar
1 tablespoon sugar
2 tablespoons water
½ teaspoon salt

Place spinach in a large heat proof bowl. Bring vinegar, sugar, water, salt and reserved bacon grease to a boil. Pour over spinach and eggs and mix. Sprinkle bacon on top.

Yield: 4 to 6 servings

Annie Patton Young
Mebane

PEANUT BROCCOLI SALAD

3 cups broccoli, chopped
2 boiled eggs, chopped
½ cup sweet pickle relish
½ cup mayonnaise
1 cup dry roasted peanuts
1 medium onion, chopped

Combine all ingredients except peanuts and onion, which are added just before serving. This is better made night before serving.

Yield: 6 servings

Hazel Bray Burleson (Mrs. P. K.)
Burlington

MRS. DULL'S TOMATO ASPIC

2 tablespoons plain gelatin
¼ cup water
2 cups cocktail vegetable juice
2 tablespoons grated onion
2 tablespoons chili sauce
1 teaspoon salt
⅛ teaspoon pepper

Dissolve gelatin in water. Pour remaining ingredients in blender and add gelatin last. Put in 4-cup dish and chill. Aspic fillers can be added as desired:

Chopped celery
Artichoke hearts
Shrimp
Water chestnuts
Avocados

Serve with homemade mayonnaise.

Yield: 4 servings

Sara Jo Barnett Blair (Mrs. Walker)
Burlington

TOMATO ASPIC

3½ tablespoons plain gelatin
3 cups tomato juice
1 cup consommé
¼ cup sugar
½ teaspoon salt
3 tablespoons apple cider vinegar

Sprinkle gelatin on 1 cup cold tomato juice. Heat remaining juice and ingredients; pour onto the gelatin. Stir to dissolve. Pour into a large mold or 6 to 8 small molds. Chill until set.

Yield: 6 to 8 servings

Bettie Kendrick Gant (Mrs. Kenneth)
Burlington

VEGETABLE SALAD

4 medium cooked potatoes, diced
3 or 4 cooked carrots, diced
2 small packages frozen sugar peas
1 large tomato
2 stalks celery
1 small head lettuce
2 cups shredded cabbage
½ cucumber, cut fine
½ green pepper, cut fine
1 onion, cut fine

Mix all ingredients for salad.

Dressing:
1 teaspoon sugar
1 teaspoon mustard
¼ cup mayonnaise, or more
2 tablespoons vinegar
3 tablespoons oil

In separate bowl, mix dressing ingredients, adding more mayonnaise if necessary to obtain a good consistency. Pour over vegetables when ready to serve. Serve on lettuce leaf.

Yield: 16 servings

Blanche Stafford Blackwelder (Mrs. Clyde W.)
Burlington

VEGETABLE SALAD WITH FRUIT

2 stems broccoli, broken
1 head cauliflower, broken
1 cup raisins
1 cup grapes, sliced in half and seeded
1 large apple, diced
8 slices bacon, cooked and crumbled
1 cup nuts, chopped
1 large onion, diced
2 tablespoons vinegar
1 cup mayonnaise
¼ cup Durkee sauce
Sugar, if desired

Mix all ingredients together and chill several hours.

Yield: 8 to 10 servings

Dell Rose Bright (Mrs. Lewis)
Burlington

CITRUS SALAD

3 envelopes plain gelatin
1 cup cold water
1 cup boiling water
1 cup sugar
Grated rind of one lemon
3 grapefruits, peeled, sectioned, drained
3 oranges, peeled, sectioned, drained
1 large can crushed pineapple, drained
Juice of 3 lemons
1 teaspoon salt
Dash cayenne

Soak gelatin in cold water. Add boiling water to dissolve. Add sugar and mix well. Add lemon rind, fruit sections and lemon juice. Pour into individual molds and refrigerate until set.

Yield: 10 servings

Barbara May McNeeley (Mrs. C. C., Jr.)
Burlington

GINGER ALE GRAPEFRUIT SALAD

1 small package lemon gelatin
½ cup boiling water
¼ cup sugar
1 cup ginger ale
½ cup grapefruit juice
2 cups grapefruit sections, fresh or canned
8 maraschino cherries
Mayonnaise

Dissolve gelatin in water. Add sugar and stir until dissolved. Cool. Add ginger ale and grapefruit juice. Mix well and chill until partially set. Pour into 5-cup mold and add grapefruit. Chill until firm. Garnish with cherries and mayonnaise.

Yield: 6 to 8 servings

Patricia Allebach Donnell (Mrs. Raymond D.)
Burlington

CRANBERRY SALAD

1 quart cranberries
2 cups sugar
3 tablespoons plain gelatin
1 cup cold water
Dash of salt
1½ cups diced celery
1 cup chopped nuts
Mayonnaise

Wash cranberries. In medium saucepan, place cranberries with just enough water to cover. Cook until tender. Add sugar. Cook five minutes. Soften gelatin in cold water. Add gelatin and salt to cranberries and stir until dissolved. Chill until partially set. Add celery and nuts. Mix well. Pour into large mold and chill until set. Serve with mayonnaise.

Yield: 8 to 10 servings

Patricia Allebach Donnell (Mrs. Raymond D.)
Burlington

BING CHERRY SALAD

¼ cup boiling water
1 envelope plain gelatin
1 (3-ounce) package black cherry gelatin
2 (18-ounce) cans Bing cherries, drained and juice reserved
1 cup pecans, broken
¼ cup sherry

Dissolve water and plain gelatin. Dissolve black cherry gelatin in boiling cherry juice, adding water to make two cups. Mix both gelatins and add cherries, pecans and sherry. Chill in individual molds or square dish.

Yield: 8 servings

Mrs. James is the great, great granddaughter of Edwin Michael Holt.

Dolores Cheatham James (Mrs. Harry C.)
Burlington

CINNAMON APPLE SALAD

2 cups sugar
½ cup water
1 cup red cinnamon candies
Few drops red food coloring
10-12 firm apples (York, Winesap, Red Delicious) peeled and cored
8 ounces cream cheese, softened
Small amount mayonnaise
Pecan halves

Set electric fry pan at 250°. Make a syrup by combining sugar, water, cinnamon candies, color and cook until dissolved and smooth. Place prepared apples in syrup and cook until transparent—test with fork. Do not cover pan or cook too fast—apples will cook to pieces. Watch constantly while spooning hot syrup over apples and turning over when each side is done—this takes a long time. Remove from pan and chill. Serve on lettuce with a small amount of cheese and pecan in center of each apple.

Yield: 10 to 12 servings

Pretty on the table at Christmas—a tradition in our family.

Lottie Sue Fesperman Arthur (Mrs. Bob)
Burlington

WHITE SALAD

4 egg yolks beaten and slightly sweetened
1 cup milk
1 teaspoon plain gelatin
Water
1 pint cream, whipped
1 (27-ounce) can pineapple chunks
1 (27-ounce) can white cherries, seeded and halved
¾ pound marshmallows, cut in quarters
Juice of 1 lemon
8 ounces blanched almonds, chopped

Mix eggs with milk and scald in a double boiler. Soak gelatin in water to moisten and add to mixture. Fold in cream and remaining ingredients. Chill for 24 hours. Garnish with lettuce.

Yield: 20 servings

Julia Atwater-Teague (Mrs. Woodrow)
Burlington

BLACK CHERRY SALAD

1 tablespoon plain gelatin
2 tablespoons warm water
1 (18-ounce) can dark, pitted cherries, drained and liquid reserved
1 cup rosé wine
1 (3-ounce) package cherry gelatin
1 (3-ounce) package strawberry gelatin
1 box frozen, sliced strawberries
1 (20-ounce) can pineapple tidbits
1 cup chopped nuts

Dissolve plain gelatin in warm water. Heat 1 cup cherry juice (water added to make 1 cup, if necessary) and 1 cup wine and pour over flavored gelatins. Add plain gelatin, fruit and nuts. Pour into 5-cup ring mold or individual molds. Chill until set. Serve with poppy seed dressing.

Dressing:
1½ cups sugar
2 teaspoons dry mustard
2 teaspoons salt
⅔ cup vinegar
2 cups salad oil
3 tablespoons poppy seeds

In small bowl, mix at medium speed all ingredients except oil and seeds. Slowly add oil and seeds and mix until thick. Refrigerate.

Yield: 8 to 10 servings

Dell Rose Bright (Mrs. Lewis)
Burlington

PINEAPPLE ORANGE SALAD

1 (15¼-ounce) can crushed pineapple
1 (6-ounce) package orange gelatin
2 cups buttermilk
1 cup flaked coconut
1 cup chopped pecans
1 (12-ounce) carton non-dairy whipped topping, thawed

Boil pineapple in medium saucepan, stirring constantly. Remove from heat, stir in gelatin until dissolved. Add buttermilk, coconut and pecans. Cool. Fold in topping. Pour into 13x9x2-inch dish. Chill until set.

Yield: 8 to 10 servings

Elinor Samons Euliss (Mrs. Wade)
Burlington

ORANGE REFRIGERATOR SALAD

1 (3-ounce) package orange gelatin
1 (12-ounce) package small curd cottage cheese
1 (11-ounce) can mandarin oranges, drained
1 (8¼-ounce) crushed pineapple, drained
1 (4½-ounce) carton whipped topping, thawed

Sprinkle dry gelatin over cottage cheese. Add oranges and pineapple. Stir gently to mix well. Fold in whipped topping. Cover and refrigerate at least 4 hours or overnight.

Yield: 6 to 8 servings

Frances Tucker Gosnell
Mebane

GRANDMOTHER'S CHRISTMAS SALAD

8 egg yolks
8 tablespoons sugar
6 tablespoons vinegar
1 (16-ounce) package marshmallows, cut in half
1 (16-ounce) can crushed pineapple
1 quart whipping cream, whipped
½ pound chopped pecans
1 (16-ounce) jar maraschino cherries, finely cut

Cream eggs and sugar. Add vinegar and cook in double boiler until thick. Beat until cool. Add marshmallows and pineapple. Mix well and let stand 30 minutes. Add whipped cream to mixture plus pecans and cherries. Freeze in ice cube trays or use ice cream freezer. Recipe can be divided in half and frozen in freezer.

Yield: 15 to 20 servings

A favorite since 1930!

Edwina G. Hughes Johnston (Mrs. Bill)
Burlington

FROZEN FRUIT SALAD WITH HONEY DRESSING

1 large can crushed pineapple, drained
1 large can fruit cocktail, drained
1 small package lemon gelatin, sugar free
½ cup water
½ pound miniature marshmallows (optional)
½ cup almonds, chopped
½ cup pecans, chopped
1 quart frozen whipped non-dairy topping

Drain pineapple and fruit cocktail, keeping juice. Bring juice to a boil. Stir in lemon gelatin, and add ½ cup water. Cool. If desired, fold in marshmallows. Add pineapple and fruit cocktail and nuts. Fold in frozen non-dairy topping. Place in paper-lined muffin tins. Freeze. Then place in freezer bags. When ready to serve, peel paper and place salads on lettuce. Sprinkle with coconut and decorate with a cherry. Serve frozen with honey dressing.

Yield: 24 to 30 servings

Honey Dressing:
⅔ cup sugar
1 teaspoon dry mustard
1 teaspoon paprika
¼ teaspoon salt
1 teaspoon celery seeds
1 tablespoon lemon juice
⅓ cup strained honey (no comb)
5 tablespoons vinegar
1 cup salad oil

Measure sugar, dry mustard, paprika, salt and celery seeds into small mixing bowl. Add lemon juice, honey and vinegar. Beat in 1 cup salad oil. Put in closed jar in refrigerator.

Yield: 2 to 4 cups

My aunt, Lucile Johnston Cullers, served this often to the Presbyterian ladies.

Mary Johnston Lindley (Mrs. J. Thomas)
Burlington

FRUIT IN SHERRY

1 (20-ounce) can pineapple chunks
1 (16-ounce) can apricot halves, cut in half
1 (16-ounce) can pear slices
1 (16-ounce) can peach slices
1 (16-ounce) can red pie cherries

Sauce:
½ cup sugar
2 tablespoons flour
1 stick butter, melted
1 cup sherry

Drain fruit well. Arrange in 2-quart casserole dish. Mix sugar and flour well, then add butter stirring until smooth. Gradually add sherry. Pour over fruit and bake 325° for 30 to 35 minutes.

Yield: 10 servings

Laura Lyle Millender (Mrs. Steve H.)
Burlington

FROZEN FRUIT SALAD

2 (3-ounce) packages cream cheese, softened
¼ cup sugar
1 cup mayonnaise
4 slices pineapple, diced
1 cup chopped nuts
1 green pepper, chopped
1 cup maraschino cherries, halved
1 cup whipping cream, whipped

Cream cheese thoroughly and add remaining ingredients except whipped cream and mix well. Fold in cream. Pour into large mold or 12 individual molds. Freeze 3 to 4 hours.

Yield: 12 servings

Mary E. McClure Phillips
Graham

PINEAPPLE CASSEROLE

3 eggs
½ cup butter, softened
1½ cups sugar
6 slices bread, cubed
1 (15¼-ounce) can crushed pineapple in its own juice

Beat eggs until fluffy. Add remaining ingredients and mix well. Bake in a 2-quart casserole at 325° for 40 to 45 minutes.

Yield: 6 to 8 servings

Cindy Browning Kearns (Mrs. Paul)
Burlington

PINEAPPLE AU GRATIN

1 (20-ounce) can pineapple chunks
1 cup shredded longhorn or Cheddar cheese
¾ cup sugar
3 tablespoons flour
25 round, buttery crackers
¾ stick butter melted

Preheat oven to 350°. Drain pineapple and reserve 3 tablespoons juice. Mix together pineapple, 3 tablespoons juice, cheese, sugar and flour. Place in 2-quart buttered, shallow casserole. Sprinkle crushed crackers on top, covering completely. Drizzle butter over crackers. Bake 25 to 30 minutes until light brown. Serve warm or cold as an accompaniment to baked ham or chicken. Can also be served as a dessert with whipped cream.

Yield: 5 to 6 servings

Margaret Nelson Patton (Mrs. H. L.)
Kerrville, Texas

PEGGY'S PICKLED PINEAPPLE

1 (29-ounce) can pineapple chunks, drained
¾ cup cider vinegar
1 cup sugar
3 whole cloves
2 (3-inch) sticks cinnamon
1 tablespoon whole mace
2 teaspoons (or more) tiny cinnamon candies

Combine ¾ cup pineapple juice, vinegar, sugar, spices and candies in a large saucepan and cook over low heat, uncovered, for 15 minutes. Add pineapple and cook an additional 5 minutes. Cool. Pour into a jar with a tight fitting lid and refrigerate 24 hours before serving.

Yield: 20 servings

Pretty served in a crystal bowl with a silver fork!

Peggy Carter Lackey (Mrs. Mack E.)
Burlington

BAKED FRUIT

1 small pineapple, prepared, and cut into bite sized pieces
2 pears cut into bite sized pieces
2 slightly tart apples cut into bite sized pieces
1 small can mandarin oranges, drained
1 medium to large bunch green or red seedless grapes
1 can cherry pie filling
2 tablespoons butter
3 tablespoons dark brown sugar
¼ cup Cointreau liqueur

Preheat oven to 325°. Layer fruit in casserole dish and spread pie filling on top to cover fruit. Dot with butter and sprinkle with 3 tablespoons of sugar. Pour liqueur on top and bake for 1 hour.

Yield: 6 to 8 servings

Mrs. Brown is the great granddaughter of Edwin Michael Holt.

Margaret Holt Brown (Mrs. Walter M., Jr.)
Burlington

BUFFET FRUIT CASSEROLE

3 (16-ounce) cans various fruit chunks (pineapple, pears, peaches)
1 cup juice, drained from pineapple
1 small package instant vanilla pudding
3 teaspoons instant orange drink mix

Mix pudding and instant orange drink mix with pineapple juice. Drain other fruits well and layer in 13x9-inch casserole dish. Pour pudding mix over fruit. Chill well and garnish with fresh strawberries in season.

Yield: 8 to 10 servings

Elizabeth Hayden Harmon
Burlington

CRANBERRY APPLE CASSEROLE

3 cups diced, unpeeled apples
2 cups raw cranberries
1 cup sugar
½ cup butter, melted
1½ cups oatmeal
1½ cups brown sugar
⅓ cup flour
⅓ cup chopped pecans

Place fruit and sugar in a 2-quart greased casserole dish. Mix remaining ingredients well and cover fruit. Bake 350° for 1 hour.

Yield: 8 to 10 servings

Jean Millikan Frissell (Mrs. Fred, III)
Whitsett

By the fall of 1853 the Holts had constructed a dye-house adjacent to the Alamance Cotton Factory. Thomas Holt states: "The Frenchman remained with me until I thought I could manage the dyeing myself. I got along very well, with the exception of dyeing indigo blue. Afterward, an expert dyer in blue came out from Philadelphia who taught me in the dyeing of that color. He then put two Negroes to work with me, and side by side I worked with them at the dye tubs for over eight years."

W.J. NICKS STORE

Graham, N.C.

Nicks Store is the second oldest commercial establishment in Graham. The three-story brick mercantile building was erected in 1851-52 by the firm of McLean and Hanner. In 1892, the building was sold to William J. Nicks, whose family continued to operate the business until 1964.

In the early 1900s the top floor of the store was used for social functions, fraternal and political meetings and, for a time, served as a dancing school. In October 1954 the third floor was destroyed by Hurricane Hazel.

CHEESE BAKE

12 salted crackers
1 cup sharp Cheddar cheese, grated
1 egg, beaten
1½ cups milk
¼ teaspoon salt
¼ teaspoon pepper

Crush crackers and add cheese then place in casserole dish. Combine egg, milk, salt and pepper and pour over cracker mixture. Bake at 350° for 20 to 25 minutes. Chopped ham or cooked sausage may be added if desired.

Yield: 4 to 6 servings

Edith Brown Isley (Mrs. Blenton)
Burlington

QUICHE LORENE

2 frozen 9-inch pie crusts, thawed
1 pound bacon, crisply cooked, drained and crumbled
6 large eggs
1 cup sour cream
½ teaspoon salt
1 cup milk
3 cups grated hoop cheese
Parsley
Paprika

Prick bottom and sides of crusts, using a little egg white to brush over crust. Place in 300° oven about 5 minutes to dry out. Cover each crust bottom with half the bacon. Blend eggs, sour cream, salt, pepper and milk with mixer. Place cheese over bacon. Ladle liquid over all. Sprinkle with parsley and paprika. Bake at 350° for 30 to 35 minutes.

Yield: 6 servings

NOTE: This can be frozen or will keep in refrigerator several days.

Lorene Turner Lyon (Mrs. James W.)
Burlington

MAPLE-BACON OVEN PANCAKE

1½ cups buttermilk baking mix
1½ cups shredded cheese
¾ cup milk
¼ cup maple syrup
1 tablespoon sugar
2 eggs
1 teaspoon salt
12 slices bacon, cooked and crumbled

Beat biscuit mix, ½ cup of the cheese, milk, syrup, sugar, eggs and salt, with a hand beater until only small lumps remain. Pour into a greased and floured 13x9x2-inch pan. Bake uncovered at 425° for 10 to 15 minutes. Sprinkle with remaining cheese and bacon. Bake uncovered until cheese is melted.

Yield: 8 to 10 servings

Good and quick for campers.

Deleano Hall Williams (Mrs. Nelson)
Burlington

COTTAGE CHEESE BAKE

2 (10-ounce) packages frozen mixed vegetables
2 cups cottage cheese
¼ cup sour cream
2 tablespoons plain flour
1 teaspoon salt
⅛ teaspoon pepper
2 eggs

Thaw and drain vegetables. Place in a shallow 1½-quart casserole dish. In a mixing bowl, beat together cottage cheese and sour cream until smooth. Add flour, salt and pepper. Add eggs and beat until thoroughly blended. Pour over vegetables. Bake at 350° for 40 minutes.

Yield: 6 to 8 servings

Holly Jill Smith
Delray Beach, Florida

EGG AND BROCCOLI BAKE

1 (10-ounce) package frozen broccoli
6 hard cooked eggs, halved lengthwise
2 (10¾-ounce) cans condensed Cheddar cheese soup
1 cup milk
¼ cup margarine, melted
¼ cup water
2 cups herb-seasoned stuffing mix

Cook broccoli, drain. Arrange broccoli and eggs in 12x8x2-inch baking dish. Stir soup until smooth; gradually blend in milk. Pour over broccoli and eggs. In bowl, combine margarine and water. Stir in stuffing mix. Sprinkle over casserole. Bake at 400° for 30 minutes or until bubbling.

Yield: 6 to 8 servings

Joy Kristen Smith
Delray Beach, Florida

EGG CASSEROLE

6 slices white bread, trimmed and buttered
½ pound sharp cheese, grated
6 eggs, beaten
Salt
Pepper
2 cups milk

Grease an 8x10-inch casserole dish. Cut bread into 1-inch cubes. Alternate bread and cheese evenly in dish. Mix eggs and milk well with mixer. Pour liquid over all. Cover and refrigerate at least 4 hours or overnight. Bake uncovered at 375° for 35 to 40 minutes.

Yield: 8 servings

NOTE: ½ pound ham, shrimp, or sausage, cooked and drained, may be added.

Virginia Rascoe Hinton (Mrs. James M.)
Burlington

EGGS IN CHEESE SAUCE

2 tablespoons butter
1 teaspoon onion, grated
2 tablespoons all-purpose flour
1½ cups light cream
¾ cup Cheddar cheese, grated
Dash of Worcestershire sauce
Pinch of cayenne pepper
½ teaspoon paprika
Salt to taste

Melt butter over medium heat; add onion and cook only until onion is golden. Stir in flour and add cream to make a cream sauce. (This can be served as a spread on toast or in place of hollandaise sauce on vegetables.)

6 hard-cooked eggs, sliced
Parsley, chopped
Paprika
Buttered toast

Gently stir sliced eggs into the hot sauce. When eggs are hot, spoon mixture over hot toast. Garnish with parsley and paprika if desired.

Yield: 2 cups of sauce

Doris Clapp Gilliam (Mrs. Emery)
Elon College

CINDY'S EGG CASSEROLE

15 slices bread, cubed
½ cup margarine, melted
1 (16-ounce) package pasteurized process cheese product
8 eggs
4 cups milk
½ cup butter, melted

Grease a 3-quart casserole dish and line with bread crumbs. Mix melted margarine and cheese together until smooth. Pour over bread cubes. Beat eggs, milk and melted butter. Pour over casserole and refrigerate overnight. Bake at 350° for 30 to 40 minutes or until set.

Yield: 18 servings

Cindy Browning Kearns (Mrs. Paul)
Burlington

BRUNCH CASSEROLE

8 slices white bread, crusts trimmed
1 pound sausage, cooked but not dry
½ pound grated sharp cheese
3-4 eggs
2 cups milk
½ teaspoon salt
1 teaspoon dry mustard
Dash of pepper

Line a greased 9x13x2-inch baking dish with bread. Sprinkle sausage and cheese evenly over bread. Mix together eggs, milk, salt, mustard and pepper. Pour egg mixture over sausage-cheese mixture. Chill overnight. Bake at 350° for 30 to 35 minutes.

Yield: 8 to 10 servings

Helen Flynn Walton (Mrs. Clarence A.)
Burlington

RICE AND SOUR CREAM

1 tablespoon butter
¾ pound Monterey Jack cheese, cut in chunks
3 cups sour cream
2 (4 or 5-ounce) cans peeled green chilies, chopped
½ cup grated Cheddar cheese
3 cups cooked rice, salted and peppered

Butter 1½-quart casserole. Cut cheese into chunks. Mix sour cream, chilies and cheese. Start with layer of the cooked rice, then layer chilies and sour cream mixture then the cheese, end with layer of the rice. Cover and bake at 350° about 30 minutes. Remove from oven and sprinkle with the Cheddar cheese. Allow cheese to melt in oven. This can be made ahead and kept refrigerated. Heat in oven and add Cheddar cheese just before serving.

Yield: 8 servings

Nancy Roney Barger (Mrs. Adrian F.)
Haw River

GREEN RICE

1 cup uncooked rice (or 4 cups cooked)
2 (10-ounce) packages frozen broccoli, chopped
1 cup chopped onion
1 stick margarine
1 (11-ounce) can cream of mushroom soup
½ cup milk
1 teaspoon salt
¼ teaspoon pepper
1½ cups grated sharp cheese

Cook rice in 2 cups water until done. Cook broccoli only slightly and drain. Sauté onions in margarine until golden brown. Combine all ingredients, saving some cheese for top. Place in greased 9x13-inch casserole and bake uncovered at 325° for 30 minutes.

Yield: 6 servings

Marie Myers Franck (Mrs. Roscoe W.)
Liberty, North Carolina

SPINACH RICE CASSEROLE

3 cups cooked rice
1 (10-ounce) package frozen, chopped spinach
1 cup milk
¼ cup butter, melted
¼ pound cheese, grated
1 to 2 teaspoons onion, minced
½ cup green pepper, minced
1 tablespoon Worcestershire sauce
1¼ teaspoons salt

Preheat oven to 300°. Combine rice and drained, cooked spinach. Add the remaining ingredients and place in a greased 1½-quart casserole. Bake for 45 minutes.

Yield: 8 servings

Dale Harris Leahy (Mrs. Charles)
Burlington

RICE SOUFFLÉ

1 cup cooked rice, cold
3 eggs, separated
2 tablespoons margarine
½ cup milk
¼ pound Cheddar cheese, grated
⅛ teaspoon salt

Combine rice and egg yolks. Add margarine, milk and cheese. Beat egg whites until stiff. Fold in egg whites and salt. Bake at 300° for 30 to 45 minutes.

Yield: 6 servings

Helen Robertson Stewart (Mrs. Buck)
Burlington

BAKED RICE

1 medium onion, diced
½ cup margarine
2 (10½-ounce) cans beef consommé
1 cup rice, uncooked

Preheat oven to 350°. Sauté onion in margarine until soft. Combine with beef consommé and rice. Bake in a 1½-quart casserole dish for 1 hour.

Yield: 6 servings

Kathleen Johnston Miles
Burlington

YORKSHIRE PUDDING

6 pats margarine
1 egg
½ cup milk
½ cup flour
Salt—dash

Melt a pat of margarine in each cup of a 6-cup muffin tin. Evenly pour batter into each cup. Bake in a preheated 400° oven for 20 minutes. Serve with beef roast and gravy.

Yield: 6 servings

Vicki Vanderberg Hightower (Mrs. William)
Burlington

FRENCH RICE

1 (10½-ounce) can onion soup, undiluted
½ cup butter or margarine, melted
1 (4½-ounce) jar sliced mushrooms
1 (8-ounce) can sliced water chestnuts
1 cup uncooked regular rice

Combine soup and butter; stir well. Drain mushrooms and water chestnuts, reserving liquid. Add enough water to reserved liquid to equal 1⅓ cups. Add mushrooms, water chestnuts, liquid and rice to soup mixture; stir well. Pour into a lightly greased 10x6x2-inch baking dish. Cover. Bake at 350° for 1 hour.

Yield: 6 servings

Frances Trax Bennett (Mrs. Howard L.)
Burlington

SPECIAL MACARONI AND CHEESE

¾ cup macaroni
1 teaspoon salt
3 cups water
3 cups grated sharp cheese
2 cups milk
⅛ teaspoon cayenne pepper
¼ teaspoon seasoned salt
¼ teaspoon prepared mustard
3 eggs

Combine macaroni, salt and water. Cook until macaroni is tender. Drain. Add remaining ingredients. Mix well and pour into a greased 1½-quart casserole. Bake at 350° for 20 to 30 minutes or until browned.

Yield: 4 to 6 servings

Kathleen Johnston Miles
Burlington

ANGEL HAIR PASTA WITH TOMATO SAUCE

Tomato Sauce:

3 ribs celery, peeled and chopped
2 medium yellow onions, peeled and chopped
1 medium red onion, peeled and chopped
2 medium green bell peppers (or 1 green and 1 red), cored and chopped
2 (16-ounce) cans peeled whole tomatoes (preferably Italian plum tomatoes without salt or other spices), strained of most juices
1 (8-ounce) can tomato purée
Oregano
1 bay leaf
Basil
1 clove garlic, chopped
Extra virgin olive oil
Salt
Pepper
1 tablespoon unsalted butter
Small jar capers

In bowl, mix celery, onions and peppers. In skillet, coat bottom liberally with olive oil, then melt butter. Add ⅓ of celery-onion-pepper mixture. Cook over low heat, stirring occasionally for 10 minutes. Add another ⅓ to pan and cook about 5 to 6 minutes. Add tomatoes, the purée, oregano, some basil (a couple sprinkles), the whole bay leaf, some ground pepper. Bring to very slow simmer. Do not let bottom of pan get too hot or the tomatoes will burn and the dish will be ruined. Simmer 10 minutes. Remove bay leaf. With spoon or fork, break up tomatoes which are still whole or in large lumps. Simmer about 30 minutes longer. Add capers. Mixture will slightly thicken as surface water evaporates. Add salt and, if you wish, a *small* pinch of cayenne pepper. If it looks like there is too much surface water, spoon off. Stir and it's ready to serve. This sauce is quite versatile and is good on fish, veal chops, steaks, etc.

1 package angel hair pasta (8 "nests" per package)
Olive oil

Bring a large pot of salted water to boil. Add a dash of oil to water. Drop in pasta. Stir and boil rapidly until done (about 3 minutes). Drain in strainer or colander. Sprinkle with olive oil and shake in the colander or strainer. Put on plate, add sauce and serve.

Yield: 8 servings

"A good wine for this will be a medium-bodied Italian red, such as a Chianti Classico or a Bardolino. The slight astringency of the red Italian wines go well with tomato sauces. Your favorite white wine will also be fine. Heavier reds such as cabernets from California are too rich for this dish, and most French Bordeaux are too subtle, although no one will complain."

David Pardue
Burlington

NOODLE CASSEROLE

8 ounces fine noodles, cooked
1 pint sour cream
1 cup small curd cottage cheese
Salt
1 onion, finely chopped
1 tablespoon Worcestershire sauce
Parmesan cheese

Mix noodles, 1 cup sour cream and cottage cheese. Add salt to taste. Mix onion and Worcestershire sauce. Place ingredients in a greased 1½-quart casserole. Spread with remaining sour cream and sprinkle generously with Parmesan cheese. Bake at 350° for 45 minutes. Do not freeze.

Yield: 8 to 10 servings

Courtesy of Lords Proprietors' Inn
Edenton, North Carolina

COMPANY MACARONI AND CHEESE

2 cups uncooked macaroni
1 pound sharp cheese, grated
1 (11-ounce) can cream of mushroom soup
1 cup mayonnaise
1 (2-ounce) jar pimentos, chopped
1 tablespoon grated onion
1 cup round, buttery cheese crackers, crushed

Preheat oven to 350°. Cook macaroni in salted water; drain. Mix remaining ingredients and pour over the macaroni which has been placed in a 9x13-inch baking dish. Top with crushed crackers. Bake until hot and slightly browned.

Yield: 8 to 10 servings

Peggy Haywood Smith (Mrs. J. Harold)
Burlington

Shortly after Thomas Holt became proficient in dyeing colorfast indigo yarn, four box-looms were installed at the Alamance Cotton Factory, and thus began the manufacture of a class of goods known as "Alamance Plaids". Concerning this event, Thomas Holt wrote: "I am reliably informed that up until that time there had never been a yard of plaid or colored cotton goods woven on a loom south of the Potomac River. If this be true, I am entitled to the honor of having dyed with my own hands and had woven under my own supervision the first yard of cotton colored goods manufactured in the South."

OFFICE, ALTAMAHAW COTTON MILL   Altamahaw, N.C.

The Altamahaw Mill office is a multi-storied vernacular brick building constructed c. 1890 by John Q. Gant. During the 1890s the office served as headquarters of Holt, Gant and Holt, a textile partnership between Gant and Laurence and L. Banks Holt; sons of textile pioneer Edwin M. Holt. In 1902, the building was incorporated into the holdings of Glen Raven Cotton Mills.

With its unique patterned brickwork, its use of Romanesque arches, stone lintels and fine interior detail, the Altamahaw Mill office represents the best in commercial construction in the late Victorian period. In its day the mill office was also the most modern building in Alamance County. The office is said to have been the first commercial structure in the county to have central heat, gas lighting and hot and cold running water.

BOEUF BOURGUIGNON
(Burgundy Beef)

4 slices bacon, cut in small pieces
3 pounds boneless chuck roast, trimmed and cut in 1-inch cubes
2 tablespoons brandy
3 medium onions, finely chopped
2 cloves garlic, finely chopped
4 tablespoons flour
1½ cups red wine, Burgundy
1½ cups beef broth
1 bay leaf
1 teaspoon thyme
Ground pepper to taste
1 cup mushrooms, if large, cut in half
3 sprigs chopped parsley

Fry bacon and set aside. Sauté the beef in the fat until brown. Add bacon to beef, heat brandy, pour over beef and bacon in a casserole which has been placed over moderately high heat. Stir in onion, garlic and flour; add the wine and bring to simmer. Add parsley, bay leaf and pepper. Bake at 300° to 325° for 1½ hours. It is good to chill this overnight, but not required. Reheat over low heat or in slow oven. Sauté mushrooms in small amount of butter and add to casserole. Serve with potatoes and carrots that have been cooked separately.

Yield: 8 to 10 servings

Robert Burns King
Burlington

CALIFORNIA CHUCK ROAST

Chuck roast, desired weight
1 large jar mustard
1 (pound) box salt

Prepare coals ready for cooking. Spread ½ jar of mustard on one side of meat. Pour salt all over. Place meat directly in hot coals. Quickly spread the other side and around edges with remaining mustard. Again coat with salt. Cook to desired doneness. The caked salt acts as a shield to keep meat tender and flavorful, so scrape off just before serving.

Yield: 3 to 4 servings

Captain Thomas J. Harper, USN RET
Burlington

BEEF BURGUNDY

3 medium onions, sliced thin
2 (4-ounce) cans mushroom pieces
½ stick margarine
1½ pounds lean beef, sliced in thin strips or 1½-inch cubes
1½ cups dry Burgundy
3 tablespoons beef bouillon
¾ cup hot water
¼ teaspoon marjoram
¼ teaspoon thyme
¼ teaspoon oregano
¼ teaspoon pepper
3 tablespoons flour
¼ cup water

In a dutch oven sauté onions and mushrooms in margarine until onions are tender. Remove to covered bowl and set aside. Add beef to pan, brown thoroughly; add 1 cup Burgundy, bouillon dissolved in ¾ cup hot water, herbs and seasonings. Cover pan and simmer over low heat for 1½ to 2 hours or until meat is tender. Add remaining Burgundy, mushrooms and onions. Cook an additional 20 minutes. To thicken sauce stir in flour mixed with water. Remove from heat. Serve over rice.

Yield: 6 to 8 servings

Shirley Barbee Fink (Mrs. Howard)
Graham

CREOLE STEAK

2 pounds round steak, cut 2 inches thick
2 tablespoons oil
½ cup vinegar
1 (16-ounce) can tomatoes
½ bunch carrots, diced
2 medium onions, diced
2 cups potatoes, cut in large cubes
1 cup celery, diced
1 green sweet pepper, diced

Salt and pepper steak. Heat oil in a skillet and brown steak on both sides quickly, place in roaster and pour vinegar and water over steak. Add vegetables. Keep covered while cooking. Bake slowly at 250° for 2½ hours, or until steak is fork tender.

Yield: 6 to 8 servings

Ann Cates Moore (Mrs. Richard J.)
Burlington

STRIPPED STEAK

4 tablespoons butter
1 medium onion, chopped
1 (4-ounce) can mushrooms, sliced and drained
1½ pounds round steak trimmed of fat and cut into bite size strips
2 tablespoons flour
1 (10-ounce) can beef consommé
1 cup water
1 tablespoon prepared mustard
2 tablespoons brown sugar
1 to 2 teaspoons Worcestershire sauce
Salt and pepper to taste
Cooked rice or noodles

Melt butter in large skillet. Add chopped onions and mushrooms; sauté for 5 minutes. Add strips of round steak and cook over medium heat until meat is brown. Blend flour into meat mixture. Remove from heat; add consommé, water, mustard and brown sugar. Return to medium heat until it reaches simmering point. Cover and simmer on low heat until steak is tender, 30 minutes to 1 hour. Thicken sauce if desired, with a small amount of flour mixed to a paste with water. Serve over cooked rice or noodles.

Yield: 4 to 6 servings

Margaret Nelson Patton (Mrs. H. L.)
Kerrville, Texas

SWISS STEAK

2 pounds round steak
1 medium onion, chopped
1 (28-ounce) can tomatoes, undrained

Cut steak in serving size pieces. Pound with a meat mallet to tenderize. Place in baking dish. Add onion and sprinkle over meat. Pour tomatoes over meat. Bake covered at 250° for 2 hours or until fork tender.

Yield: 6 to 8 servings

This is very good served with noodles.

Frances Alexander Campbell (Mrs. Bob)
Chapel Hill, North Carolina

SHISH KABOBS

1 pound beef filet loin, cut 1-inch thick
1 pound boneless leg of lamb, cut 1-inch thick
1 pound pork tenderloin, cut ½-inch thick
1 eggplant
4 apples
1 green pepper, seeded
12 large mushrooms
½ pound bacon, sliced

Place meat in a shallow dish, keeping each type separate.

Marinade:
½ cup vegetable oil
¼ cup soy sauce
½ cup red wine
1 teaspoon ground ginger
1 small clove garlic, minced
1½ teaspoons curry powder
2 tablespoons ketchup
¼ teaspoon pepper
¼ teaspoon TABASCO pepper sauce

Prepare the marinade by blending all ingredients in a blender or food processor with the metal blade. Set aside. Pour ¾ of the marinade over the meat. Cover and refrigerate 24 hours, stirring once or twice. A few hours before serving, peel and slice eggplant ½-inch thick; cut into 1½-inch squares. Peel apples and cut into 6 wedges. Cut green pepper in 1½-inch squares. Place eggplant, apple, green pepper and mushrooms in a medium bowl and add remaining marinade. Let set 2 to 3 hours at room temperature, stirring occasionally. To cook kabobs, wrap a half slice of bacon around each piece of lamb. On large skewers, alternate beef, mushrooms, lamb, eggplant, pork, green pepper and apple. Barbecue or broil 5 to 10 minutes on each side.

Yield: 8 servings

Eda Contiguglia Holt (Mrs. Ralph M., Jr.)
Burlington

CROCK POT BEEF STEW

1½ pounds stew beef
4 carrots, sliced
4 medium potatoes, cubed
1 medium onion, chopped
1 (8-ounce) bottle Russian salad dressing

Combine all ingredients in a crock pot. Cook 8 to 10 hours on low.

Yield: 4 to 6 servings

Cleo Rumbley Smith (Mrs. Richard H.)
Burlington

SAUERBRATEN

2 pounds boneless beef roast

Marinade:
1 onion, sliced
½ lemon, sliced
4 peppercorns
4 cloves
1 bay leaf
1 teaspoon salt
1 tablespoon sugar
2 cups cider vinegar
2 cups water
½ lemon, sliced
6 gingersnaps or rye bread crumbs

Wash meat, drain well and put in an earthenware bowl with onion, lemon and spices. Cover with vinegar and water, let stand 3 or 4 days in a cool place, turning daily. Remove meat from the marinade and dry before cooking. Melt 2 ounces oil until hot. Brown meat quickly on all sides in an uncovered pan. Add all the liquid and spices to the pan with 6 gingersnaps or crusts of rye bread. Simmer gently with lid on. Turn from time to time. Cook until tender. Remove meat, strain gravy, then return to pan, thicken with flour or cornstarch. Return meat to pan and cook 5 minutes.

Yield: 4 to 6 servings

Potato dumplings go very well with this dish.

Grace Kusenberg Sailer (Mrs. Kenneth)
Burlington

QUICK STROGANOFF

1½ pounds trimmed stew beef
½ (10¾-ounce) can mushroom soup
½ (10¾-ounce) can onion soup
1 pint sour cream
1 can sliced buttered mushrooms, drained
Pepper

Place uncooked beef and mixed soups in a 1½-quart covered deep dish casserole. Pepper well. Bake at 250° for four hours. Remove from oven and add mushrooms and sour cream. Stir carefully. Cover to keep hot. Serve over rice or noodles.

Yield: 3 to 4 servings

Elizabeth Pruitt Dunn (Mrs. James)
Baltimore, Maryland

BARBECUED SPARERIBS

1 clove garlic, peeled and mashed
1 tablespoon soy sauce
⅓ cup sugar
6 tablespoons orange juice
¼ teaspoon pepper
1 tablespoon grated orange rind
2½-3 pounds tender spareribs, whole pieces
½ teaspoon candied ginger, finely cut

Mix first 6 ingredients, for sauce, together. Rinse meat, drain and pat dry. Trim fat away. Do not separate ribs. Place meat in a shallow baking dish and spread with sauce, covering well. Let stand in refrigerator 45 minutes to 1 hour, turning in sauce 2 to 3 times. Bake at 325° for 1 hour.

Yield: 4 servings

Great cooked on the grill!

Ann Birmingham Flagg (Mrs. Raymond)
Burlington

GROUND BEEF AND SAUSAGE CASSEROLE

1 (8-ounce) package spaghetti, cooked according to package directions
2 cups shredded Cheddar cheese
1 pound lean hamburger
1 pound hot sausage
½ cup chopped onion
1 clove garlic or dry minced garlic
1 (15-ounce) can tomato sauce
½ cup catsup
3 tablespoons Worcestershire sauce
¼ teaspoon salt
1 teaspoon basil

Place spaghetti in buttered 2-quart casserole dish. Add shredded cheese on top. Cook hamburger, sausage, onion and garlic until done. Drain and stir in tomato sauce, catsup, Worcestershire, salt and basil. Simmer 5 minutes, stirring occasionally. Spread over cheese. Cover with foil and refrigerate overnight. Bake uncovered at 350° for 25 to 30 minutes. Very good and different.

Yield: 4 to 6 servings

Hazel Swanson Roney (Mrs. James A.)
Mebane

BURGER CASSEROLE

1 pound ground beef
½ cup diced celery
¼ cup chopped onion
1 (10¾-ounce) can vegetable soup
¼ teaspoon salt
1 cup mashed potatoes

Brown beef and drain off fat. Cook celery and onion until tender and add to beef and mix well. Add soup and salt. Spoon into a 1-quart casserole dish; mound potatoes around edge of casserole. Bake at 425° for 15 minutes.

Yield: 3 to 4 servings

NOTE: May substitute another soup, such as chicken noodle.

Constance Cates Isley
Burlington

MACARONI ONE DISH DINNER

1 (pound) package macaroni, cooked and drained
2 tablespoons vegetable oil
1 pound ground beef
1 medium onion, diced
1 rib celery, diced
½ green pepper, diced
Salt to taste
Pepper to taste
1 (15½-ounce) jar homestyle spaghetti sauce
7½ ounces water
1 teaspoon commercial herb seasoning mix
1 cup grated cheese

Brown meat, vegetables and seasonings in oil until done. Add sauce and water, blending well. Mix with macaroni and pour into a large baking dish and top with cheese. Bake at 350° for 20 minutes or until cheese melts and casserole is bubbly.

Yield: 4 to 6 servings

Francine Holt Swaim (Mrs. D. Cletus)
Liberty, North Carolina

PENNSYLVANIA GOULASH

1 cup chopped celery
½ cup chopped onion
½ cup chopped green pepper
3 teaspoons cooking oil
1 pound ground beef
2 (10¾-ounce) cans tomato soup
¼ teaspoon cinnamon
2½ cups macaroni
1½ cups grated cheese

Sauté vegetables in oil and add meat. Cook until color is gone, then add soup and cinnamon, salt and pepper to taste. Cook macaroni according to directions, drain and add to sauce. Pour ½ mixture in 13x10x2-inch baking dish and sprinkle cheese evenly over top. Add remaining mixture on top. Bake at 350° for 30 to 40 minutes or until brown on top.

Yield: 12 servings

Elizabeth Hayden Harman
Burlington

MOTHER'S CREAMED HAMBURGER

2 medium onions, chopped
2 tablespoons margarine
1 pound ground round or chuck
2 tablespoons flour
1 cup milk
Salt
Pepper

Cook onions in margarine until soft. Add meat and cook until brown. Sprinkle flour over meat, add milk and cook until thickened. Add more milk, if necessary. Season with salt and pepper to taste. Serve over mashed potatoes or toast.

Yield: 4 to 5 servings

Elaine Frissell Neese (Mrs. L. E., Jr.)
Whitsett, North Carolina

HAMBURGER CASSEROLE

1 pound ground meat
1 small onion, chopped
1 (8-ounce) can tomato sauce
1 (10¾-ounce) can Cheddar cheese soup or cheese slices
½ cup macaroni, cooked

Brown meat and onion in a skillet. Add tomato sauce and simmer 10 minutes. Oil a 1-quart casserole, spoon in ⅓ of meat mixture. Add cooked macaroni, then remainder of meat mixture. Spread cheese soup or cheese slices over top. Cover casserole tightly. Bake at 400° until bubbly.

Yield: 4 to 6 servings

Mary Robertson Vaughn (Mrs. Homer)
Graham

BEEF AND NOODLES

1 pound lean hamburger
2 tablespoons cooking oil
1 medium onion, chopped
½ green pepper, chopped
1 tablespoon Worcestershire sauce
¼ teaspoon garlic salt
1 (8-ounce) can tomato sauce
1 (8-ounce) package cream cheese
1½ cups egg noodles, broken into small pieces and cooked

Brown hamburger, onion and pepper in oil in a frying pan. Add Worcestershire sauce and garlic salt. Cook 5 to 10 minutes. Add tomato sauce; cook an additional 10 minutes. Turn heat down. Add cream cheese and cooked noodles. Stir until cheese is well blended.

Yield: 6 to 8 servings

Martha Ann Shaw
Burlington

CHARCOAL LEG OF LAMB

Leg of Lamb, any weight desired

Marinade:
1 cup oil
1 cup vinegar
2 cups red wine
Leeks, diced
3 cloves garlic, crushed
½ cup brown sugar
1 tablespoon rosemary
1 tablespoon tarragon

Have butcher butterfly a leg of lamb. Mix all ingredients and marinate lamb overnight. Grill over hot coals that have rosemary sprinkled over them.

Sauce:
Heat equal amounts of honey and spicy mustard with a dash of rosemary added. Add drippings from lamb.

Yield: 4 to 5 cups marinade

Jan Sellars Scott
Burlington

JOE'S SPECIAL

⅓ pound ground round steak
Olive oil
1 teaspoon minced onion
1 teaspoon salt
1 teaspoon Accent
Dash TABASCO pepper sauce
1 teaspoon Worcestershire sauce
4 eggs, well beaten
2 large handsful of spinach, washed and drained or ¾ package frozen spinach, defrosted and drained

Brown meat in a skillet with olive oil. Add the 5 seasonings. Toss spinach with meat. Beat eggs with a fork and add to meat and spinach mixture; salt and pepper to taste, mixing well. Serve with French bread, sprinkled with Parmesan cheese.

Yield: 4 servings

Bettie Kendrick Gant (Mrs. Kenneth)
Burlington

SPAGHETTI BEEF CASSEROLE

2 (10-ounce) packages long noodles
1 teaspoon garlic salt
2 pounds ground beef
1 stalk celery, chopped
1 pound onions, diced
1 pound green pepper, chopped
1 (10¾-ounce) can tomato soup
1 (12-ounce) can tomato paste
2 (8-ounce) cans tomato sauce
1 (13-ounce) can olives with liquid, green or black
1 (6-ounce) can mushrooms, with liquid
1 pound grated sharp cheese

Cook noodles with garlic salt according to directions and drain. Brown meat, drain, leaving some drippings to sauté celery, onions and pepper until tender. Mix all remaining ingredients in a large bowl. This recipe can be divided into 4 small casseroles; 2 medium or 1 large square casserole. Cover with grated cheese. Bake at 325° for 1 hour.

Yield: 20 servings

Dale Harris Leahy (Mrs. Charles)
Burlington

EASY MEAT LOAF

1½ pounds ground chuck
1 cup spaghetti sauce
1 envelope onion-mushroom soup, dry
1 (5¾-ounce) can evaporated milk
2 slices bread, crumbled
3 tablespoons Worcestershire sauce
½ teaspoon salt
½ teaspoon onion salt
½ teaspoon garlic powder
½ teaspoon black pepper

Mix all ingredients well. Shape into loaf in baking dish and cover with foil. Bake approximately 1½ hours at 350°. Remove foil and cook 15 minutes or until top is brown.

Yield: 6 to 8 servings

Mildred Spoon Alexander (Mrs. Carl B.)
Burlington

REDUCED CALORIE SPAGHETTI SAUCE

¾ pound extra lean ground beef
2 tablespoons chopped parsley
1 small onion, diced
1 medium carrot, shredded
½ rib celery, diced
1 (28-ounce) can tomatoes
1 (6-ounce) can tomato paste
¾ teaspoon salt
½ teaspoon fennel seeds
¼ teaspoon pepper
½ cup dry red wine

In a saucepan cook ground beef, parsley, carrot, onion and celery stirring often until meat is brown. Add tomatoes, tomato paste and remaining ingredients. Heat to boiling, stirring to break up tomatoes. Cover and simmer 30 minutes. Stir occasionally.

Yield: 5½ cups sauce

Ann Dean Honeycutt (Mrs. Chester)
Burlington

SPAGHETTI SAUCE

1 pound ground beef
2 teaspoons seasoned salt
¼ teaspoon pepper
1 (28-ounce) can crushed tomatoes
1 (8-ounce) can tomato sauce
1 package spaghetti sauce mix

Brown beef in dutch oven or heavy iron skillet. Add salt and pepper; cook slowly uncovered, for 10 minutes. Stir in tomatoes, tomato sauce and spaghetti mix. Cover and simmer 30 minutes.

Yield: 6 servings

Carolyn Penelope Weatherly
Burlington

SPAGHETTI SAUCE

2 pounds ground round or sirloin steak
1 cup chopped onion
1 chopped green pepper
2 (28-ounce) cans tomatoes
1 (15-ounce) can tomato sauce
1½ teaspoons salt
1½ tablespoons sugar
2 teaspoons Worcestershire sauce
2 tablespoons chili powder
2 tablespoons flour

Brown beef and onions. Drain and put in a large pan. Add green pepper. Cook about 10 minutes. Put tomatoes in a processor or blender and chop 3 to 5 seconds. Add remaining ingredients, except flour, to beef mixture. Simmer 1 hour. Dissolve flour in a little water. Stir into sauce and let come to a boil to thicken.

Yield: 8 to 12 servings

This is a 35 year old recipe.

Jeanette Zimmerman Newlin (Mrs. Thomas)
Haw River

MY SPAGHETTI SAUCE

2 pounds extra lean hamburger
4 tablespoons oil
4 (5-ounce) cans tomato sauce
1 tablespoon Italian seasoning
1 whole bay leaf
½ teaspoon garlic salt
1 teaspoon basil leaves
½ teaspoon red pepper
½ teaspoon lemon pepper
3 tablespoons minced onion
1 teaspoon oregano

Brown hamburger in oil. Add all of the spices and cook together 5 to 10 minutes. Add the tomato sauce; let simmer 30 to 60 minutes. Serve hot over spaghetti. Taste sauce as it simmers; add more spices if needed.

Yield: 10 to 15 servings

Carlton Jackson Shaw
Burlington

LASAGNA

1 pound hamburger
1 pound hot sausage
1 clove garlic, minced
1 tablespoon basil
1½ teaspoons salt
1 (16-ounce) can tomatoes
1 (12-ounce) can tomato paste
2 eggs
½ cup grated Parmesan cheese
2 tablespoons parsley flakes
1 teaspoon salt
½ teaspoon pepper
1 (10-ounce) package lasagna noodles
3 cups Ricotta cheese
1 pound Mozzarella cheese

Brown meat slowly and spoon off fat. Add next 5 ingredients. Simmer uncovered 30 minutes. Stir occasionally. Cook noodles in water until tender. Drain and rinse. Beat eggs. Add remaining ingredients (except noodles and cheeses). Layer in 13x10x2-inch pan, ½ each of noodles, Ricotta cheese, Mozzarella cheese, meat mixture; repeat layers. Bake at 375° for 30 minutes. Let stand 15 minutes before serving.

Yield: 6 to 8 servings

Beth Elder Ellington (Mrs. Jeff)
Burlington

LASAGNA

1 pound lasagna noodles
1½ pounds pizza or Mozzarella cheese, sliced
1 cup Ricotta or cottage cheese
½ cup grated Parmesan cheese

Cook noodles until just tender. Drain and dry well on paper towels. Spread a thin layer of sauce on bottom of a 2-quart rectangular casserole dish, cover with a layer of noodles (cut to fit). Spread with a layer of sauce, dot with spoonfuls of Ricotta or cottage cheese, and a sprinkling of Parmesan, cover with 1 or 2 slices of pizza or Mozzarella cheese. Repeat these layers until all ingredients are used, ending with sauce and Mozzarella. Bake at 350° for 30 minutes until golden hot and bubbly. Allow to cool for 5 to 10 minutes before cutting to serve.

Sauce:
1 tablespoon cooking oil
1 cup minced onion
1 clove garlic, minced
2 pounds ground beef
2 (16-ounce) cans tomatoes
1 (8-ounce) can tomato paste
½ cup red wine
1 teaspoon oregano
2 tablespoons Worcestershire sauce
2 teaspoons salt
1 teaspoon seasoned salt
1 teaspoon sugar
1 teaspoon basil
TABASCO pepper sauce to taste

Heat oil, add onion and garlic, sauté until golden. Stir in beef, cook until brown. Add tomatoes, tomato paste, tomato sauce, wine and seasonings, mix well. Cover and cook over low heat 1 hour or until sauce thickens. This freezes well.

Yield: 16 servings

Barbara May McNeely (Mrs. C. C., Jr.)
Burlington

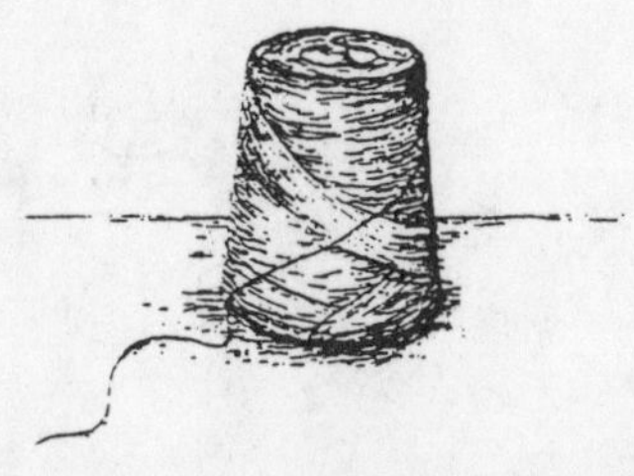

LASAGNA

1 package lasagna noodles, cooked according to package directions.

Sauce:
2 tablespoons oil
1 pound ground beef
½ cup chopped onion
1 (15-ounce) can tomato paste, plus 1 can water
1 teaspoon sugar
1 teaspoon salt
1 teaspoon pepper
1½ teaspoons garlic powder
3 tablespoons Parmesan cheese
1 tablespoon oregano
1 (12-ounce) carton creamed cottage cheese
1 pound Mozzarella cheese

Beginning with sauce, cover bottom of large oven proof baking dish. Add a thin layer each of noodles, sauce, cottage cheese and Mozzarella cheese. Repeat layers, but do not end with cottage cheese on top. Bake at 350° for 20 minutes, covered with heavy foil. Remove foil and bake an additional 5 minutes.

Yield: 10 to 12 servings

Burlington caterer, creator of wedding cakes and party fare, both beautiful and delicious.

Edith Brown Isley (Mrs. Blenton)
Burlington

QUICK CHILI CON CARNE

1 pound ground beef
1 cup chopped onions
2 cloves garlic, chopped
2 (15½-ounce) cans kidney beans, undrained
1 (10¾-ounce) can tomato soup
½ cup water
2 tablespoons chili powder
1 tablespoon vinegar
1 teaspoon salt

In a 2-quart pan, brown ground beef, stirring to break up meat as it cooks. Add onions and garlic. Pour off excess grease. Add beans, soup, water, chili powder, vinegar and salt. Stir well. Heat to boiling, reduce heat, cover and simmer 30 minutes. Stir occasionally. Serve over rice with a tossed salad. Makes a complete meal.

Yield: 8 servings

Margarett Sullivan Warren (Mrs. William G.)
Mebane

GREAT CHILI

3 pounds ground beef
3 medium onions, chopped
2 cups chopped celery
1 (28-ounce) can tomatoes
2 (15-ounce) cans kidney beans
Salt to taste
2 teaspoons chili powder
Cayenne pepper, optional

Cook beef, chopped onions and celery together until onions are transparent, about 10 minutes. Add other ingredients. Cover and cook slowly, stirring occasionally, for at least an hour. The cayenne pepper determines the hotness of the chili, so use as much as desired. This can be added at the table. The flavor of this chili improves with long cooking and is just as good or better reheated. Can be frozen.

Yield: 10 servings

Evelyn Davis Slott
Burlington

LIVER WITH MUSTARD CREAM WITH BROILED ONIONS

1½ pounds calves' liver, cut in thin slices
Salt and freshly ground black pepper
½ cup all-purpose flour
3 tablespoons butter
3 tablespoons olive oil
¼ cup dry white wine or beef broth
2 tablespoons imported mustard
½ cup heavy cream

Sprinkle liver on both sides with salt and pepper. Dip in flour and shake off excess. In a heavy, 10-inch skillet, heat butter and oil over moderately high heat until hot but not smoking. Add a few pieces of liver—taking care not to touch in skillet. Cook about 2 minutes on each side. As liver is done, remove to a serving platter. Add wine to skillet and increase heat to high. Stir in the mustard and cream. Boil 1 to 2 minutes, until slighty thickened. Pour over liver.

Yield: 4 servings

Broiled Onions: For each serving, cut a medium-sized onion in half. Brush cut surfaces with vegetable oil. Broil on a foil-lined pan 2 to 3 inches from heat source for 5 to 10 minutes until cut surfaces are dark brown and onions are tender. Check frequently to make sure that the onions don't burn.

Mary Carter Hudgins
Burlington

DELICIOUS HAM SALAD

1½ cups small elbow macaroni, cooked and drained
1 cup diced ham
1 (15½-ounce) can pineapple tidbits, reserve juice
1 cup diced celery
½ cup chopped nuts
2 tablespoons cornstarch
½ cup mayonnaise

Mix macaroni and ham, tidbits, celery and nuts. Add cornstarch to the pineapple juice, cook over low heat until thickened. Cool. Add mayonnaise to juice mixture, mix well. Add to macaroni-ham mixture.

Yield: 4 to 6 servings

Cleo Rumbley Smith (Mrs. Richard H.)
Burlington

HAM LOAF

1½ pounds smoked ham, ground
1 pound ground pork or veal
½ teaspoon salt
2 eggs
½ cup milk
½ cup tomato juice
1 cup bread or cracker crumbs

Mix all ingredients together. Put in loaf pan and bake at 350° for 1½ hours.

Glaze:
½ cup brown sugar
⅓ cup vinegar
½ cup water
1 teaspoon prepared mustard

Mix all ingredients together, spread on loaf the last 15 minutes of baking.

Yield: 6 to 8 servings

Karen Gregory Powell (Mrs. Sam C.)
Burlington

HAM AND MUSHROOM NEWBURG

16 slices thin boneless ham pieces, about 5x2½-inches
1 pound fresh mushrooms, cleaned and stems removed
1 tablespoon flour
2 tablespoons margarine
1½ cups half and half
¼ cup dry sherry
3 egg yolks, beaten
⅛ teaspoon nutmeg
8 slices French bread, cut 1-inch thick

Sauté ham, keep warm. Slice mushroom caps, coat with flour. Melt margarine. Add mushrooms, brown lightly, about 5 minutes. Remove from heat. Add all remaining ingredients except egg yolks. Cook, uncovered, simmering 2 minutes. Add a small amount of the hot sauce to egg yolks. Remove pan from heat. Add warmed egg yolks. Cook, stirring until bubbly about 5 minutes. Put ham on bread slices. Pour Newburg over ham.

Yield: 4 servings

Vicki Burton Vernon (Mrs. John H., III)
Burlington

PORK CHOP DELIGHT

8 boned pork chops
1 (16-ounce) package frozen potato puffs
1 (10¾-ounce) can chicken soup
1 cup sour cream
1½ cups chopped onions
1½ cups chopped green peppers

Salt and pepper chops to taste. Sauté on both sides to brown lightly. Arrange chops in very large casserole dish. Place frozen potato puffs over chops. Mix soup, sour cream, onions and spread over potatoes. Reserve green pepper. Bake at 375° for about 20 minutes. Remove from oven, sprinkle green pepper over top, return to oven for an additional 10 to 15 minutes or long enough to bake onions and blend ingredients.

Yield: 6 to 8 servings

Lorene Turner Lyon (Mrs. James W.)
Burlington

BOURBON-BRAISED PORK CHOPS

⅓ cup plain flour
½ teaspoon salt
¼ teaspoon pepper
4 pork chops, 1-inch thick
1 tablespoon vegetable oil
4 orange slices
2 tablespoons brown sugar
2 tablespoons corn starch
⅛ teaspoon ground allspice
1 cup hot water
¼ cup orange juice
2 tablespoons bourbon
¼ cup currants or raisins

Combine flour, salt and pepper. Dredge chops in flour mixture. Heat oil in a large skillet over medium heat; brown chops on both sides. Place an orange slice on top of each chop. Combine brown sugar, cornstarch and allspice in small saucepan; gradually stir in water. Cook over medium heat, stirring constantly until mixture thickens and comes to a boil. Cook 1 minute stirring constantly. Remove from heat; stir in orange juice, bourbon and currants. Spoon over pork chops. Cover, reduce heat and simmer 1 hour or until tender.

Yield: 4 servings

Sherry Faulkner Scott (Mrs. Don E., III)
Elon College

RICE-SAUSAGE CASSEROLE

1 (6½-ounce) box long grain and wild rice, cooked
1 pound sausage, cooked and drained
1 (16-ounce) carton sour cream
2 cups chicken or turkey, cooked and chopped
1 (3-ounce) can mushrooms, drained
1 (6-ounce) can Durkee French Fried Onions

Mix first 5 ingredients together. Pour into a greased 2-quart rectangular casserole. Bake at 350° for 25 minutes. Place onions on top and bake an additional 5 minutes. This may be frozen without the onions.

Yield: 6 to 8 servings

Barbara May McNeely (Mrs. C. C., Jr.)
Burlington

SWEET AND SOUR PORK

2 pounds lean pork, cut in 1-inch pieces
¼ cup margarine
1 (4-ounce) can mushrooms, drained and liquid reserved
1 (14-ounce) can pineapple chunks, drained and liquid reserved
1 (5-ounce) can water chestnuts
1 (5-ounce) can bamboo shoots
2 tablespoons sugar
1 tablespoon soy sauce
1 tablespoon vinegar
2 medium green peppers, cut in strips
2 medium onions, sliced
2 tablespoons cornstarch
4 cups cooked rice

Brown pork strips in margarine in a skillet. Combine liquid and add water, if necessary, to make 1 cup. Add to skillet and bring to boil. Cover and reduce heat; simmer for 30 minutes. Add water chestnuts and bamboo shoots. Stir in sugar, soy sauce and vinegar. Add mushrooms, pineapple chunks, green peppers and onions. Cook an additional 15 minutes. Blend cornstarch with small amount of cold water and stir into hot mixture; continue stirring while cooking until slightly thickened. Serve with hot rice.

Yield: 6 to 8 servings

Nancy Roney Barger (Mrs. Adrian F.)
Haw River

SAUSAGE CASSEROLE

2 packages chicken noodle soup mix
4½ cups boiling water
1½ to 2 pounds sausage, mixing half hot and half mild
4 or 5 spring onions including tender tops, chopped
1 large green pepper, chopped
1 cup celery including tender tops, chopped
1 cup uncooked brown rice
1 cup drained sliced water chestnuts
Salt and pepper to taste
Curry powder—optional
¼ cup slivered almonds

Mix 2 packages of soup in boiling water and boil for 7 minutes. Cook sausage until done, then drain. Sauté onions, pepper and celery in 3 tablespoons sausage drippings. Add soup, rice and chestnuts. Mix together. Pour into 2-quart casserole dish. Bake covered at 350° for 1 to 1½ hours.

Yield: 10 to 12 servings

Virginia McPherson Hamby (Mrs. Clayton)
Mebane

Early Alamance Plaids, now called "First Generation Plaids", were produced in varying patterns of indigo blue and white. The indigo used for dyeing the cotton was brought by wagon load into Alamance County from the coastal areas of North and South Carolina. Between 1853 and 1861 more than twenty-five patterns of blue and white Alamance Plaids were produced.

FIRST REFORMED
UNITED CHURCH OF CHRIST

Burlington, N.C.

Designed in the 1920s and erected in 1940-41, the First Reformed United Church of Christ is among the most distinctive religious edifices in Burlington. Built from plans drawn by the Greensboro, N.C. architectural firm of Benton and Benton, the church exhibits elements of the Romanesque style as employed in northern Italy in the Middle Ages. The church is most notable for its three-part facade and its six-stage campanile or bell tower.

The congregation was organized in 1889 as the German Reformed Church, and later was known as the First Evangelical and Reformed Church.

LEMONY ALMOND TOPPED FILLETS

1 pound skinless fish—flounder, orange roughy, sole or trout fillets
½ cup fine, dry breadcrumbs
2 tablespoons margarine, melted
1 teaspoon grated lemon peel
⅓ cup almonds, toasted and sliced

Measure thickness of fish. For large fillets, place in a single layer on lightly greased microwave safe 10x6x2-inch dish, tucking under the edges. For small fillets, layer evenly in dish. Mix crumbs, margarine and lemon peel. Sprinkle over fish, then top with almonds. Cover with plastic wrap folding back one corner. Cook on high power 3 minutes; rotate dish ½ turn and continue cooking 2 to 4 minutes or until done.

Yield: 4 servings

Frances Anderson Johnson (Mrs. Eldridge, Jr.)
Greensboro, North Carolina

BAKED SHAD WITH NO BONES

1 (3-6 pound) roe Shad, cleaned with head, tail and fins attached
2 tablespoons vinegar

Place Shad on large sheet of heavy-duty aluminum foil sprayed lightly with vegetable spray. Sprinkle vinegar over entire fish. Seal foil around fish in airtight drugstore fold. Place on roaster and bake 6 hours at 200°. Serve very warm on platter with lemon slices and fresh dill to garnish. NOTE: If this fish is seasoned before cooking it becomes very strong; therefore, season after cooking. The roe is in the fish the entire time. It may be necessary to sew or skewer the fish to hold roe inside.

Yield: 4 to 6 servings

Helen Moseley Gant (Mrs. Cecil, Jr.)
Burlington

MARINATED BAKED FISH

1/4 cup butter or margarine
1/4 cup lemon juice
1/4 cup chopped green onions
2 tablespoons water
1/2 teaspoon garlic salt
1/4 to 1/2 teaspoon dill weed
1 pound fish steaks or fillets, fresh or frozen, thawed

Preheat oven to 350°. In a 12x7-inch dish, combine all ingredients except fish. Add fish and marinate 1 hour. Bake, in marinade, for 15 to 20 minutes or until fish flakes. Garnish as desired. Serve immediately.

Yield: 2 to 4 servings

Anne Patterson Miller (Mrs. Jesse)
Burlington

GRILLED FISH CAPE COD STYLE

Fish—Blue, Haddock, Halibut, Sword or Tuna, your choice.
Mayonnaise

Brush one side of fish with mayonnaise and place on foil. Place on charcoal grill, cover and cook 5 minutes. Turn. Brush other side with mayonnaise; cover and cook 7 minutes.

Yield: 2 to 4 servings

A professional fisherman on Cape Cod gave me this recipe.

Captain Thomas Harper, USN RET
Burlington

TUNA CASSEROLE

1 (10 3/4-ounce) can mushroom soup
1 soup can milk
2 (4-ounce) packages saltine crackers
1 (9 1/4-ounce) can tuna

Heat soup and milk until smooth. Make 2 layers each of tuna and crackers and pour soup mixture over all. Bake at 325° for 20 minutes or until bubbly.

Yield: 4 to 6 servings

Martha Ann Shaw
Burlington

SALMON LOAF

1 can Red Sockeye Salmon (drained and all bones and skin removed)
2 egg whites, beaten
½ cup stuffing mix, dry
¼ cup oat bran
½ teaspoon salt
¼ teaspoon paprika
3 tablespoons minced parsley
2 tablespoons chopped onion
2 tablespoons chopped green pepper
½ tablespoon chopped chives
White pepper to taste
Garlic to taste
¼ cup milk or fish stock
2 teaspoons lemon or lime juice
1 teaspoon Worcestershire sauce

Mix all ingredients together well. Bake at 400° for 30 minutes in greased glass loaf pan. Option: Microwave to internal temperature of 170° or about 10 minutes.

Yield: 6 to 8 servings

Helen Moseley Gant (Mrs. Cecil, Jr.)
Burlington

CRAB BAKE

6 ounces shell shape macaroni
8 ounces cream cheese, softened
1 cup sour cream
1 cup cottage cheese
½ cup green onions, chopped
½ cup fresh parsley, chopped or 2 dried tablespoons
2 (6-ounce) cans crabmeat
1½ cups Cheddar cheese, shredded
2 medium tomatoes, sliced

Cook macaroni 5 minutes; rinse and drain. Combine cream cheese, sour cream, cottage cheese, onions and parsley. Arrange half the macaroni in a greased 2-quart casserole. Spoon half the cheese over all and top with tomato slices. Bake at 350° for 30 minutes.

Yield: 8 to 10 servings

This is one of my favorite dishes to serve at our annual family reunion.

Jessie Ormond Pyne (Mrs. Minetree)
Burlington

MARYLAND'S EASTERN SHORE CRAB CAKES WITH TARTAR SAUCE

3 eggs, beaten
2 tablespoons heavy cream
1 tablespoon Dijon mustard
1 teaspoon Worcestershire sauce
2 teaspoons seafood seasoning
⅛ teaspoon cayenne pepper
Freshly ground black pepper
3 tablespoons minced scallions
2 tablespoons minced fresh parsley
½ cup mayonnaise
2 pounds crabmeat, picked of shell and cartilage
1 cup fine breadcrumbs
1 stick butter
4 tablespoons oil
½ cup finely chopped parsley

Beat eggs in large bowl then add cream, mustard, sauce, seasoning, cayenne and black pepper. Mix well. Add scallions, minced parsley, and mayonnaise until mixture is well blended. Gently fold in crabmeat. Form 8 crab cakes of equal size and coat with breadcrumbs. Place cakes on baking sheet, cover with plastic wrap and chill 1 hour.

Tartar Sauce:
2 tablespoons wine vinegar
1 tablespoon Dijon mustard
4 teaspoons salt
Freshly ground black pepper
TABASCO pepper sauce to taste
1 cup mayonnaise
1 medium onion, finely chopped
¼ cup finely chopped dill pickles
¼ cup finely chopped chives
2 tablespoons chopped capers

Mix vinegar, mustard, salt and pepper until well blended. Add TABASCO pepper sauce, mayonnaise, onion, pickles, chives and capers. Beat until all ingredients are well blended. Cover and chill until ready to use.

Now, melt half the butter and half the oil in a large, heavy skillet. Sauté 4 cakes 3 to 4 minutes on each side, drain on paper towels and keep warm. Repeat with remaining cakes. Sprinkle chopped parsley on each cake and serve with tartar sauce and lemon wedges.

Yield: 8 servings

Sherry Faulkner Scott (Mrs. Don E., III)
Elon College

CRAB IMPERIAL

1 pound backfin crab
½ cup onion, minced
½ cup pepper, red and green, minced
½ cup mayonnaise
Dash dry mustard
Dash seafood seasoning
Salt to taste
Pepper to taste
6 tart shells, baked

Carefully mix all ingredients and fill tart shells. Broil 6 to 8 minutes.

Yield: 6 servings

Sherry Gail Moses
Graham

CRABMEAT CASSEROLE

6 slices bread, cut into halves
1 pound crabmeat
3 eggs
2 cups milk
½ pound Old English cheese, grated
½ cup butter
Salt to taste
Pepper to taste

In casserole dish layer bread, grated cheese and crabmeat. Beat eggs and milk and pour over mixture. Add melted butter then season lightly on top. Refrigerate 3 hours. Bake at 350° for 1 hour.

Yield: 6 to 8 servings

Eugenia Goley Pruitt (Mrs. Ronald)
Burlington

SHRIMP IN CREAM

2 tablespoons butter
2 pounds raw shrimp, cleaned
1 cup heavy cream
1 teaspoon chopped chives
2 teaspoons lemon juice
1 teaspoon Worcestershire sauce
TABASCO pepper sauce to taste

Heat butter in heavy saucepan. Add shrimp and cream. When cream boils add other ingredients and boil 3 to 5 minutes. Serve over rice.

Yield: 4 to 6 servings

Laura Lyle Millender (Mrs. Steve H.)
Burlington

CRAB QUICHE

1 (10½-ounce) can she crab soup
3 eggs, beaten
Milk, enough to thin slightly
1 (8-ounce) can crab meat, picked of shell or ½ pound fresh crab, picked
Lemon juice to taste
⅛ teaspoon mace
Pie crust, unbaked and buttered

Mix all ingredients well and pour into pie shell. Bake at 375° about 30 minutes or until firm.

Yield: 4 to 6 servings

Helen Moseley Gant (Mrs. Cecil, Jr.)
Burlington

ENJOY A SHRIMP ENTRÉE

9 cups water
3 pounds medium-sized fresh shrimp
1 tablespoon lemon juice
½ cup chopped green pepper
¼ cup chopped onion
½ cup chopped celery
1 cup sliced mushrooms
4 tablespoons butter or margarine, melted
1 (10¾-ounce) can cream of celery soup, undiluted
1 cup half and half
¼ cup dry sherry
½ teaspoon salt
½ teaspoon white pepper
3 cups cooked rice
1 (8-ounce) can sliced water chestnuts
Paprika
Fresh parsley sprigs

Bring water to a boil; add shrimp, and cook 3 to 5 minutes. Drain well; rinse with cold water. Chill. Peel and devein shrimp. Set 6 shrimp aside for garnish. Combine shrimp and lemon juice; set aside. Sauté green pepper, onion, celery and mushrooms in butter in a small skillet until tender. Combine soup, half and half, sherry, salt and pepper. Stir in shrimp, vegetables, rice and water chestnuts. Spoon into lightly greased individual au gratin dishes. Bake at 350° for 15 to 20 minutes or until bubbly. Garnish with paprika, reserved shrimp and fresh parsley.

Yield: 6 servings

Ed Hudgins
Burlington

SESAME SHRIMP AND ASPARAGUS

2-2½ pounds shrimp, measured with heads off, but shells on
1½ pounds fresh asparagus
2 ounces soy sauce (the low sodium type is fine)
3 ounces oil (preferably ½ sesame oil and ½ liquid corn or peanut oil, but all corn or peanut oil may be used.)
2 teaspoons sesame seeds

Clean shrimp. Break off and discard tough ends of asparagus, wash, then cut into one-inch pieces. Blanch asparagus for 60 seconds. This is done by bringing a pot of water to a boil, then dropping in asparagus and boiling for one minute. Drain asparagus in colander or a strainer, and run cold water over it for a few seconds. Mix together the soy sauce and oil. Put *all* ingredients into a bowl and stir. At this point, the dish can be cooked and served immediately, or it can marinate in the refrigerator for up to several hours. Ideally, the dish should marinate about one hour refrigerated. To cook, heat skillet or wok to medium or slightly hotter. Stir in all ingredients. Stir constantly until shrimp turn pink. This will only take a few minutes. An attractive presentation is to serve over a small bed of lettuce or serve over rice for a more hearty dish.

Yield: 8 servings

A perfect wine with this is a California or Alsace Gewürztraminer, but make sure it is a dry one and not a "late harvest," as the late harvest wines are for dessert. Beer is good, too, and most any dry white wine will be suitable.

David Pardue
Burlington

SHRIMP RICE SALAD

6 cups cooked rice
2 cups diced celery
4 tablespoons onions, minced
3 cups mayonnaise
1 cup Catalina dressing
2 teaspoons salt
1 teaspoon pepper
3 tablespoons curry powder
4 pounds shrimp, cleaned and cooked

Mix all ingredients except shrimp. Add shrimp. Chill.

Yield: 10 to 12 servings

Grace Lane Mitchell
Greensboro, North Carolina

SCAMPI

½ stick butter
½ cup vegetable oil
1 or 2 cloves garlic, minced
1 bay leaf
2 green onions, minced
2 or 3 tablespoons chopped fresh parsley
Juice of ½ lemon
Dash of Worcestershire sauce
1 teaspoon salt
½ teaspoon pepper
3 teaspoons sugar
½ cup white wine
1½ to 2 pounds shrimp, cleaned and peeled

Mix all ingredients, except shrimp, in saucepan and simmer about 10 minutes. Cool slightly. Place shrimp in single layer in a large baking pan. Pour sauce over all and refrigerate. This can be made early in the day and kept refrigerated. Bring to room temperature and broil about 10 to 15 minutes or until shrimp are bright pink and begin to curl. Serve shrimp and spoon some of sauce over rice.

Yield: 6 servings

Denise Clark Gant (Mrs. Allen E., Jr.)
Burlington

SHRIMP CREOLE

4 pounds raw shrimp, cleaned
2 medium onions, sliced
1 green pepper, sliced
1 cup celery, sliced
½ cup vegetable oil
2 (27-ounce) cans tomatoes
1 (8-ounce) can tomato sauce
½ cup water
⅛ teaspoon garlic powder
1 bay leaf
2 teaspoons salt
2 teaspoons sugar
4 teaspoons chili powder
3 dashes TABASCO pepper sauce
2 packages frozen peas

Place shrimp in boiling salted water to cover and simmer, covered 5 minutes; drain. In dutch oven, sauté onions, pepper and celery in oil until tender. Add next 9 ingredients and simmer 30 minutes. Add shrimp. Cook peas according to package directions; drain. Just before serving, add peas. Serve over rice.

Yield: 6 to 8 servings

Mary Helen Wilson Long (Mrs. Robert)
Burlington

SHRIMP CREOLE

2 pounds shrimp, shelled
1½ cups each carrots, celery, green pepper, chopped
¾ cup chopped onion
Small amount of butter
Cayenne pepper to taste
Paprika
2 cloves garlic, chopped or a sprinkle garlic salt
1 (8-ounce) can tomato sauce
1 small can tomato paste
1 (10½-ounce) can beef consommé
TABASCO pepper sauce to taste
Small amount of flour to thicken

Cook shrimp until they turn pink. Sauté the vegetables in butter until crunchy and add seasonings to taste. Stir once and add canned ingredients and TABASCO pepper sauce. Stir to combine. Simmer for a few minutes. Thicken with a small amount of flour, blending well to avoid lumps. This may be served with sour cream on the side.

Yield: 8 to 10 servings

Jacqueline Garrison Powell (Mrs. William C.)
Burlington

INA'S SHRIMP CREOLE

¼ pound bacon, cooked until crisp and crumbled
3 green peppers, cut into strips
1 regular size bottle ketchup
3 tablespoons Worcestershire sauce
4 drops TABASCO pepper sauce
Black pepper
½ teaspoon salt
1 teaspoon sugar
2 pounds shrimp, cooked and deveined

Mix pepper, ketchup, sauces and seasonings in saucepan and simmer 45 minutes. Add shrimp and simmer an additional 15 minutes. Serve over hot rice and sprinkle with bacon.

Yield: 4 to 6 servings

A dear friend gave me this recipe and it is so easy but so good!

Frances Ray Reed (Mrs. Donald)
Burlington

SHRIMP CREOLE

2 large green peppers
2 medium onions
2 (28-ounce) cans tomatoes
Salt and pepper
Worcesterhire sauce
Paprika
TABASCO pepper sauce
3 pounds cooked shrimp, cleaned
2 cups cooked rice
2 strips bacon, cooked and crumbled
Grated Parmesan cheese

Finely chop green peppers and onions. Sauté in olive oil until golden. Add tomatoes and season highly with all seasonings. Cook until slightly thickened, 20 to 30 minutes. At last minute add shrimp and cook slowly only until shrimp is hot. Pour into the middle of a deep ring of cooked rice. Sprinkle shrimp sauce with crumbled bacon and freshly grated Parmesan cheese. Serve immediately.

Yield: 12 servings

Frances Glass Erwin (Mrs. Jesse Harper, III)
Burlington

CURLY'S BOILED SHRIMP

5 pounds raw shrimp
3 quarts cold water
½ cup salt
3 teaspoons pepper
20 whole allspice berries
1 teaspoon cayenne pepper
6 bay leaves
1 stalk of celery tops, cut to first joint
Juice and rind of 1 lemon
1 clove garlic
3 medium onions, whole

Rinse shrimp and drain. Combine all other ingredients in large kettle and boil for 3 minutes. Place shrimp carefully in kettle and boil slowly for 10 to 15 minutes. Test after 10 minutes for tenderness. When tender, pour cold water into kettle until shrimp sink to bottom and let stand 3 to 5 minutes. Drain. Allow shrimp to cool and peel.

Yield: 10 to 12 servings

May serve with a sauce but Curly always thought it an insult to the shrimp!

Mary Maude Sanders Cockman
Burlington

GILLIAM'S SPRING SHRIMP CASSEROLE

2-3 pounds shrimp, cleaned, peeled, cooked
1 cup wild rice, cooked
1 cup white rice, cooked
1 cup grated sharp cheese
½ cup bleu cheese
1 (10¾-ounce) can mushroom soup
1 stick butter
½ cup chopped green pepper
½ cup chopped onions
½ cup chopped celery
8 lemons, sliced very thin

Mix first six ingredients well. Sauté vegetables in butter just until limp and add to shrimp mixture. Place into a well greased long casserole and completely cover top with sliced lemons. Bake at 375° for 20 to 25 minutes.

Yield: 6 to 8 servings

N. Jane Iseley
Burlington

QUICK SHRIMP BISQUE

2 tablespoons butter
2 tablespoons raw rice
1 medium onion, chopped
2 cups water
1 large can tomato sauce
1 teaspoon curry powder
1 tablespoon water
Salt to taste
Pepper to taste
1 large can shrimp, cut in small pieces (or 1 pound cooked, cut in small pieces)

Melt butter and add rice and cook until rice is yellowed. Add onions, water and tomato sauce. Mix curry powder and 1 tablespoon water until well blended. Stir all ingredients together and season to taste. Simmer 25 minutes. Add shrimp and simmer an additional 10 minutes.

Yield: 8 to 10 servings

Sara Shaw Young
Burlington

SHRIMP AND MUSHROOM POLONAISE

1 pound fresh shrimp
1 pound fresh mushrooms
4 tablespoons butter
2 tablespoons olive oil
6 to 8 shallots, chopped
¼ cup chopped parsley
¼ cup Madeira
Freshly ground pepper
Paprika
1 cup sour cream

Clean shrimp. Remove stems from mushrooms. Melt butter and add oil. Sauté shallots gently for 2 minutes. Add mushrooms and sauté gently for 10 minutes, tossing frequently. Add parsley and wine. Let come to a boil and add shrimp. Cook 4 to 5 minutes or until shrimp turn pink. Season with salt, pepper and paprika. Stir in sour cream. Heat but do not boil. Serve with rice pilaf.

Yield: 4 servings

Ed Hudgins
Burlington

SHRIMP AND CRAB CASSEROLE

2 pounds shrimp, cleaned and cooked
2 pounds crabmeat, picked of shell
2 medium onions, chopped fine
2 medium green peppers, chopped fine
1½ pints mayonnaise
1 bottle Durkee Famous Sauce
Salt to taste
Pepper to taste
TABASCO pepper sauce
Toasted breadcrumbs

Mix all ingredients except breadcrumbs. Place in large greased casserole dish and spread breadcrumbs on top. Bake at 400° for 20 minutes.

Yield: 10 servings

Catherine Holt McCormick
Burlington

SEAFOOD CASSEROLE

2 (6-ounce) packages wild and white rice mix
1 pound crabmeat
4 (4½-ounce) cans shrimp, drained
3 (10¾-ounce) cans cream of mushroom soup
⅓ cup grated onion
1 cup chopped green pepper
1 cup chopped celery
1 (4-ounce) jar pimento drained and chopped
3 tablespoons lemon juice

Preheat oven to 325°. Cook rice mix according to package directions. Pick crabmeat of shell and cartilage. Rinse shrimp in cold water and drain again. Lightly grease a 4-quart casserole and combine all ingredients right in the casserole. Stir to mix well. Reserve a few shrimp and crabmeat for garnish. Sprinkle with paprika. Bake uncovered 1 hour.

Yield: 10 to 12 servings

Gilberta Jeffries Mitchell (Mrs. R. G.)
Mebane

SEAFOOD NEWBURG A LA SUSAN

1 pound scallops
½ pound deveined raw shrimp
½ pound crabmeat
2 quarts boiling water
1 tablespoon shrimp spice and 2 teaspoons salt in cheesecloth bag
3 egg yolks, beaten
2 cups half and half
6 tablespoons butter or margarine
2 tablespoons flour
⅛ teaspoon nutmeg
1 teaspoon salt
3 tablespoons sherry

Combine first 6 ingredients in pot. Bring to boil and cook 2 to 3 minutes. Drain. Combine egg yolks and half and half. Melt butter in blazer of chafing dish. Add flour, nutmeg, salt and sherry. Stir until blended. Add seafood mixture, stirring until heated. Slowly, add egg and cream mixture stirring constantly until thickened and smooth. Serve as a dip with crackers or on English muffins.

Yield: 4 to 6 servings

Evelyn Moss Brassington
Burlington

TAKE-YOUR-CHOICE CHOWDER

¼ cup sliced celery
2 tablespoons chopped onion
1 tablespoon margarine
1 (10½-ounce) can condensed cream of potato soup
½ soup can milk
½ soup can water
1 (7-ounce) can minced clams, drained

Cook celery and onion in margarine. Add soup, milk, water and clams. Heat well and serve.

Variations: omit clams; add one of the following:
1 (7-ounce) can crabmeat, drained and flaked
1 (6-ounce) can shrimp, drained
1 (7-ounce) can tuna, drained and flaked or
1 cup flaked cooked fish

Yield: 4 to 6 servings

Joy Kristen Smith
Delray Beach, Florida

LINGUINI WITH CLAM SAUCE

8 ounces uncooked linguini
2 (6½-ounce) cans minced clams, undrained
½ medium onion, chopped
1 clove garlic, minced
¼ cup olive oil
1 tablespoon chopped fresh parsley (or 2 tablespoons dried)
⅛ teaspoon black pepper
⅓ cup grated Parmesan cheese

Cook linguini in heavy pot according to package directions. Drain, return to pot; set aside. Drain clams, reserving liquid; set clams aside. Sauté onion and garlic in hot oil in a saucepan until tender. Add clam liquid and simmer 15 minutes. Stir in clams, parsley, pepper and cheese. Heat thoroughly. Add clam mixture to linguini, tossing well. Cook over medium heat until thoroughly heated. Serve immediately.

Yield: 4 servings

Frances Trax Bennett (Mrs. Howard L.)
Burlington

JANSON'S TEMPTATION

Irish potatoes, enough to fill pan of choice
1 (4.4-ounce) can anchovies
1 large onion, chopped
Salt
1 quart cream
Fresh breadcrumbs
Butter

Wash, peel and cut potatoes into french fry shape. Layer bottom of greased pan to make 1-inch deep. Spread anchovies then onion over potatoes. Place remaining potatoes on top and cover with cream. Sprinkle a thin layer of breadcrumbs over all and lightly salt. Dot with small amounts of butter. Bake at 350° for 45 to 50 minutes or until potatoes are done.

Yield: 6 to 8 servings

Britt Älander Nordh (Mrs. Jan)
Örebro, Sweden

OYSTER PIE

1 stick butter, melted
1 teaspoon Worcestershire
½ cup dry breadcrumbs
1 cup round buttery cracker crumbs
1 pint oysters
Salt to taste
2 tablespoons heavy cream
2 tablespoons oyster liquid

Mix butter, Worcestershire, bread and cracker crumbs together. Put ⅓ of the crumb mixture in a buttered shallow baking dish and cover with ½ the oysters. Sprinkle with seasonings. Add ½ each of oyster liquid and cream. Repeat. Cover top with remaining crumbs. Bake at 400° for 30 minutes.

Yield: 4 servings

This recipe can be doubled—it goes fast!

Pamela Anne Morrison
New York, New York

TIG HUGHES' SCALLOPED OYSTERS

1 pound box saltine crackers or round buttery crackers
1 stick butter or margarine
1 pint standard oysters, drained of liquid, but reserved
Salt to taste
Pepper to taste
2 to 3 cups milk

Butter 2-quart casserole. Crumble half of crackers on bottom of dish. Sprinkle half of oysters on top of crackers and dot with half of butter. Sprinkle salt and pepper to taste. Repeat layer. Cover with milk. Bake at 350° about 30 minutes or until brown.

Yield: 6 to 8 servings

Holt Hughes McQueen (Mrs. Robert B.)
Graham

Lottie Sue Fesperman Arthur (Mrs. Bob)
Burlington

DADDY'S OYSTER STEW

½ pint select oysters
1 or 2 rounded tablespoons butter
1 teaspoon minced onion
½ teaspoon Worcestershire sauce
1 cup half and half

In saucepan, cook oysters, butter, onions and Worcesterhire until oysters begin to curl. In another pan, heat cream. Pour oysters into cream and season to taste.

Yield: 2 servings

Elaine Frissell Neese (Mrs. L. E., Jr.)
Burlington

Poultry and Game

Following the Civil War, the production of blue and white Alamance Plaids was gradually supplanted as other dyes and colors gained popularity. These "Second Generation Plaids" included varying shades of brown and yellow, achieved through the use of synthetic dyes, as well as natural organic coloring agents made from onion skins and walnut hulls. Throughout the late 1800s the variously colored Alamance Plaids were shipped throughout the United States, where they gained favor as a popular dress material.

CHARLES T. HOLT HOUSE

Haw River, N.C.

With its picturesque massing of peaks, turrets and decorative chimneys, the Charles T. Holt house is the most ornate early textile mansion still standing in Alamance County. Completed in September, 1897, the house was designed by architect George F. Barber of Knoxville, Tennessee.

The house was built for Charles T. Holt, son of N.C. Governor Thomas Michael Holt and grandson of textile pioneer Edwin Michael Holt. It sits atop a hill overlooking the Granite and Tabardrey Mills in Haw River, and is presently owned by Mr. and Mrs. Clyde R. Teague.

CHICKEN BONNE FEMME

2 whole large chicken breasts
2 egg yolks
2 tablespoons dry white wine
1 tablespoon lemon juice
1¾ sticks butter or margarine
¼ teaspoon tarragon
⅛ teaspoon ground red pepper
¼ teaspoon salt
2 tablespoons salad oil
1 (10 to 12-ounce) bag spinach
½ pound mushrooms, thinly sliced
1 carrot, cut into 2" by ⅓" strips

Cut each chicken breast in half, remove skin and bones. With meat mallet, pound each breast half to ¼ inch thickness; set aside. In double boiler over hot, not boiling, water, with wire whisk, beat egg yolks, wine, and lemon juice until mixture thickens slightly. Add ¾ cup butter or margarine (1½ sticks), 1 tablespoon at a time, beating constantly with whisk until butter melts and mixture thickens. Stir in tarragon, ground red pepper, and ¼ teaspoon salt. Cover and keep sauce warm. In a 5 quart Dutch oven or saucepot over high heat, in hot salad oil, cook spinach and ¼ teaspoon of salt just until wilted, stirring constantly. Arrange spinach on platter; cover and keep warm. In a 12-inch skillet over medium high heat, in 2 tablespoons hot butter or margarine (¼ stick), cook chicken breasts until fork-tender and lightly browned on both sides, about 5 to 7 minutes. Arrange chicken on spinach. In drippings in skillet over medium heat, cook mushrooms and carrot until tender, stirring occasionally. Pour sauce over chicken. Top with mushroom and carrot mixture.

Yield: 4 servings

Mary Carter Hudgins
Burlington

CHICKEN PARMESAN

2 whole chicken breasts, skinned and split
½ stick margarine, melted
½ teaspoon salt
¼ teaspoon black pepper
½ cup flour
½ cup Parmesan cheese

Dip chicken in melted butter. Mix dry ingredients in a bowl. Coat chicken in dry ingredients. Bake in a lightly oiled baking dish at 325° for 1 hour.

Yield: 4 servings

Ann Dean Honeycutt (Mrs. Chester)
Burlington

SUPREMES DE VOLAILLE A LA MOUTARDE
(Chicken Breasts With Mustard Sauce)

4 whole, skinless, boneless chicken breasts
Salt to taste, if desired
Freshly ground pepper to taste
3 tablespoons butter
2 tablespoons finely chopped shallots
½ cup dry white wine
1 cup heavy cream
3 tablespoons imported mustard
3 tablespoons finely chopped chives, optional

Split the chicken breasts in half lengthwise. Cut away and discard any cartilage and connecting tissues. Sprinkle the breasts with salt and pepper. Heat the butter in a large, heavy skillet and add the breasts in one layer. Cook over moderately low heat three to four minutes or until lightly browned. Turn the pieces and continue cooking seven to eight minutes. Transfer the pieces to a warm platter. Add the shallots to the skillet and cook, stirring, about 30 seconds. Add the wine and cook, stirring, about one minute. Add the cream and cook down until reduced to about ¾ cup. Stir in the mustard; return the chicken breasts to the skillet and turn them in the sauce. Bring to a boil. Sprinkle with chives and serve. Rice goes well with this dish.

Yield: 4 servings

Mary Carter Hudgins
Burlington

BARBEQUE CHICKEN

2 chickens, cut up, or chicken breasts
1½ cups vinegar
2 cups water
1½ sticks margarine
4 medium onions
4 tablespoons Worcestershire sauce
Salt and pepper, to taste

Combine all ingredients except Worcestershire sauce in roasting pan. Cook 1 hour or until tender on top of stove. Uncover and bake at 350° or until golden brown, basting with sauce every 5 to 10 minutes.

Yield: 8 to 10 servings

Mary E. McClure Phillips
Graham

BAR-B-Q CHICKEN

1 frying size chicken, cut up
1 bottle chili sauce
½ cup vinegar
½ stick margarine
2 tablespoons Worcestershire sauce
1 lemon, sliced thinly

Batter and fry chicken until light brown. Place in baking dish. Combine remaining ingredients except lemon. Bring mixture to boil. Pour over chicken. Place lemon slices over top. Cover with foil and bake at 375° for 1 hour. Delicious served with rice.

Yield: 6 servings

Eunice Evans Carden
Mebane

BAKED MUSTARD CHICKEN

4 boneless chicken breast halves
¼ cup spicy brown mustard
½ cup herb seasoned breadcrumbs
¼ cup margarine
2 tablespoons lemon juice
2 tablespoons white wine (dry sherry)
Paprika

Brush chicken with mustard, dredge with bread crumbs. Place in an 8-inch square baking dish. Combine margarine, lemon juice and wine; drizzle 1 tablespoon over each piece of chicken. Pour remainder in dish. Cover and bake at 350° for 45 minutes. Remove cover, sprinkle with paprika and bake an additional 15 minutes. Freezes well and reheats well in microwave.

Yield: 4 servings

Margaret Long Beatty (Mrs. Hayden)
Burlington

BAKED CHICKEN IN SHERRY

6 chicken breasts halved and salted or 1 large fryer cut up and salted
1 medium onion, diced
1/4 teaspoon pepper
1 teaspoon salt
1 (10 3/4-ounce) can cream of mushroom soup
1/2 (14 1/2-ounce) can evaporated milk
1/4 cup butter
1/2 cup cooking sherry
1 tablespoon flour
Chopped parsley

Dredge chicken lightly in flour; brown on all sides in butter or oil. Heat soup, milk and remaining ingredients, pour over chicken. Cover with foil, cook at 350° for 1 hour, basting often. Remove foil to allow to brown the last few minutes, or turn broiler on for a few minutes. Add chopped parsley to serve.

Yield: 10 to 12 servings

Eunice Evans Carden
Mebane

BAKED CHICKEN

1 stick butter
1 cup sour cream
1 can mushroom soup
2 teaspoons Worcestershire sauce
Salt and pepper to taste
4 chicken breasts, cut in half

Melt butter in casserole. Roll chicken breasts in butter and bake at 400° for 45 minutes, turning frequently. Mix sour cream, soup, salt, pepper and Worcestershire sauce. Pour over chicken. Reduce heat to 375°. Bake 15 minutes.

Yield: 8 servings

The Brannock sisters, Edith and Madge, have catered many special receptions throughout Alamance County.

Edith Ruth Brannock
Elon College

CHICKEN JUBILEE

4-6 chicken breasts
1 teaspoon salt
¼ teaspoon pepper
¼ cup margarine
1 (8-ounce) can sweet and sour sauce
1 cup drained, sliced peaches
1½ cups drained, dark pitted sweet cherries
1 onion sliced thinly
½ cup chili sauce

Place chicken in baking dish. Sprinkle with salt and pepper, drizzle with melted margarine. Mix other ingredients and pour over chicken. Bake at 350° until tender, about 1 hour.

Yield: 4 to 6 servings

Martha Young Clark (Mrs. T. N.)
Burlington

SEDGEFIELD CHICKEN

4 chicken breasts, cut in half
1 jar or package dried beef
½ cup sour cream
1 cup cream of mushroom soup
¼ cup milk
1 cup grated sharp Cheddar cheese

Place dried beef in a layer in a large baking dish. Place chicken side by side on top of beef. Mix sour cream, soup and milk. Spoon over chicken. Bake at 350° for 1 hour. Remove from oven, sprinkle with cheese, bake 30 minutes longer. Good with rice or green noodles.

Yield: 8 servings

Ann Spoon Cooper (Mrs. Collins)
Windsor, North Carolina

CHICKEN SUPREME

8 whole chicken breasts, halved, skinned and boned
4 small cloves garlic, minced
10 tablespoons butter or margarine
4 (10¾-ounce) cans cream of chicken soup
1 cup water
1 package slivered almonds, toasted
3 tablespoons parsley flakes

In a skillet, brown chicken in butter and garlic. Cover and cook over low heat 45 minutes or until tender. Combine soup, water and parsley flakes. Stir 1 cup soup mixture into chicken, brown slightly. Heat remainder of soup mixture to pour over chicken before serving. Top with almonds and serve over rice. Can be prepared a day ahead and reheated.

Yield: 14 to 16 servings

Ann Birmingham Flagg (Mrs. Raymond)
Burlington

JOHN'S LEMON CHICKEN

1 large whole fryer
1 lemon, perforated
Softened butter

Stuff lemon into cavity of chicken. Sew up neck and end with twine. Rub chicken with butter and place breast side down on parchment paper on a large cookie sheet. Bake on middle rack of oven at 350° for 45 minutes. Remove from oven, and carefully turn over so as not to puncture the skin. Bake this breast side for an additional 30 minutes. Turn oven up to 400° and bake an additional 15 minutes. Remove from oven, then remove twine and with a long spoon "squash" the lemon in the chicken then remove the lemon. NOTE: Total baking time is 90 minutes.

Yield: 3 to 4 servings

Eda Contiguglia Holt (Mrs. Ralph M., Jr.)
Burlington

CHICKEN SCALA

3 whole chicken breasts, halved and deboned
2 tablespoons flour
¼ cup butter
1 (10¾-ounce) can beef bouillon
1 cup sour cream
1 teaspoon salt
½ teaspoon pepper
1 tablespoon grated Parmesan cheese

Flour chicken, sauté in butter until brown, about 15 minutes. Add bouillon and simmer 45 minutes. Stir in sour cream, salt and pepper. Simmer 10 minutes. Remove chicken to casserole dish. Stir sauce to mix well and strain over chicken. Refrigerate overnight in sauce to improve flavor. Heat slightly just before serving. Sprinkle cheese on top and put under broiler until golden brown.

Yield: 6 servings

Martha Curtis Hudgins (Mrs. Ed)
Burlington

SOUR CREAM MARINATED CHICKEN BREASTS

5 whole chicken breasts, halved
¼ cup lemon juice
2 teaspoons Worcestershire sauce
2 teaspoons celery salt
1 teaspoon paprika
2 cloves garlic minced, if desired
2 teaspoons pepper
Breadcrumbs, day old French bread is good
½ cup melted margarine
¼ cup melted shortening

Combine sour cream, lemon juice, Worcestershire sauce, celery salt, paprika, garlic and pepper; blend well. Sprinkle chicken with salt and coat with sour cream mixture. Cover with plastic wrap and refrigerate for at least 12 hours. Remove chicken from refrigerator and coat with bread crumbs. Place in single layer in a lightly greased 9x13x2-inch baking dish. Combine margarine and shortening, pour half of mixture over chicken. Bake at 350° for 45 minutes. Pour remaining mixture over chicken, continue baking an additional 15 minutes or until tender.

Yield: 10 servings

Frances Anderson Johnson (Mrs. Eldridge J.)
Greensboro, North Carolina

MARINATED CHICKEN BREASTS

4 to 6 chicken breasts, halved

Marinade:
1 cup pineapple juice
1/3 cup teriyaki sauce
1/4 cup Italian dressing
1 tablespoon lemon juice

Mix marinade ingredients well and marinate chicken 6 to 24 hours. Cook on grill about 10 to 15 minutes. Do not overcook. Variation: Delicious cut in strips and served on top of a bed of lettuce, cucumbers and tomatoes. Sprinkle with toasted almonds and honey mustard dressing.

Dressing:
Equal parts of mayonnaise, mustard, honey and a small amount of lemon juice.

Yield: 4 to 6 servings

Jeanette Zimmerman Newlin (Mrs. Thomas)
Haw River

CHICKEN BREASTS BAKED IN WINE

8 chicken breasts, deboned
2 (10 3/4-ounce) cans cream of chicken soup
2 (10 3/4-ounce) cans cream of mushroom soup
4 tablespoons minced parsley
3 cloves garlic, slivered
4 tablespoons slivered, blanched almonds
3/4 cup sherry or white wine

Place 1/2 the chicken breasts in casserole. Mix soups together, add sherry and garlic. Pour 1/2 the mixture over chicken breasts, and sprinkle parsley and almonds on top. Add remaining breasts, repeat, placing parsley and almonds on top. Cover and bake at 350° for 1 1/2 hours. Serve with wild rice.

Yield: 8 to 10 servings

Lucille Paschal Wofford
Burlington

CHICKEN PICCATA

4 whole chicken breasts, skinned, boned, and halved
½ cup flour
1½ teaspoons salt
¼ teaspoon freshly ground pepper
Paprika
¼ cup clarified butter
1 tablespoon olive oil
5 tablespoons dry Madeira or sherry
3 tablespoons fresh lemon juice
Lemon slices
3 to 4 tablespoons capers, optional
¼ cup minced fresh parsley, optional

Pound chicken breasts between 2 sheets of waxed paper until thin, about ¼ inch. Combine flour, salt, pepper and paprika in bag. Add chicken and coat well. Shake off excess. Heat butter and olive oil in large skillet until bubbling. Sauté chicken breasts, a few at a time, 2 to 3 minutes on each side. Do not overcook. Drain on paper towels and keep warm. Drain all but 2 tablespoons of butter and oil. Stir Madeira or water into drippings, scraping bottom of skillet to loosen any browned bits. Add lemon juice and heat briefly. Return chicken to skillet, interspersing with lemon slices, and heat until sauce thickens. Add capers. Sprinkle with minced parsley.

Yield: 4 to 5 servings

Peggy Jones McCuiston (Mrs. John)
Burlington

QUICK CHICKEN PIE

4 cups chicken or 4 chicken breasts, uncooked
1 cup celery soup
1 cup chicken broth
1½ cups buttermilk baking mix
1½ cups milk
1 stick butter

Combine chicken soup and broth into casserole. Mix buttermilk baking mix with milk in bowl and pour over chicken mixture. Bake at 350° for 35 to 40 minutes or until brown.

Yield: 6 to 8 servings

Foy Elder Lane (Mrs. V. Wilton)
Burlington

GINNY'S CHICKEN AND RICE

4 whole chicken breasts, deboned
1 (10¾-ounce) can cream of chicken soup
1 (10¾-ounce) can cream of celery soup
½ cup butter
¼ cup sherry
3 ounces grated Parmesan cheese
¼ cup slivered almonds
1¼ cups wild rice

Mix soups and heat. Add butter and sherry. Mix half of soup mixture with rice and put in bottom of 1½-quart casserole. Top with chicken breasts and cover with remaining soup mixture. Sprinkle with Parmesan cheese and almonds. Bake uncovered at 275° for 2½ hours.

Yield: 8 to 10 servings

Sue McKee Watson (Mrs. Robert A.)
Elon College

CAPITAL CHICKEN DEVINE

6 chicken breasts
4 tablespoons butter
1 tablespoon cooking oil
½ stick butter
8 ounces fresh mushrooms
1 tablespoon flour
1 (10¾-ounce) can cream of chicken soup
1 cup dry white wine
1 cup water
½ cup cream
1 teaspoon salt
½ teaspoon pepper
2 (15-ounce) cans artichoke hearts
6 green onions, chopped, with green stems
2 tablespoons chopped parsley

In a large frying pan, heat butter and oil to medium temperature. Add chicken and cook about 10 minutes, turning until golden brown on all sides. Remove chicken, place in casserole. In the same frying pan, after it has been cleaned, add 4 tablespoons butter. Sauté mushrooms, caps and stems until tender. Remove mushrooms. Stir in flour and add soup, wine and water stirring until this reaches a sauce consistency. Pour over chicken in casserole. Bake at 300° for 1 hour uncovered. Stir in cream, salt and all seasonings. Arrange artichoke hearts around chicken. Sprinkle green onions and parsley over all. Bake an additional 5 minutes.

Yield: 6 servings

Dorothy Ruffin Scott (Mrs. Don E., Jr.)
Burlington

BUTTERMILK FRIED CHICKEN

3 pounds chicken legs and breasts
2 cups plain flour
1 tablespoon salt
1 teaspoon paprika
½ teaspoon black pepper
1 cup buttermilk
1 teaspoon baking powder
Vegetable oil

Combine flour, salt, pepper and paprika in a plastic or paper bag; shake to mix and set aside. Combine buttermilk and baking powder in a bowl and mix well. Dip 2 pieces chicken in buttermilk mixture; place chicken in bag and shake to coat. Repeat with remaining chicken. Place chicken in a shallow pan; cover and refrigerate at least 1 hour. Heat 1 inch oil in a large skillet to 325°; add chicken and fry 30 to 35 minutes or until golden brown, turning once. Drain on paper towels.

Yield: 8 servings

Sherry Faulkner Scott (Mrs. Don E., III)
Elon College

CHICKEN CAGNEY

6 large tomatoes, sliced
¾ cup round, buttery crackers, crumbled
1½ cups Parmesan cheese
Onion salt to taste
6 chicken breasts, skinned and boned
½ cup wine (white)
2 tablespoons butter

Cover bottom of 7½x11½-inch baking dish with sliced tomatoes. Sprinkle with onion salt and crumble crackers over that. Then sprinkle 1 cup Parmesan cheese over tomatoes. Place chicken on top of tomatoes and pour the wine over the chicken. Add more onion salt and the remaining Parmesan cheese. Dot with butter. Bake at 350° covered for 1 hour and uncovered for ½ hour.

Yield: 6 servings

Variation: Flounder fillets may be substituted in place of chicken. If so, bake for 10 minutes covered and 10 minutes uncovered.

Patsy Slate Burke (Mrs. Bill)
Burlington

CHICKEN TETRAZZINI

¾-1 pound cooked chicken, diced
1 (4-ounce) jar chopped pimento
4 ribs celery, diced
1 medium onion, diced
1 small green pepper, diced
¼ stick margarine
3 cups milk
4 tablespoons cornstarch
1½ tablespoons chicken bouillon
½ pound pasteurized process cheese
2 tablespoons dry sherry, optional
8 ounces medium-wide noodles, cooked

Combine chicken and pimentos in large bowl. Set aside. Sauté celery, onion and pepper in margarine until tender. Combine in bowl with chicken. Whisk together in a saucepan, milk, bouillon, and cornstarch; cook over medium heat stirring frequently until thick and bubbly. Remove from heat. Stir in sherry and cheese until cheese melts. Stir sauce into chicken mixture. Add noodles, mix well. Pour into a quart size casserole. Bake at 350° 30 to 45 minutes.

Yield: 8 to 10 servings

Shirley Barbee Fink (Mrs. Howard)
Graham

CHICKEN TETRAZZINI

3 pounds chicken
1 small green pepper, chopped
½ cup chopped onion
½ cup chopped celery
1 tablespoon oil
1 (7-ounce) package vermicelli, cooked in chicken broth
2 (10¾-ounce) cans cream of mushroom soup
½ cup grated sharp cheese

Boil chicken about 1 hour; cut in bite size pieces and reserve broth. (This step could be done a day ahead and refrigerated until ready to make casserole.) Sauté pepper, onion and celery in oil. Layer ½ of the vermicelli in casserole; layer ½ each of onion mixture, chicken and 1 can of soup. Repeat layers. Top with the grated cheese. Bake at 350° until bubbly and cheese is melted. Freezes well but must be thawed before baking. Additional broth may be added if casserole seems too dry.

Yield: 8 to 10 servings

Marianne Salogga Roarick (Mrs. Richard)
Burlington

CHICKEN TETRAZZINI

½ cup butter
½ cup chopped onions
¼ cup flour
2 cups chicken stock
Salt and pepper
2-3 cups diced cooked chicken
1 cup canned tomatoes
½ cup grated cheese
½ pound spaghetti, cooked
½ cup buttered crumbs
Paprika

Heat butter, add onions and cook until tender. Add flour and blend. Slowly add stock and stir until smooth. Season to taste. Add chicken, tomatoes and cheese. Stir in spaghetti and pour into a greased casserole. Top with crumbs and dash of paprika. Bake at 350° for about 30 minutes.

Yield: 6 to 8 servings

Helen B. Long (Mrs. George A.)
Burlington

OUR FAVORITE TETRAZZINI

1 large fryer
3 or 4 chicken breast halves
3 cups hot water
½ teaspoon celery salt
1 teaspoon onion salt
¾ teaspoon salt
3 tablespoons butter
3 tablespoons flour
¼ teaspoon pepper
¼ teaspoon paprika
½ teaspoon salt
⅛ teaspoon nutmeg
2½ cups chicken stock
1 cup half and half
½ pound box thin spaghetti
Salt to taste
2 cups mushrooms
3 tablespoons butter
1 tablespoon lemon juice
⅔ cup Parmesan cheese

Combine first 6 ingredients in pot and cook until tender. Debone in large pieces and reserve stock. Place in large baking dish. Melt butter and remove from heat. Add next 5 ingredients. Slowly stir in broth and cook until thickened. Add half and half. Pour over chicken and refrigerate overnight. Next day, cook spaghetti in stock and add enough water to cover. Add salt and cook until tender. Drain. Sauté 2 cups mushrooms in 3 tablespoons butter and 1 tablespoon lemon juice. Add spaghetti to mushroom mixture. Place spaghetti in 14x9-inch baking dish. Add chicken and sauce mixture. Top with ⅔ cup Parmesan cheese. Bake at 350° for about 25 minutes or until bubbly.

Yield: 8 to 12 servings

Jean Millikan Frissell (Mrs. Fred, III)
Whitsett, North Carolina

CHICKEN CASSEROLE

2 cups (or more) diced, cooked chicken
3 eggs, boiled and chopped
1 cup diced celery
1 tablespoon lemon juice
1 (10¾-ounce) can cream of chicken soup
Salt to taste
1 cup potato chips

Mix all ingredients except potato chips. Place in casserole then top with potato chips. Bake at 350° for 30 minutes or until bubbly.

Yield: 4 servings

Elizabeth Newlin Newlin (Mrs. Harvey R.)
Burlington

CREAMED CHICKEN

1 cup diced, cooked chicken
2 ounces mushrooms
¼ cup chopped green pepper
¼ cup butter
1 teaspoon salt
1 teaspoon pepper
¼ cup flour
1 cup chicken broth
1 cup half and half
¼ cup chopped pimento

Sauté mushrooms and green pepper in butter. Blend in salt, pepper and flour. Slowly stir in chicken broth and half and half. Let thicken. Add chicken and pimento.

Yield: 4 to 6 servings

Nice to serve in patty shells.

Dorothy Mae Brittle
Burlington

CHEESEY CHICKEN

Chicken breasts (3 or 4), cooked and cut in strips
1 package frozen crescent rolls
Grated sharp Cheddar cheese
1 can cream of chicken soup, diluted with ½ can water

Roll chicken strips and cheese in crescent rolls. Place in baking pan and cover with soup mixture. Bake at 350° for 40 minutes. Sprinkle top with additional cheese. Bake an additional 5 minutes.

Yield: 6 to 8 servings

Aundree Bryant Price (Mrs. William)
Elon College

HOT CHICKEN SALAD

2 cups chopped cooked chicken
2 cups chopped celery
½ cup slivered, blanched almonds
½ teaspoon grated onion
2 tablespoons fresh lemon juice
1 cup mayonnaise
½ teaspoon salt
½ cup grated sharp Cheddar cheese
⅔ cup potato chips, broken

Combine all ingredients except cheese and potato chips. Spoon into lightly greased dish. Combine cheese and potato chips, sprinkle over top. Bake uncovered at 400° for 20 minutes.

Yield: 6 servings

Ethel Boone Gant (Mrs. Allen E.)
Burlington

CRUNCHY HOT CHICKEN SALAD CASSEROLE

3 cups diced, cooked chicken
1 cup chopped celery
½ cup chopped onion
½ cup almonds and/or water chestnuts
1½ cups cooked rice
1 tablespoon lemon juice
Salt and pepper to taste
2 hard-boiled eggs, chopped
¾ cup mayonnaise
¼ cup water
2 cups crushed potato chips
1 cup sharp cheese, grated

Combine first 8 ingredients. Mix mayonnaise and water and beat with wire whisk. Pour over chicken mixture. Toss lightly. Place in greased casserole. Cover, refrigerate overnight. Bake at 450° for 15 minutes. Top with chips and cheese mixed together. Return to oven for 5 minutes.

Yield: 6 to 8 servings

Alene Stonestreet Ventura
Burlington

CHICKEN AND DUMPLINS

1 cup flour
Pinch salt
1 tablespoon shortening
1 egg plus 2 tablespoons water
1 fryer size chicken cooked, skinned and deboned
3-4 cups chicken broth

Mix flour and salt, cut in shortening with a pastry blender. Beat egg with water, mix into flour. Flour board and roll as thin as possible. Cut in desired width, hang on pastry rack to dry, 2 or 3 hours. Bring broth to boiling, drop in pastry strips. Cook until desired doneness, about 10 to 15 minutes. Add cooked chicken.

Yield: 8 to 10 servings

Agnes Compton Allen
Mebane

CHICKEN CASSEROLE

¼ cup melted butter
1 cup cracker crumbs
1 (8-ounce) carton sour cream
1 (10¾-ounce) can cream of chicken soup
¼ cup chicken broth
Salt and pepper to taste
3 whole chicken breasts, cooked and cut into bite sized pieces
½ cup grated Cheddar cheese

Combine cracker crumbs and butter. Mix well. Spoon half the crumbs into a shallow, 2-quart casserole then cover with chicken. Combine sour cream, soup, broth, salt and pepper. Mix well. Pour over chicken, top with grated cheese and remaining crumbs. Bake at 350° for 20 to 25 minutes.

Yield: 6 servings

Beth Elder Ellington (Mrs. Jeff)
Burlington

CURRIED CHICKEN CASSEROLE

4 chicken breasts, halved, cooked and deboned
2 packages frozen broccoli, cooked
2 cups cream of chicken soup
2 tablespoons chicken broth
1 cup mayonnaise
1 cup grated sharp Cheddar cheese
3 tablespoons lemon juice
½-1 tablespoon curry powder
3 tablespoons butter, melted
½ cup breadcrumbs

Line casserole dish with cooked broccoli. Place chicken on top of broccoli. Mix together the mayonnaise, broth, soup, cheese, lemon juice and curry powder. Spread evenly on top. Cover with breadcrumbs. Bake at 350° for 35 to 40 minutes or until bubbly.

Yield: 8 servings

Nancy Matthews Slott (Mrs. Steven D.)
Burlington

EASY CHICKEN PIE

4 chicken breasts, cooked, skinned and halved
2 (10¾-ounce) cans onion soup
½ cup broth from cooked chicken
1 package frozen English peas
1 (6-ounce) can sliced mushrooms
1½ cups buttermilk baking mix
1½ cups milk

Place cooked chicken breasts in oven proof baking dish. Combine soup, peas and mushrooms. Pour over chicken. Mix baking mix and milk, pour over chicken, dot with butter. Bake at 350° for 30 minutes or until crust is brown.

Yield: 6 to 8 servings

Claiborne Sellars Young
Burlington

VEGETABLES ORIENTAL WITH TURKEY OR CHICKEN

½ cup sliced onion
2 tablespoons vegetable oil
2 cups diagonally cut celery
1 cup green peas
2 (3-ounce) cans mushrooms with broth, sliced
1⅓ cups chicken broth
3 tablespoons cornstarch
1 teaspoon salt
1 teaspoon brown bouquet sauce
½ teaspoon ginger (crystallized-diced)
½ pound sliced turkey or chicken, cooked

Cook onion in oil; add celery, cook 1 minute, then add peas and cook 4 minutes. Combine broth from one can mushrooms, chicken broth, cornstarch, salt, bouquet sauce and ginger. Add liquid to skillet and cook until sauce thickens. Stir in mushrooms. Add meat, cover and heat thoroughly, for 5 minutes. Serve with rice.

Yield: 4 servings

Beulah Pritchard Wilson (Mrs. John J.)
Burlington

CHICKEN OR SALMON A LA KING

2 tablespoons butter
1 green pepper, minced
1 cup sliced mushrooms
2 tablespoons flour
1 cup chicken stock
2 cups diced, cooked chicken or boned canned red salmon
1 cup sour cream or evaporated milk
2 egg yolks
1 pimento, diced
Salt and pepper
4 teaspoons sherry

Melt butter. Add green pepper and mushrooms. Sauté until tender. Lift out. Add flour to butter. Add stock and cook until thickened. Add chicken or salmon, cooked pepper and mushrooms. Heat thoroughly. Remove from heat and add cream mixed with beaten egg yolks and remaining ingredients. Do not boil after adding egg yolks. Serve at once or keep hot over boiling water.

Yield: 4 servings

Lucille Oakley Langston
Burlington

CRUNCHY CHICKEN BAKE

2 cups cooked, cubed chicken
1½ cups chopped celery
½ cup grated American cheese
2 teaspoons grated onion
2 tablespoons lemon juice
2 tablespoons slivered almonds, toasted
½ teaspoon salt
1 cup potato chips

Combine all ingredients except cheese and chips. Mix well and turn into baking dish. Sprinkle top with cheese—then chips. Bake at 350° for 30 minutes or until hot through and cheese is melted.

Yield: 4 to 6 servings

Grace Anderson Thompson (Mrs. A. G. Jr.)
Burlington

MOIST TURKEY BREAST

1 turkey breast
½ lemon, juiced
1 cup chopped onion
1 cup chopped celery
1 (8-ounce) package herb stuffing
1 (10¾-ounce) can cream of chicken soup (dilute with 1½ cans water)

Preheat oven to 325°. Soak turkey breast overnight in salt water with lemon juice. Cook onions and celery. Drain. Place foil in bottom of pan with 1 cup water underneath. Place breast side down on foil. Mix herb stuffing with onions and celery. Add ½ of diluted soup and enough water to moisten well. Put into ribcage and close with skewer. Put remaining soup mixture into gravy. Cover with foil. Cook until thermometer registers 180°. Add water to bottom of pan as needed. Partially cool before carving.

Yield: 4 to 6 servings

Elizabeth (Beth) Gatewood Neal (Mrs. Tom)
Burlington

HOT TURKEY SALAD

2 cups diced turkey or chicken, cooked
3 cups diced celery
½ cup chopped walnuts
2 tablespoons chopped onion
1 cup mayonnaise
1 teaspoon salt
2 tablespoons lemon juice
⅔ cup grated cheese
1½ cups crushed potato chips

Mix all ingredients well, except cheese and potato chips. Pour into greased baking dish. Sprinkle with cheese and top with potato chips. Cook at 400° for 20 minutes.

Yield: 4 to 6 servings

Essie Cofield Norwood (Mrs. Ralph)
Burlington

TURKEY PARMESAN SANDWICHES

½ small yellow onion—coarsely chopped
1 clove garlic
1 pound turkey breast, cooked and coarsely chopped
¼ cup Parmesan cheese plus a little extra for sprinkling finished sandwich
Dijon mustard
Mayonnaise
Salt and freshly ground black pepper
Pumpernickel bread
Alfalfa sprouts

In a food processor, grind together onion and garlic—add turkey and pulse to finely chop. Stir in ¼ cup Parmesan. Add mustard and mayonnaise, salt and pepper to taste. Spread on pumpernickel bread—sprinkle with extra Parmesan cheese and broil until browned. Top with alfalfa sprouts and serve.

Yield: 3 cups

A different and delicious sandwich and also good on miniature pumpernickel as an hors d'oeuvre.

Suzanne Reed Martin
Burlington

PHEASANT

1 pheasant
1 medium onion, chopped
1 clove garlic, minced
½ cup white wine
1 (10¾-ounce) can chicken gumbo soup
½ cup mushrooms, fresh or canned
2 tablespoons oil
2 tablespoons butter

Using sharp knife, remove breast from bone. Remove legs and thighs. Discard carcass. In skillet, place 2 tablespoons oil and 2 tablespoons butter and sauté pheasant parts to light brown. Remove from pan. Add chopped onions, garlic clove, minced, season to taste and sauté until tender. Reduce heat to simmer and add wine, chicken gumbo soup, mushrooms and pheasant parts. Cook uncovered for 2 hours. Serve over rice, wild rice or pasta.

Yield: 2 servings

W. Walt Brown, Jr.
Burlington

HENS IN THE POT

4 Cornish game hens, 1 pound each
3 tablespoons butter or margarine
1 teaspoon salt
¼ teaspoon pepper
1 teaspoon thyme
1 tablespoon flour
1 tablespoon Worcestershire sauce
2 tablespoons lemon juice
1 cup red wine
8 small onions
3 tablespoons butter
8 small mushrooms
Fresh parsley

Thaw hens in refrigerator the day before cooking. In a large dutch oven, melt butter. Add hens and brown on all sides. Add salt, pepper and thyme. Stir in flour and Worcestershire sauce, lemon juice and wine. Cover and simmer 40 to 50 minutes. About 25 minutes before hens are done, sauté onions in 3 tablespoons butter until golden. Add mushrooms and cook lightly. Add mixture to hens. Sprinkle with parsley and serve with steamed rice or noodles.

Yield: 8 servings

Elsie Pentecost Clapp (Mrs. W. Keith)
Saxapahaw

DUCK OR CHICKEN WITH WINE AND GINGER SAUCE

6 chicken breast halves or 1 cut-up fryer or 2 ducks
½ cup oil
¼ cup soy sauce
¾ cup rosé wine
1 clove garlic, chopped
1 teaspoon ginger
1 tablespoon brown sugar

Place chicken or duck in large pan with skin up. Combine remaining ingredients and pour over chicken. Cover and bake at 325° for 1½ hours or until done. Serve over fluffy rice. Sauce is enough for 1 chicken or 2 ducks.

Yield: 6 servings

Dorothy Ruffin Scott (Mrs. Don E., Jr.)
Burlington

SMOTHERED MARSH HENS

8 marsh hens
6 tablespoons bacon drippings
6 tablespoons flour
2 cups chicken stock or 1 (10¾-ounce) can chicken soup
Salt and pepper to taste

Parboil eight skinned birds in salt water just long enough to take out the blood and keep the shape. Drain and put in deep frying pan on top of stove. In separate pan, add bacon drippings and flour, stirring constantly until browned. Add stock (or soup), salt and pepper and cook until smooth. Pour over hens and simmer for 1 hour, then uncover and broil 15 minutes.

Yield: 8 servings

My husband enjoyed hunting and fishing in every season of the year and the bounty from Currituck game was traditionally shared by family and friends on his December 6th birthday.

Grace Lane Cook (Mrs. Staley A.)
Burlington

CREAMED QUAIL

12 quails, cleaned and dressed
Salt and pepper
Seasoned herb mix
1 pound margarine
4 cups sweet cream
1½ cups toasted breadcrumbs

Salt, pepper and season the quail. Simmer slowly in margarine in cooker until tender. Add cream and continue simmering until done. Remove quail to a hot platter. Sprinkle toasted breadcrumbs over quail. Pour cream gravy over all.

Yield: 12 servings

Harriett Eiler Copland (Mrs. James R. III)
Burlington

BROILED GOOSE FILETS

4 goose breast filets
1 bottle Italian dressing
2 teaspoons Worcestershire sauce
Salt and pepper to taste

Marinate filets with other ingredients for 12 hours. Cook on hot grill: 3 minutes skin side, 2 minutes other side. Slice like London Broil. Good served with wild rice and marinated mushrooms.

Yield: 4 servings

Harriett Eiler Copland (Mrs. James R. III)
Burlington

VENISON ROAST

1 3-5 pound venison roast
1 (10¾-ounce) can onion soup
1 medium onion, sliced
3-4 medium potatoes, diced
Salt and pepper to taste

Soak roast in cold water 3 hours. Place roast and remaining ingredients in a browning bag. Bake at 325° for 3 hours.

Yield: 6 to 8 servings

Harriett Eiler Copland (Mrs. James R., III)
Burlington

VENISON STEW

2-3 pounds venison, cut in 2-inch cubes
Oil
¼ pound salt pork, diced, cooked; reserve drippings
¼ cup flour
Water
1 large can tomatoes, chopped
Salt to taste
Pepper to taste
3 carrots, diced large
2 Irish potatoes, diced large
1 cup celery, diced large

Sauté venison in oil until browned. Remove and place in crock pot. To remaining oil, add salt pork drippings; stir in flour and enough water to make a thin sauce. To crock pot, add sauce, salt pork, tomatoes, salt and pepper. Stir well. Start crock pot on high and let stew come to a bubble, then immediately turn to low and cook 14 to 16 hours or until venison is tender. To prevent vegetables from becoming mushy, add to the stew the last 4 to 6 hours of cooking. Freezes well.

Yield: 6 to 8 servings

H. Clay Hemric
Burlington

VENISON WITH SPRING ONIONS

Dijon mustard
6 (4-ounce) venison steaks, cubed
6 spring onions
½ cup all-purpose flour
3 tablespoons vegetable oil

Spread mustard lightly over each piece of venison. Place whole spring onions in middle and roll. Fasten with toothpicks. Dust roll-ups lightly with flour and brown in oil. Remove and make gravy. Place meat back in gravy. Cook on medium heat until meat is tender.

Yield: 4 to 6 servings

Harriett Eiler Copland (Mrs. James R., III)
Burlington

The success of Alamance Plaids not only gave impetus to the North Carolina textile industry, but it also firmly established the Holt family as a leading force in textiles in the Piedmont area. By the early 1900s, twenty-five of the County's twenty-nine cotton mills were controlled by members of the Holt family.

SOUTHERN RAILWAY DEPOT

Burlington, N.C.

In continual service from 1892 until its closing in 1962, the Southern Railway Passenger Depot is a reminder of the important role which railroads played in the history and formation of Burlington, North Carolina. Once the hub of a thriving railroad and textile manufacturing center, the depot was restored in 1979 and is now used by the Burlington Recreation Department as an art gallery and civic center.

ASPARAGUS AND EGG CASSEROLE

1 (14-ounce) can asparagus spears
3 hard-boiled eggs, sliced
1 (11-ounce) can cream of mushroom soup
Salt and pepper
Breadcrumbs or canned onion rings
1 tablespoon butter

In a 1-quart casserole place one half the asparagus spears. Cover with one half the egg slices and one half of the soup. Repeat the 3 layers. Sprinkle salt and pepper on top and cover with breadcrumbs. Dot with butter. Bake at 250° for 25 minutes.

Yield: 6 servings

Dianne Simpson Gerlach (Mrs. John)
Burlington

FRESH ASPARAGUS AND GREEN ONION PIE

1½ pounds fresh asparagus
3 tablespoons margarine
3 tablespoons green onions cut in pieces, including green tops
4 eggs
1 teaspoon salt
½ teaspoon black pepper
¾ cup grated cheese
¾ cup evaporated milk
1 cup milk
1 (9-inch) unbaked pie shell

Wash asparagus; trim and cut into ½-inch pieces. Melt margarine in a skillet and cook green onions over low heat. In a large bowl beat eggs with salt, pepper, cheese and milk. Add asparagus and onions. Turn into the pie shell. Bake at 425° for 10 minutes. Reduce heat to 350° and bake an additional 30 minutes.

Yield: 6 to 8 servings

Annie Patton Young
Mebane

BIG DADDY'S STRING BEAN CASSEROLE

1 package frozen French-style green beans
2 tablespoons butter
1 tablespoon flour
1 teaspoon sugar
½ teaspoon salt
½ teaspoon pepper
1 cup sour cream
2 long slices aged Swiss cheese
1 small onion, chopped
Corn flakes

Cook green beans in boiling water according to directions on package. Combine butter, flour, sugar and salt in a double boiler and mix well. Add the sour cream and mix well. Crumble cheese into sour cream mixture and continue cooking, stirring occasionally until cheese melts. In a skillet sauté onions in 1 teaspoon of butter until tender. Stir cooked onions into sour cream mixture. Drain green beans and combine with sour cream mixture. Pour into a medium casserole and top with corn flakes. Bake at 350° for about 30 minutes. May be doubled.

Yield: 2 servings

Claiborne Sellars Young
Burlington

CLASSIC COMPANY GREEN BEANS (MICROWAVE)

2 (9-ounce) packages frozen French-style green beans or
2 cans French-style green beans, drained
1 (10¾-ounce) can cream of mushroom soup or
1 (10¾-ounce) can cream of celery soup
1 (3-ounce) can French fried onions

Place beans in 2-quart glass casserole. Cover and cook on high 9 to 11 minutes or until beans are tender, stirring twice. Stir in soup and half of onions. Top with remaining onions. Cook on high 5 to 6 minutes. Let stand 3 minutes before serving.

Yield: 4 to 6 servings

Helen Rumley Cleek (Mrs. Robert)
Elon College

GREEN BEAN CASSEROLE

2 (16-ounce) cans French-style green beans, drained (or 4 cups any cooked vegetables)
1 (10¾-ounce) can cream of mushroom soup
1 (2.8-ounce) can French fried onions
½ teaspoon salt
⅛ teaspoon black pepper

Combine beans, soup, seasonings and half the can of onions; pour into a 1½-quart greased casserole. Bake uncovered at 350° for 30 minutes. Top with remaining onions and bake an additional 5 minutes.

Yield: 6 servings

Violet Hoffman Daniel (Mrs. Mack T.)
Winston-Salem, North Carolina

SWEET AND SOUR GREEN BEANS

2 strips bacon
⅓ cup onion, finely diced
1 (15½-ounce) can cut green beans, reserve liquid
1 tablespoon sugar
⅛ teaspoon salt
Dash of pepper
1 tablespoon vinegar

Cut bacon into ½-inch pieces and brown lightly with onion. In same pan add the liquid drained from the beans and cook down to about ½ cup. Add beans and remaining ingredients. May be prepared a day ahead and heated slowly to serve.

Yield: 4 servings

Claire deHart Lewis (Mrs. Cruse)
Burlington

MARINATED BEANS

2 (16-ounce) cans French cut green beans
1 (16-ounce) can tiny green peas
1 small jar pimento
1 cup celery, chopped
¾ cup vinegar
¾ cup sugar
½ cup vegetable oil
1 teaspoon salt
Dash of pepper

Drain beans, peas and pimentos. Place in bowl. Combine remaining ingredients and pour over bean mixture. Refrigerate 24 hours.

Yield: 12 to 14 servings

Nancy Kernodle Sain (Mrs. Tom)
Burlington

RANCH STYLE BEANS

1 pound lean ground beef
2 tablespoons vegetable oil
1 package onion soup mix
½ cup water
1 cup ketchup
2 tablespoons vinegar
2 tablespoons prepared mustard
1 (29-ounce) can pork and beans
1 (16-ounce) can kidney beans, drained

Brown beef in oil in large skillet. Stir in remaining ingredients and let simmer about 30 minutes. Stir occasionally.

Yield: 4 to 6 servings

Martha Ann Shaw
Burlington

BAKED BEANS

6-8 slices bacon
1 onion
2 jars baked beans
1 tablespoon ketchup
2 teaspoons mustard
1 tablespoon molasses
1 tablespoon brown sugar
4 ounces of a cola soda

Fry bacon, remove. Sauté onion in drippings. Crumble bacon and add with onion to the remaining ingredients. Bake in casserole at 325° for 45 to 60 minutes.

Yield: 4 to 6 servings

Dale Harris Leahy (Mrs. Charles)
Burlington

TASTY BEETS

1 (16-ounce) can beets
¼ cup sugar
⅓ cup vinegar
½ teaspoon pickling spices

Pour all ingredients into a saucepan and bring to a full boil. May be served hot or cold.

Yield: 4 servings

Willis Thompson Durham
Burlington

HARVARD BEETS

2 tablespoons butter
½ cup sugar
1½ tablespoons flour
¼ cup vinegar
2 cups beets, sliced
¼ cup beet juice

Melt butter in a saucepan; add sugar and flour which have been mixed together. Stir in the vinegar, beet juice and salt. Cook to a boil, stirring until thick and smooth. Add the sliced, cooked beets and let stand for at least 30 minutes. Reheat just before serving.

Yield: 4 servings

Norma Robertson Smith (Mrs. Banks)
Graham

SAVORY FRESH MUSHROOMS

1 teaspoon margarine
1 pound fresh mushrooms, sliced and whole
¼ teaspoon paprika
¼ teaspoon seasoned salt
⅛ teaspoon pepper
¼ cup chopped fresh parsley
2 tablespoons dry sherry

Melt margarine in large skillet and add remaining ingredients. Cover and cook over medium heat, stirring occasionally. Do not overcook—5 or 6 minutes should be enough.

Yield: 4 to 6 servings

Betsy Liles Gant (Mrs. Edmund R.)
Burlington

SESAME BROCCOLI

1 pound fresh broccoli
2 tablespoons vegetable oil
2 tablespoons vinegar
2 tablespoons soy sauce
8 teaspoons sugar
2 tablespoons sesame seeds

Cook broccoli until tender. Combine remaining ingredients and heat. Pour over the cooked broccoli and serve while hot.

Yield: 4 to 5 servings

Dorothy Bowden Shoffner
Burlington

BROCCOLI WITH CHEESE SAUCE

2 (10-ounce) packages frozen broccoli or cauliflower
1 (11-ounce) can Cheddar cheese soup
¼ cup milk
¼ cup buttered breadcrumbs

Place cooked and drained broccoli in shallow baking dish. Blend soup and milk; pour over broccoli. Top with the crumbs. Bake at 350° about 30 minutes or until hot and bubbly.

Yield: 6 to 8 servings

Vera Whitesell Howard (Mrs. Wade)
Burlington

GANT FAMILY CORN PUDDING

2 eggs
2 cups tender corn cut from cob
1 cup medium or heavy cream
Salt to taste
2 teaspoons sugar
1 teaspoon butter (rounded)

Preheat oven to 350°. Beat eggs and add remaining ingredients. Bake about 30 minutes. This will have a custard-like consistency.

Yield: 4 to 6 servings

Betsy Liles Gant (Mrs. Edmund R.)
Burlington

BUSY DAY CORN DISH

2 cups (16½-ounce) can cream style corn
1 cup cooked rice
1 stick melted margarine
1 (2-ounce) jar pimentos
1 small onion, chopped
1 small green pepper, chopped
½ cup grated cheese

Combine all ingredients and pour into 1½-quart casserole. Bake at 300° for 30 minutes. Top with the cheese and bake until melted.

Yield: 6 servings

Daisie Holt Schwartz
Paris, Texas

CORN PUDDING

2 cups fresh corn or frozen
½ cup sugar
1½ tablespoons flour
Dash nutmeg
2 eggs
1 cup half and half
¼ cup butter, melted
Salt and pepper to taste

Mix corn, sugar, flour and nutmeg. Beat eggs lightly and add to corn mixture. Add milk and mix. Add butter, mixing thoroughly. Pour into a 1-quart greased baking dish. Bake at 350° for 30 minutes. Reduce heat to 325° for 10 minutes or until custard is firm.

Yield: 6 servings

Ruth Gilliland Kent
Burlington

CORN PUDDING

1 egg
2 tablespoons flour
2 tablespoons sugar
2 tablespoons butter, melted
½ cup milk
½ cup corn

Preheat oven to 350°. Beat egg. Mix flour and sugar together and add to the egg. Add melted butter and then milk. Add corn last and pour into a small greased baking dish. Bake for 30 minutes.

Yield: 2 servings

Dorothy Mae Brittle
Burlington

CORN PUDDING

2 heaping tablespoons butter
2 tablespoons sugar
2 tablespoons all purpose flour
2 eggs
½ cup milk
¼ teaspoon salt
1 (20-ounce) can creamed corn

Preheat oven to 350°. Cream butter and sugar and set aside. In another bowl mix flour, eggs and milk. Add corn, undrained, and salt. Blend. Add butter and sugar to this and blend together. Place in ungreased 2-quart rectangular glass baking dish and bake 45 minutes or until set and lightly browned.

Yield: 4 to 6 servings

Barbara May McNeely (Mrs. C. C., Jr.)
Burlington

PIMENTO CORN

2 heaping tablespoons butter
2 heaping tablespoons flour
1¼ cups milk
3 eggs, beaten
2 cups corn
½ pound Cheddar cheese
1 cup red and green peppers, chopped
Salt to taste

Preheat oven to 325°. In a saucepan work together the butter and flour; add gradually the beaten eggs and milk. Cook over medium heat until thick, stirring constantly. Remove from heat; add corn, peppers and ½ of the cheese. Cook all slowly about 5 minutes, stirring constantly. Add pinch of salt. Pour into a greased 1½-quart casserole and top with remaining cheese. Bake for 45 minutes.

Yield: 6 servings

Peggy Howe Helms (Mrs. Steve T.)
Burlington

ORANGE CARROTS

1 cup orange juice
½ cup sugar
2 tablespoons cornstarch
3 cups carrots, sliced and cooked
2 tablespoons margarine, melted

Preheat oven to 350°. In a 2-quart casserole combine orange juice, sugar and cornstarch mixing well. Stir in carrots and margarine. Cover and bake for 30 minutes.

Yield: 4 servings

Norma Campbell Moore (Mrs. Vernon)
Burlington

MARINATED CAULIFLOWER

4 cups cauliflower, thinly sliced
1 cup ripe olives, sliced
⅔ cup green pepper, chopped
1 (4-ounce) jar pimentos, drained and diced
½ cup minced onion
½ cup vegetable oil
3 tablespoons wine vinegar
1 teaspoon sugar
½ teaspoon salt
½ teaspoon pepper

Combine, in a large bowl, all the vegetables; toss to mix. Combine oil, vinegar, sugar, salt and pepper in a covered jar, shaking vigorously. Pour over vegetables and toss lightly. Chill overnight. Toss again before serving.

Yield: 8 to 10 servings

Ann Dean Honeycutt (Mrs. Chester)
Burlington

CHOU FARCI CASSEROLE

1 large head cabbage
1 pound pork sausage
2 large onions, chopped
4 slices white bread, crumbled and soaked in milk
Garlic, if desired
Cracker crumbs

Cut cabbage into bite size pieces. Parboil in salted water and drain well. Slowly brown sausage and onions. Remove from heat. Add the bread and milk paste which should be about the consistency of thick cream. Mix well. Butter a large 3-quart baking dish and layer with cabbage then with sausage and bread mixture. Repeat, ending with cabbage on top. Cover with cracker crumbs. Bake uncovered at 350° until hot and bubbling.

Yield: 6 to 8 servings

Patricia Allebach Donnell (Mrs. Raymond D.)
Burlington

SLAW NANCY

1 medium cabbage, shredded
1 medium onion, chopped
12 green olives, sliced
1 green pepper, chopped
¾ cup, or less, sugar
¾ cup white vinegar
1 teaspoon celery seed
1 teaspoon salt
1 teaspoon prepared mustard
⅛ teaspoon black pepper
½ cup vegetable oil

In bowl combine cabbage, onion, olives and green pepper. Pour sugar on top. In a pan, boil together the remaining ingredients for 3 minutes. Pour over the vegetable mixture. Refrigerate 24 hours before serving.

Yield: 6 to 8 servings

Madge O'Kelly Brannock
Elon College

STUFFED CUCUMBERS

3 medium sized cucumbers
1 cup chopped tomato
1 onion, minced
1½ cups chicken, cooked and minced
1 tablespoon ketchup
1 teaspoon salt
¼ teaspoon pepper
½ teaspoon sugar
¼ teaspoon paprika
1 cup thin white sauce
½ cup buttered crumbs, browned

Preheat oven to 350°. Cut cucumbers lengthwise into halves. Scoop out pulp and reserve. Salt cucumber shells lightly and place close together in a buttered pan. Mix pulp with remaining ingredients except for the crumbs. Bake 20 to 25 minutes. Top with browned crumbs.

Yield: 6 servings

Lucille Oakley Langston
Burlington

BAKED EGGPLANT

1 large eggplant, peeled and cut in ½-inch slices
1 egg, beaten
1 cup dried breadcrumbs
1 small onion, chopped
¾ cup celery, chopped
¼ cup milk
4 tomatoes, sliced
½ teaspoon salt
¼ teaspoon pepper
¼ cup cheese, grated

Dip eggplant into egg then breadcrumbs. Sauté on both sides in cooking oil. Arrange slices in a 9x13-inch shallow baking dish. Cook celery and onions until tender and add the milk, salt and pepper. Place a thick slice of tomato on each slice of eggplant and then top with celery, and onion mixture. Sprinkle cheese over top and bake at 350° for 30 minutes.

Yield: 6 servings

Mary Helms Harden (Mrs. Junius)
Graham

EGGPLANT CASSEROLE

1 large eggplant
2 cups chopped tomatoes
1 tablespoon butter
2 tablespoons brown sugar
3 tablespoons flour
½ cup sugar
1 cup green pepper, chopped
Breadcrumbs
Butter

Peel and dice eggplant and cook in salted water for 10 minutes. Drain and place in bottom of casserole. Cook together the remaining ingredients, except the crumbs and butter, until thick. Pour over eggplant. Top with crumbs and dots of butter. Bake at 400° for 30 minutes.

Yield: 4 to 6 servings

Betty Kichline Gerow (Mrs. James A.)
Burlington

SCALLOPED EGGPLANT

1 large eggplant
2 tablespoons butter
1 (11-ounce) can cream of mushroom soup
½ cup breadcrumbs
1 teaspoon sugar
3 tablespoons grated cheese

Slice eggplant and soak in salt water. Drain and drop into boiling water. Cook until tender. Arrange in baking dish and dot with butter and pour can of soup over it. Sprinkle with breadcrumbs, sugar and cheese. Bake at 350° for 30 minutes.

Yield: 4 servings

Julia Atwater-Teague (Mrs. Woodrow)
Burlington

FRENCH FRIED ONION RINGS

¾ cup sifted flour
½ teaspoon salt
½ cup milk
2 tablespoons vegetable oil
1 egg
2 large Bermuda onions
1 quart oil for deep frying

Sift flour and salt into a bowl. Add milk, 2 tablespoons oil and egg; beat until smooth. Cut onions into ¼-inch slices and separate into rings. Dip each ring into the batter. Drain excess batter over bowl. Meanwhile, place oil in a 3 quart saucepan and heat to 380°. Drop a few rings at a time into the hot oil. Do not crowd. Fry 3 to 4 minutes. turning occasionally until golden brown. Drain on absorbent paper.

Yield: 4 to 6 servings

Donna Thompson Bonds (Mrs. John E.)
Kernersville, North Carolina

GLAZED VIDALIA ONIONS

6 Vidalia onions
Vegetable oil to rub on onions
6 tablespoons brown sugar
1-2 tablespoons crystalized ginger, crushed
2 tablespoons butter
¾ cup white wine
2 tablespoons fresh parsley

Clean and peel onions. Make a small hole in top of each onion. Rub onions with a small amount of vegetable oil and place in a lightly greased baking dish. Mix sugar, ginger, butter, wine and parsley together and beat about 10 minutes in a saucepan. Spoon small amount of liquid into the center of each onion, then pour remainder over the onions. Bake at 350° for 60 minutes basting as the onions cook.

Yield: 6 servings

Denise Clark Gant (Mrs. Allen E., Jr.)
Burlington

VIDALIA ONION CASSEROLE

4 medium onions, sliced
3 tablespoons butter
2 tablespoons flour
Salt and pepper
¾ cup beef bouillon
¼ cup sherry
1½ cups plain croutons
2 tablespoons melted butter
½ cup shredded Swiss cheese
3 tablespoons Parmesan cheese, optional

Cook onions in 3 tablespoons butter until tender. Blend in flour, salt and pepper. Add bouillon and sherry. Cook and stir until thickened and bubbling. Turn into casserole dish. Toss croutons with 2 tablespoons butter and sprinkle over onion mixture. Top with cheeses. Broil about 1 minute.

Yield: 4 servings

Jessie Ormond Pyne (Mrs. Minetree)
Burlington

VIDALIA ONION PIE

3 tablespoons butter
2½ cups chopped Vidalia onions
1 frozen 9-inch pie crust
2 eggs, slightly beaten
¼ cup evaporated milk
Salt and pepper
1 cup grated sharp Cheddar cheese
Paprika

Sauté onions in melted butter until almost tender. Pour into pie crust. Mix in a bowl eggs, salt, pepper, milk and ½ cup of the cheese. Pour over onions and stir slightly. Bake at 425° for 15 minutes. Remove from oven and top with remaining cheese and paprika. Return to oven and bake 8 to 10 minutes.

Yield: 6 servings

Aundree Bryant Price (Mrs. William)
Elon College

LEBANESE GREEN PEAS AND RICE

2 tablespoons olive oil
1½ pounds chicken breasts, boned, skinned and cut into large strips
1¼ cups onion, chopped
1 clove garlic, minced
1 cup chicken broth
1 (8-ounce) can tomato sauce
2 cups fresh or canned tomatoes, chopped
1 teaspoon salt
½ teaspoon pepper
½ teaspoon sugar
2 (10-ounce) packages frozen green peas

In dutch oven, heat oil and sauté chicken until lightly browned, but *not cooked through.* Remove chicken from pan, set aside and lightly brown onions and garlic. Add broth, tomato sauce, tomatoes, salt, pepper and sugar. Bring to a boil, reduce heat and simmer 15 minutes. Add chicken and peas to tomato sauce and cook on low 20 minutes or until chicken is done.

Lebanese Rice:

2 tablespoons spaghetti, broken into small pieces
2 tablespoons butter
1 cup rice
1 teaspoon salt
2 dashes cinnamon
2 cups water

Fry spaghetti in butter over medium heat until brown. Add rice, salt, cinnamon and sauté 5 minutes longer. Add water and bring to a boil. Cover tightly and cook over low heat for 15 minutes.

Yield: 4 to 6 servings

Marie's Lebanese and Greek specialties appear in four local cookbooks.

Marie Koury (Mrs. Ernest A.)
Elon College

MARINATED ROASTED PEPPERS

4 red bell peppers
Vinegar and oil dressing to taste

Roast peppers, by placing them on a foil-lined pan under oven broiler, turning often. Remove when charred all over. Place in brown paper bag. Close tightly and allow them to steam 15 minutes. Peel and cut into strips and marinate in the oil and vinegar dressing.

Yield: 4 to 6 servings

Sandra Elder Harper
Burlington

GREEN PEA CASSEROLE

1 (10-ounce) package frozen green peas
1 (7-ounce) can water chestnuts
1 (11-ounce) can cream of mushroom soup
1 teaspoon soy sauce
1 (4-ounce) can sliced mushrooms
½ teaspoon monosodium glutamate

In a greased 2-quart baking dish layer frozen peas, water chestnuts and mushrooms. Mix soup with soy sauce and monosodium glutamate. Bake at 350° for 30 minutes.

Yield: 6 servings

Ethel Boone Gant (Mrs. Allen E.)
Burlington

BLACK-EYED PEA SKILLET DINNER

1 pound ground beef
1¼ cups onion, chopped
1 cup green pepper, chopped
2 (16-ounce) cans black-eyed peas, drained
1 (16-ounce) can whole tomatoes, undrained and coarsely chopped
¾ teaspoon salt
½ teaspoon pepper

Cook ground beef, onion and green pepper over medium heat until browned, stirring to crumble meat; drain. Add remaining ingredients and bring to a boil. Reduce heat and simmer 30 minutes, stirring often.

Yield: 8 to 10 servings

Elizabeth Hoffman Pleasant (Mrs. Thomas)
Burlington

POTATO CASSEROLE

3 or 4 boiled potatoes—diced large
¼ cup margarine
3 tablespoons sour cream
1 (11-ounce) can cream of chicken soup
1 tablespoon grated onion
1 cup Cheddar cheese, grated
Round buttery crackers, crushed

Combine all ingredients except crackers. Place in 2-quart casserole and top with the crushed crackers. Bake at 350° for 35 to 40 minutes.

Yield: 4 servings

Betty Robertson Murray (Mrs. Homer B.)
Burlington

POTATOES BAKED IN CREAM

1 tablespoon butter
1 clove garlic, minced
3 large baking potatoes, scrubbed but not peeled
2 cups heavy cream
½ teaspoon salt
Black pepper, freshly ground
Nutmeg, freshly grated
⅓ cup Parmesan cheese, freshly grated

Preheat oven to 400°. Butter a 2-quart casserole dish and sprinkle in the garlic. Slice potatoes into ⅛-inch slices and arrange in the prepared dish. In a saucepan combine salt, cream, black pepper and nutmeg. Heat to a simmer and pour over potatoes. Top with cheese and bake for 40 to 45 minutes. Potatoes will be thickened, brown and bubbling.

Yield: 6 servings

Susan Dawson Sterken (Mrs. John)
Burlington

POTATOES ROMANOFF

6 medium potatoes
1 pint sour cream
½ pint whipping cream
1½ cups shredded sharp cheese
Salt
Pepper
Paprika

Boil potatoes in skins, cool, peel and shred into a bowl. Add remaining ingredients, mixing lightly but thoroughly. Place in casserole and refrigerate overnight. Sprinkle top with additional cheese and paprika. Bake at 350° for 30 to 40 minutes.

Yield: 6 to 8 servings

Linda Whisnant Irwin
Burlington

HASH BROWN POTATO CASSEROLE

1 (32-ounce) package frozen hash brown potatoes, thawed
¾ cup butter, melted
½ cup chopped onion
8 ounces sour cream
1 (11-ounce) can cream of chicken soup
1 cup shredded Cheddar cheese
2 cups corn flakes

Combine potatoes, ½ cup butter, onions, soup, sour cream and cheese. Stir well. Spoon into greased 9x12-inch casserole. Crush corn flakes and mix with remaining butter. Place corn flakes on top. Bake at 350° for 50 minutes.

Yield: 8 to 10 servings

Mildred Scott Robertson
Burlington

SQUASH CAKES

3 large yellow squash
1 cup Cheddar cheese, grated
1 large onion, finely chopped
2 eggs, beaten
1 cup flour
Salt and pepper to taste
Oil

Combine squash, cheese, onion and beaten eggs; mix. Stir in the flour, salt and pepper. With floured hands make into cakes and fry in oil until brown on both sides.

Yield: 6 to 8 servings

Lucy Clapp Wagoner (Mrs. John)
Burlington

SQUASH SOUFFLÉ

2 pounds of yellow squash, peeled and sliced
1 medium onion, chopped
Salt to taste
½ teaspoon sugar
2 eggs, slightly beaten
3 tablespoons margarine, melted
3 tablespoons flour
1 cup milk
½ pound sharp Cheddar cheese, grated
Seasoned salt to taste
Buttered breadcrumbs

Combine squash, onion, salt and sugar in a small amount of water and simmer until soft. Drain well. Mash thoroughly and add eggs, margarine, flour, milk and cheese. Stir to combine all ingredients. Add cheese and seasoned salt to taste. Pour into a well greased 1½-quart casserole and bake at 350° 35 to 40 minutes. Top with crumbs and bake until brown, watching carefully.

Yield: 6 to 8 servings

Mildred Jones Brown (Mrs. Clarence J.)
Burlington

SQUASH AU GRATIN

6 medium yellow squash, sliced
½ cup onion, chopped
2 tablespoons butter
2 tablespoons flour
½ cup milk
½ cup squash liquid
¾ cup grated cheese
½ cup green pepper, chopped
½ teaspoon salt
1½ cups breadcrumbs, buttered
Paprika

Cook squash and onion in salted water until tender. Drain well and save liquid. Melt butter, add flour and stir. Gradually add milk and squash liquid, stirring until smooth. Cook over medium heat until thick as heavy cream, stirring constantly. Remove from heat. Add cheese, green pepper, squash and onions. Pour into large buttered casserole dish. Top with buttered breadcrumbs and sprinkle with paprika. Bake at 350° for 20 minutes or until brown.

Yield: 4 to 6 servings

Virginia May Corbett (Mrs. Clyde E.)
Burlington

SQUASH CAKES

1 cup squash, cooked, mashed and strained
2 eggs, slightly beaten
2 tablespoons milk
1 teaspoon salt
1 teaspoon baking powder
½ cup sifted flour

Mix cooked squash, eggs and milk together. Add salt and baking powder to flour. When griddle is hot, blend squash mixture with flour. Cook like pancakes, turning when brown. Serve immediately with butter and syrup.

Yield: 2 to 3 servings

Lucy Wilson Kernodle (Mrs. Donald R.)
Burlington

SQUASH CASSEROLE

2 pounds yellow squash
2 tablespoons butter
1 beaten egg
½ cup medium white sauce
2 tablespoons brown sugar
½ cup buttered crumbs
1 teaspoon nutmeg
Paprika

Cook squash until tender. Drain and mash. Add butter, egg, white sauce and brown sugar. Season to taste. Pour into greased casserole. Top with buttered crumbs. Sprinkle with nutmeg and paprika. Bake at 350° for 25 to 30 minutes.

Yield: 6 to 8 servings

Helen B. Long (Mrs. George A.)
Burlington

SQUASH CASSEROLE

¼ pound margarine
1 (8-ounce) package prepared herb stuffing
2½-3 cups yellow squash, cooked and drained
1 medium onion, grated
1 carrot, grated
Salt and pepper to taste
1 (8-ounce) carton sour cream
1 (11-ounce) can cream of chicken soup

Preheat oven to 350°. Melt margarine and mix with stuffing; set aside. Blend together the remaining ingredients. In a greased 9x13-inch baking dish spread half the stuffing mix. Spread squash mixture over the stuffing mix and top with remaining stuffing mix. Bake at 350° for 25 to 30 minutes.

Yield: 8 servings

Beulah Pritchard Wilson (Mrs. John J.)
Burlington

SWEET POTATO PUDDING

4 eggs
2 cups sugar
¼ cup flour
1 cup coconut
¼ pound margarine, melted
2 cups milk
2 teaspoons vanilla
4 or 5 medium sweet potatoes, shredded or finely grated

Preheat oven to 350°. Beat eggs then add sugar and beat until stiff. Add, except the sweet potatoes, the remaining ingredients and mix well. Add potatoes and mix again. Bake in a well-greased 9x13-inch baking dish 50 to 60 minutes.

Yield: 8 to 10 servings

Elizabeth Hayden Harman
Burlington

SWEET POTATO PUDDING

4 medium sweet potatoes
1 (13-ounce) can evaporated milk
2 cups sugar
2 tablespoons flour
3 eggs, beaten
Dash salt
½ stick margarine, melted
1 teaspoon vanilla extract
½ teaspoon lemon extract

Peel and grate potatoes. Add milk. Mix remaining ingredients and combine with potatoes. Pour into greased baking dish and bake at 375° about 40 minutes or until brown. Coconut or raisins may be added for variation.

Yield: 4 to 6 servings

Esther Neely Stadler (Mrs. Charlie W.)
Elon College

CARYL'S SWEET POTATOES

1 (28-ounce) can sweet potatoes
1 (16-ounce) can apricots
1 (16-ounce) can freestone peaches
1 (12-ounce) can mandarin oranges
1 (16-ounce) can pineapple chunks
1 cup brown sugar
2 tablespoons butter

Use half of juice from all cans. Place juice, sweet potatoes and all fruits in 3-quart baking dish. Sprinkle sugar over top and dot with butter. Bake at 275° for 2 hours or all day if desired.

Yield: 12 servings

Pattie Fayle Sowder
Burlington

SWEET POTATO CASSEROLE

1 (24 or 32-ounce) can sweet potatoes
1 cup sugar
1 cup milk
2 eggs
½ stick margarine
¼ teaspoon allspice
¼ teaspoon cinnamon
¼ teaspoon nutmeg

Preheat oven to 275°. Mix all ingredients together. Pour mixture into a greased 9x13-inch baking dish.

Topping:
1 stick margarine
½ cup sugar
¾ cup flour

Mix together and crumble mixture over potato mixture. Bake at 275° for 1¼ hours.

Yield: 8 servings

Cynthia Kuepferle Lindley (Mrs. Tom, Jr.)
Burlington

MIXED VEGETABLE CASSEROLE

1 (12-ounce) can cream of mushroom soup
2 (14-16-ounce) cans mixed, diced vegetables
1 medium onion, chopped
2 stalks celery, chopped
½ cup grated cheese
1 (4-ounce) can mushrooms, drained
20 round buttery crackers
½ stick melted margarine

Place mushroom soup in a large bowl. Add remaining ingredients except for crackers and butter. Fold together gently. Pour into a large greased baking dish. Mix crackers and margarine. Sprinkle over top. Bake at 350° until hot and bubbling. May vary by adding 1 (12-ounce) can water chestnuts and/or 1 cup mayonnaise.

Yield: 4 to 6 servings

Helen Robertson Stewart (Mrs. Buck)
Burlington

Grace Anderson Thompson (Mrs. A. G., Jr.)
Burlington

STIR FRY VEGETABLE MIX

3 tablespoons vegetable oil
2 medium carrots, cut into match stick strips
1 medium onion, sliced thinly and separated into rings
1 small bunch broccoli, cut into 2x½-inch pieces
½ teaspoon salt
½ teaspoon sugar
1 (4-ounce) can mushrooms, whole or sliced
2 teaspoons soy sauce

In a 12-inch skillet or wok heat oil over high heat; add carrots, onions and broccoli stirring quickly and frequently for 3 to 4 minutes. Add mushrooms, with their liquid and soy sauce, salt and sugar. Stir to coat vegetables. Cover and cook an additional 5 minutes, stirring occasionally.

Yield: 4 to 6 servings

Sue McKee Watson (Mrs. Robert A.)
Burlington

By the 1880s the production of Alamance Plaids spread from its origins in Alamance County to other parts of the Southeast. In the spring of 1884 representatives of eight Alamance County mills met in Greensboro, N.C. with delegates from seven other North Carolina mills to organize the Cotton Plaid Manufacturers' Association. Thomas Holt, son of textile pioneer Edwin Michael Holt, was elected president of the Association, which represented a total of 2300 looms.

ALAMANCE BUILDING

Elon College, N.C.

Constructed in 1923, Alamance Building was erected to house classrooms and administrative offices of Elon College. The building rests on the site of the former "Old Main" (c. 1889-90), an original structure razed by fire on January 18, 1923.

Elon College is a liberal arts institution founded in 1889 by the Christian Church in the South. The College is the direct outgrowth of Graham Institute, incorporated July 16, 1851. Elon College now boasts an enrollment of over 3300, and attracts students from throughout the United States and several foreign countries.

TANGERINE ICE

3 tangerines, grated
3 cups tangerine juice (approximately 1 dozen medium-sized)
3¼ cups water
2 cups sugar
¾ cup Temple orange juice
¼ cup lemon juice
Salt

Prepare rind and juices. (I put peeled, halved and seeded tangerines in a potato ricer to squeeze). Boil water and sugar for five minutes. Add rind; set aside; let steep until cooled to room temperature. Strain sugar water mixture, add juices and salt. Place into freezer. Stir once or twice during freezing to fluff.

Yield: 10 to 12 servings

"Good with small chocolate cakes or cookies."

Olivia Rhodes Woodin (Mrs. Raye)
Burlington

STRAWBERRY ICE

3 pint baskets of ripe firm straw-berries, puréed, then sieved to remove seeds (approximately 3 cups)
2 cups sugar
1 cup water
¾ cup fresh orange juice
⅔ cup orange juice plus ⅓ cup water
5 teaspoons Cointreau or triple sec

Boil together the sugar, 1 cup water, ¾ cup orange juice for about 3 minutes. Pour into mixing bowl and cool before adding berry essence. Add the cup of orange juice and water. Stir. Add liqueur. Pour into ice trays or shallow dish and freeze. Stir well before hard frozen and cover with plastic wrap.

Yield: 10 to 12 servings

Olivia Rhodes Woodin (Mrs. Raye)
Burlington

SORBET

2 cups water
1 cup plus 2 tablespoons sugar

Combine water and sugar. Bring to boil, stirring. Simmer 5 minutes. Cool. Add puréed fruit or liquid flavoring, as desired. Pour into freezer trays. Stir occasionally to make it mushy.

Suggested flavors:
Blueberry—purée fruit, ½ cup Kirsch, 1 tablespoon lemon juice
Peach—4 peaches puréed, 1 tablespoon Kirsch
Apple—3 cups fruit purée, 1 tablespoon lemon juice, 1 cup apple cider, ¼ cup Calvados brandy
Coffee—2 cups, strong dark
Lemon/Ginger—⅛ teaspoon ground ginger, 1 cup lemon juice, 1½ tablespoons grated lemon rind, ¼ cup brandy, ¼ cup minced crystallized ginger

Yield: 10 to 20 servings

Sandra Elder Harper
Burlington

MY MOTHER'S ICE CREAM

4 eggs, well beaten
2 heaping tablespoons flour
2 cups sugar (2½ if making vanilla)
1 pint half and half
1 tablespoon vanilla extract
Whole milk

Beat eggs, flour and sugar together. Add cream and vanilla. Pour into freezer and add whole milk to within 3 inches of top. Freeze according to manufacturer's direction.

Yield: 12 to 15 servings

NOTE: For peach, banana, strawberry or other fruit, add 2 cups of mashed fruit mixed with juice of ½ lemon.

Anne Sapp Morrison (Mrs. D. Baker)
Burlington

HOMEMADE STRAWBERRY ICE CREAM

5 cups fresh strawberries, capped, and puréed in blender
4 cups sugar
4 eggs
1 can sweetened condensed milk
1 teaspoon vanilla extract
½ pint whipping cream
1 pint half and half
Approximately 1 quart milk

Beat eggs lightly with electric mixer. Pour into large saucepan. Add about 3 cups milk and mix again. Slowly add sugar, mixing well as you go. Add sweetened condensed milk and mix again. Heat over low heat, beating occasionally with electric mixer until slightly warm. Remove from heat immediately and add vanilla. Pour into 5-quart ice cream freezer. Add strawberries, cream and half and half. Add enough milk to fill the freezer just over "Fill Line." If electric freezer is used, place ice cream in freezer until frozen harder.

Yield: 5 quarts

This was a favorite of my father, Claiborne Clark Young

Claiborne Sellars Young
Burlington

FROZEN MOCHA DESSERT

1 cup chocolate wafer crumbs
¼ cup melted butter
½ cup pecans, chopped
2 (8-ounce) packages cream cheese
1 (14-ounce) can sweetened condensed milk
½ cup chocolate syrup
2 teaspoons instant coffee
1 tablespoon hot water
1 (8-ounce) carton non-dairy whipped topping
¼ cup pecans, chopped

Mix first 3 ingredients. Press firmly into bottom of 10-inch springform pan. Beat cream cheese until fluffy. Add milk and syrup. Beat until smooth. Mix coffee and water in small bowl and add to cream cheese mixture. Fold in topping. Pour into prepared crust. Sprinkle pecans on top. Freeze overnight.

Yield: 15 to 16 servings

Marilyn Crouse Lanier (Mrs. Thomas)
Burlington

ALMONDRADA

1 tablespoon plain gelatin
6 egg whites
1½ cups sugar
½ cup chopped almonds
1 teaspoon almond extract

Mix gelatin with ¼ cup cold water. Pour over this ¼ cup boiling water. Dissolve mixture. Let cool. Beat egg whites stiff and gradually add sugar and almond flavoring. Slowly add melted gelatin. Add almonds and a few drops of food coloring, if desired. (I usually add just a hint of green.) Freeze and serve with custard sauce.

Custard Sauce:
3 cups milk
6 egg yolks
½ teaspoon salt
6 tablespoons sugar
¾ teaspoon vanilla extract

Scald milk in double boiler. Beat eggs slightly with sugar and salt. Add hot milk to mixture and cook until egg coats spoon. DO NOT OVERCOOK. Add vanilla. Refrigerate.

Yield: 6 servings

Cecelia Black Corbett (Mrs. R. E., Jr.)
Burlington

ALWAYS A DELIGHT

1 (12-ounce) package cream cheese
1 stick butter
½ cup sour cream
½ cup granulated sugar
1 envelope plain gelatin
¼ cup cold water
½ cup seedless golden raisins
1 cup slivered almonds
Grated rind of 2 lemons (no juice)

Cream cheese, butter and sour cream well. Add sugar. Soften gelatin in cold water and dissolve over hot water. Add to creamed mixture. Add remaining ingredients. Pour into 1-quart mold and chill overnight. Unmold and spread on saltine crackers, no substitute. Can be frozen after unmolded. Good with sherry or fruit.

Yield: 8 to 10 servings

Vicki Burton Vernon (Mrs. John H., III)
Burlington

SISTER CHRIS' COLD LEMON SOUFFLÉ

5 large eggs, separated
1½ cups sugar
7 ounces fresh lemon juice
2 cups heavy cream, partially whipped
2 packages plain gelatin
½ cup water
1 to 2 tablespoons lemon rind, grated
¼ teaspoon cream of tartar
Pinch salt

Beat egg yolks with sugar. Add strained lemon juice and rind. Beat until thick and "mousse" like. Add half of the cream. Melt gelatin in water over low heat and add to mixture. Beat egg whites stiff, but not dry, with cream of tartar and salt. Add remaining cream. Prepare soufflé dish with a 2" collar of waxed paper. Spoon mixture into dish. Chill until set. (2 hours at least). When firm, remove collar and sprinkle with macaroon crumbs or toasted slivered almonds, if desired. Freezes well.

Yield: 8 to 10 servings

Pattie Fayle Sowder
Burlington

BAKED ALASKA

1 9" cake layer
1 quart very firm ice cream
4 egg whites
½ cup granulated sugar

Preheat oven to 500°. Cut brown paper ½ inch larger than cake layer. Place on cookie sheet. Place cake in center and chill in freezer. Remove from freezer and quickly top cake with ice cream. Freeze until firm. Beat egg whites with electric mixer until peaks form when beater is raised. Slowly add sugar 2 tablespoons at a time, beating until glossy and stiff. Quickly spread meringue with spatula over cake and ice cream. Return to freezer. About 15 minutes before serving time, remove Alaska from freezer and bake 4 or 5 minutes or until delicate brown. Transfer to chilled serving dish using 2 spatulas (one on each side).

Yield: 10 to 12 servings

Mary Helms Harden (Mrs. Junius)
Graham

FRUIT PIZZA

½ package sugar cookie dough, sliced
1 (8-ounce) cream cheese, softened
½ cup sugar
Pineapple chunks, drained, as needed
Strawberries, as needed
Mandarin oranges, drained, as needed
Seedless grapes, as needed
Peaches, dewberries, blueberries, etc. in season
1 (12-ounce) jar apricot preserves

Preheat oven to 350°. Place sliced dough in pizza pan. Pat to make a solid crust. Bake. Cool. Whip cream cheese and sugar, beating until smooth and sugar is dissolved. Spread over crust. Top with fruits, covering completely. Over low heat, soften preserves and drizzle over fruit. Chill and serve in slices. Freezes well. Serve frozen or thawed.

Yield: 8 to 10 servings

Anne Hyde Fortner (Mrs. C. H.)
Burlington

CHOCOLATE SANDWICH COOKIE DESSERT

16 chocolate sandwich cookies
1 can cherry pie filling
2 cups small marshmallows
1 small carton non-dairy whipped topping

Place crushed cookies into a square dish. Add cherry pie filling and marshmallows. Top with non-dairy whipped topping. Place in refrigerator overnight. Cut in squares to serve.

Yield: 6 to 8 servings

This is a recipe of Jeanette Mast.

Mary Maud Sanders Cockman (Mrs. Richard)
Burlington

CHOCOLATE MINT DESSERT

Cake Layer:

1 cup all purpose flour
1 cup sugar
½ cup butter or margarine, softened
4 eggs
1 (16-ounce) can chocolate syrup

Heat oven to 350°. Grease 13x9x2-inch pan. Combine flour, sugar, butter, eggs, syrup in large mixer bowl. Beat until smooth. Bake until top springs back when lightly touched, 25 to 35 minutes. Cool in pan.

Mint Cream Center:

2 cups powdered sugar
½ cup butter or margarine, softened
1 tablespoon water
½ to ¾ teaspoon mint extract
3 drops green food color

Combine all ingredients in small bowl. Beat until smooth. Spread on cake in pan. Cover and chill.

Topping:

6 tablespoons butter or margarine
1 cup semi-sweet chocolate chips

Combine in small saucepan over very low heat. Stir until smooth. Cool slightly. Pour over mint layer and spread. Cover and chill 1 hour before serving. Cut into squares.

Yield: 12 large or 48 small servings

Frances Lee Gillespie (Mrs. James W.)
Burlington

CHOCOLATE DELIGHT

2 cups vanilla wafer crumbs
½ cup butter, melted
½ cup butter, softened
1¼ cups sifted powdered sugar
2 eggs
1 cup whipping cream
2 tablespoons cocoa
¼ cup sugar
1 cup nuts, chopped
1 ripe banana, mashed
¼ cup sliced cherries
1 cup marshmallows

Mix crumbs and melted butter. Press into pan. Reserve some for top. Cream butter and sugar. Add eggs, one a time, beating well. Spread over crumb mixture. Whip cream. Add cocoa and sugar. Fold in nuts, bananas, cherries and marshmallows. Chill 24 hours. Cut into squares to serve.

Yield: 8 to 10 servings

Linda Whisnant Irwin
Burlington

HEAVENLY DELIGHT

1 cup flour, unsifted
1 stick butter or margarine, melted
1 cup pecans

Mix with hands and press in pan. Bake 20 minutes at 350°. Do not overbake. Cool thoroughly. Mix the following and spread over crust:

1 (8-ounce) carton non-dairy whipped topping
1 (8-ounce) package cream cheese
1 cup powdered sugar

Mix the following and spread over previous layer:

1 can sweetened condensed milk
½ cup lemon juice
1 egg yolk

Beat egg yolk and stir in milk to avoid hardening of egg before adding lemon juice. Top with non-dairy whipped topping. Can be frozen or served as is.

Yield: 10 to 12 servings

Dorothy Sellars Brawley
Burlington

FLOWER POT DESSERT

1 (16-ounce) package chocolate sandwich cookies
1 (11-ounce) package cream cheese, or 1 (3-ounce) and 1 (8-ounce)
1 cup powdered sugar
½ cup margarine, softened
1 (medium) carton non-dairy whipped topping
2 (3-ounce) packages instant vanilla pudding
1 teaspoon vanilla extract
3 cups milk

Crush cookies in blender or food processor. Cream the cheese, sugar, margarine. Fold in non-dairy whipped topping. Combine pudding, vanilla, milk and add, using wire whip. Use small clay flower pots (or styrofoam cups covered with tissue paper secured with rubber band.). Layer crushed cookies and cream mixture, alternating, ending with cookies (dirt). Refrigerate or freeze. Before serving, wrap stems of real flowers in foil and insert in center. Serve immediately.

Yield: 10 to 16 servings

Helen Flynn Walton
Burlington

STRAWBERRY MARLOWE

2 pints strawberries
½ pint whipped cream
½ pound marshmallows
Powdered sugar to taste

Mash strawberries with sugar to sweeten. (With frozen strawberries, omit sugar.) Cut marshmallows into very small pieces. Mix with strawberries. Place in refrigerator and mix frequently. Before serving, fold in whipped cream and chill. Better if made a day before serving.

Yield: 6 to 8 servings

Carolyn Penelope Weatherly
Burlington

CHARLOTTE RUSSE

2 envelopes gelatin
½ cup cold milk
1 quart whipping cream, beaten stiff
½ to ¾ cup sugar
1 cup sherry to taste
6 egg whites, beaten stiff
Package of ladyfingers
Slivered toasted almonds

Pour gelatin into a measuring cup; add ½ cup cold milk. Place the container over hot water until gelatin dissolves. In a large mixing bowl, beat the cream, stir in the sugar, cooled gelatin and sherry. Fold in the beaten egg whites. Line pan (pound cake steeple pan works well) with split ladyfingers, turning the crust side to the side of the pan. Pour mixture in pan and chill until firm. Sprinkle toasted almonds on top. Left-over Russe may be frozen.

Yield: 12 to 14 servings

"A Christmas tradition"

Agnes Ravenel Gant (Mrs. Roger, Sr.)
Burlington

CHARLOTTE RUSSE

1½ envelopes plain gelatin
¼ cup water, cold
⅓ cup milk, scalded
⅓ to ½ cup powdered sugar
½ pint half and half
½ pint whipping cream
1 package plain lady fingers
1 teaspoon vanilla extract, if desired
½ teaspoon almond extract, if desired
1 tablespoon sherry, if desired

Soak gelatin in water 3 to 5 minutes. Dissolve in scalded milk. Add powdered sugar and cool. Add to half and half, pouring through fine strainer to eliminate lumps, if necessary. Whip cream until stiff. Add with wire whisk. Add desired flavoring. Place ladyfingers (opened) around edge of bowl. Pour mixture into bowl. Top with almonds.

Yield: 6 servings

Dolores Cheatham James (Mrs. Harry C.)
Burlington

SWEET COUNTRY CHEESE WITH STRAWBERRIES

1 (8-ounce) softened cream cheese
4 egg yolks
1 teaspoon lemon rind
2 tablespoons lemon juice
1 cup sugar
1 envelope gelatin
¼ teaspoon salt
1 cup light cream
1 pint sour cream
3 pints strawberries—sugar

Beat cream cheese, egg yolks, rind and juice in large mixing bowl until fluffy. Mix 1 cup sugar, gelatin and salt in top of double boiler. Blend in light cream, then sour cream. Stir over low heat until gelatin dissolves. Remove from heat; gradually stir 1 cup of this mixture in beaten cheese. Return all to double boiler. Place over simmering water and stir constantly for about 2 minutes. Pour into oiled 6-cup ring mold. Chill overnight. Unmold on pretty plate. Sprinkle strawberries with sugar and pile into center mold. Add a few strawberries on plate with strawberry leaves for garnish.

Yield: 6 to 8 servings

Frances Ray Reed (Mrs. Donald)
Burlington

BAVARIAN CREAM

1 envelope plain gelatin
4 egg yolks
Dash salt
½ cup sugar
1 cup milk
1 cup whipping cream, whipped
2 teaspoons vanilla extract

Soften gelatin in ¼ cup cold water. Mix egg yolks, salt and sugar in top of double boiler. Gradually blend in milk and cook over hot water, stirring constantly until thick and smooth. Add softened gelatin, stirring until dissolved. Cool whipped cream, add vanilla and fold in gently. Spoon into 1-quart mold or 4 or 5 sherbet or parfait glasses. Chill.

For a lighter Bavarian Cream, beat 4 egg whites and add before the whipped cream.

To make chocolate Bavarian Cream, follow instructions above. Decrease vanilla to 1 teaspoon. Before cooling the egg gelatin mixture, add 2 ounces unsweetened melted chocolate.

Yield: 8 servings

Doris Clapp Gilliam (Mrs. Emery)
Elon College

BREAD PUDDING

1 (8-ounce) loaf French or Italian bread
2½ cups milk
2 cups sugar
1 cup butter
1 (13-ounce) can evaporated milk
1½ teaspoons nutmeg
2 tablespoons vanilla extract
1 cup seedless raisins

Preheat oven to 350°. Tear bread into pieces. Pour milk over bread. Mix sugar, butter, evaporated milk, nutmeg and vanilla. Add to bread and milk. Add raisins. Pour into baking pan and place on a baking tray with sides to catch spills. Bake 1 hour. Stir and continue cooking for 40 minutes. Add marmalade and nuts, if desired. Serve with hard sauce made by thoroughly mixing 8 tablespoons butter, 1 cup powdered sugar and 3 tablespoons rum. Chill.

Yield: 10 to 12 servings

If you like bread pudding, throw away all other recipes!

Elizabeth Cheek Elder (Mrs. W. Clifton)
Burlington

BANANA PUDDING

3 small boxes instant vanilla pudding
5 cups milk
1 (8-ounce) carton sour cream
1 (9-ounce) carton non-dairy whipped topping
Ripe bananas, as needed
Vanilla wafers, as needed

Layer sliced bananas and vanilla wafers in a round bowl. Mix pudding and milk. Add sour cream and ½ of non-dairy whipped topping. Put ½ of pudding mixture over bananas and vanilla wafers. Repeat procedure. Add remaining pudding mixture on top. Cover with remainder of non-dairy whipped topping.

Yield: 10 to 12 servings

Dorothy Sellars Brawley
Burlington

PERSIMMON PUDDING

2 cups persimmon pulp
3 eggs
1¼ cups sugar
1½ cups flour
2 teaspoons cinnamon
1 teaspoon ginger
½ teaspoon nutmeg
1½ cups flour
1 teaspoon baking powder
1 teaspoon soda
2½ cups milk
½ cup butter, melted

Preheat oven to 325°. Mix first 3 ingredients. Sift flour with cinnamon, ginger and nutmeg. Mix baking powder and soda with milk. Add melted butter to pulp mixture. Add flour mixture and milk alternately to pulp mixture, beating well. Bake in greased 9x9-inch baking dish 1 hour or until firm.

Yield: 10 to 12 servings

Lyda Lee Miller (Mrs. Glenn R.)
Burlington

PERSIMMON PUDDING NEWLIN

½ gallon persimmons
½ gallon milk
1 teaspoon baking soda
1 teaspoon nutmeg
Salt
1½ cups sugar
2 eggs
Butter, size of large egg
Flour to make consistency of cake batter
1 large sweet potato, grated

Preheat oven to 350°. Mash persimmons with potato ricer using milk to help for pulp. Mix all ingredients. Bake in buttered casserole about 1 hour.

Yield: 24 to 30 servings

This is a favorite recipe of my mother, Annie Morrow Newlin

Elizabeth Newlin Newlin (Mrs. Harvey R.)
Burlington

PERSIMMON PUDDING

2 cups persimmon pulp
3 eggs
1¾ cups milk
2 cups sifted flour
½ teaspoon baking soda
1 teaspoon salt
1 teaspoon cinnamon
½ teaspoon nutmeg
1½ cups sugar
3 tablespoons butter, melted

Combine pulp, eggs and milk. Sift dry ingredients and add to pulp mixture. Pour into greased pan about 2 inches deep. Add butter. Bake 1 hour at 300° or until firm. Cut into squares. Serve with whipped cream, if desired.

Yield: 8 to 10 servings

Ruth Ferree Samuels (Mrs. Judson)
Burlington

BUTTERNUT SQUASH PUDDING

2 eggs
2 cups squash, cooked
1 cup sugar
2 cups milk
¼ stick butter, melted
1 teaspoon vanilla extract
1 teaspoon cinnamon
1 cup chopped raisins
½ cup chopped nuts

Preheat oven to 350°. Beat eggs until light. Add to squash. Combine all ingredients, mixing well. Bake in casserole 45 or 50 minutes or until golden brown and slightly candied. Cool. Serve plain or with whipped cream.

Yield: 6 to 8 servings

Margarett Sullivan Warren (Mrs. William G.)
Mebane

BAKED FRUIT DESSERT

1 can dark pitted cherries, drained
1 can sliced peaches, drained
1 can apricot halves, drained
Rind of ½ orange, grated
Rind of ½ lemon, grated
Juice of ½ orange
Juice of ½ lemon
¾ cup brown sugar

Preheat oven to 350°. Combine all ingredients and put in casserole. Bake 1 hour. Serve warm with cream or non-dairy whipped topping.

Yield: 8 servings

Julia Atwater-Teague (Mrs. Woodrow)
Burlington

PEACH DESSERT

2 (3-ounce) packages peach or apricot gelatin
1 (8¼-ounce) can crushed pineapple with juice
3 tablespoons sugar
2 cups buttermilk
1 (8-ounce) carton non-dairy whipped topping
½ cup pecans, chopped

Mix first 3 ingredients in saucepan. Bring to boil. Cool. Mix buttermilk and topping. Add pecans and combine with gelatin mixture. Pour into mold or glass dish and refrigerate. Garnish with sliced peaches, apricot halves and maraschino cherries, if desired.

Yield: 6 to 8 servings

Melva Gray Foster
Burlington

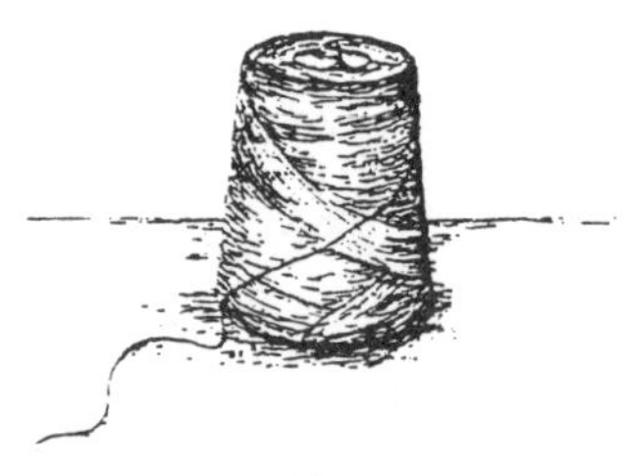

WINE JELLY

1 envelope plain gelatin
1/4 cup cold water
1/2 cup water plus 1/4 cup orange juice
1/2 cup sugar
3/4 cup wine (sweet sherry or Madeira)
1/4 cup orange juice
1 tablespoon lemon juice
Pinch of salt

Dissolve gelatin in a bowl with 1/4 cup cold water. Add 1/2 cup water plus 1/4 cup orange juice *boiling* hot and stir. Add sugar, stirring to dissolve. Add wine, 1/4 cup orange juice, salt and lemon juice. Stir again and chill in refrigerator. Serve with slightly sweetened whipped cream with a few drops of vanilla added, if desired.

Yield: 4 generous servings

Olivia Rhodes Woodin (Mrs. Raye)
Burlington

MOTHER'S MERINGUES

4 egg whites
1 teaspoon vanilla
2 cups sugar

Preheat oven to 250°. Beat egg whites until stiff. Gradually add 2/3 of the sugar. Continue beating until mixture is stiff. Add vanilla and fold in remaining sugar. Shape with spoon on cookie sheet covered with brown wrapping paper or letter paper. Bake 50 minutes and remove from paper. If desired, fill with whipped cream, ice cream or fruit.

Yield: 8 servings

This recipe never fails. They were always served at Christmas in the Sellers' home.

June Sellers Harris (Mrs. William B.)
Burlington

MIRIAM SPOON ALEXANDER'S APPLE PIE

Crust:

2 cups flour
½ teaspoon salt or to taste
⅔ cup shortening
5 to 6 tablespoons ice water

Sift flour and salt into mixing bowl. Cut in shortening, using a pastry blender or knife, until mixture is the size of small peas. Sprinkle water a little at a time, over mixture, stirring lightly with fork, until dough is just moist enough to hold together. Divide in half. Form into balls. Roll out one portion on floured surface to circle 1½ inches larger than inverted 8-inch pie plate.

Filling:

6 large sour green apples
¾ cup sugar
2 tablespoons flour
1 teaspoon cinnamon
¼ teaspoon allspice
¼ teaspoon nutmeg
2 to 3 tablespoons butter or margarine
Dash of salt

Peel and slice apples. Put in crust. Mix sugar, flour and spices and sprinkle over the apples. Dot with butter and dash of salt. Roll out remaining dough. Cut slits for escape of steam. Place top crust over filling and trim ½ inch beyond rim of pan. Seal edge by folding top crust under bottom crust. Flute edge. Bake at 400° for 45 to 60 minutes untl juices are bubbling and crust is brown. (Do not overbrown crust).

Yield: 6 to 8 servings

My mother made these pies in "dirt" dishes. Good with sharp Cheddar cheese or vanilla ice cream.

Frances Alexander Campbell (Mrs. Bob)
Chapel Hill, North Carolina

CANDIED APPLE PIE

4 large tart apples
Nutmeg to taste
Lemon juice
½ cup butter or margarine
1 cup light brown sugar
1 cup flour

Peel and slice apples and place in pie casserole dish. Sprinkle apples with nutmeg and lemon juice. Mix butter, sugar and flour together and cream well. Spread this mixture over apples. Bake at 325° for about 50 minutes. Let cool before slicing. Top with ice cream.

Yield: 6 to 8 servings

Frances Whitted White (Mrs. Bob)
Burlington

MOM'S CHERRY PIE

4 cups pitted fresh pie cherries
1¼ cups sugar
⅛ cup flour
⅛ teaspoon salt
2 tablespoons butter or margarine
1 (9-inch) unbaked double-crust pie shell

Combine cherries, sugar, flour and salt. Fill pie pan. Dot with butter. Adjust top crust; make a few slits through top crust for steam to escape. Bake at 450° for 15 minutes. Reduce heat to 350° and continue baking for 30 minutes.

Yield: 6 to 8 servings

Lynn Johnson Moseley (Mrs. W. Phillip)
Graham

PIE CRUST

4 cups plain flour
1¾ cups shortening
2 tablespoons white vinegar
2 tablespoons sugar
2 teaspoons salt
1 egg
½ cup cold water

Mix all ingredients together. Dough will be sticky. Put in refrigerator until thoroughly chilled. Roll out. Freezes well.

Yield: 5 (9-inch) crusts

Josephine Graham Umstead
Burlington

CHOCOLATE MERINGUE PIE

2½ cups sweet milk
1 cup sugar
½ cup cocoa
½ cup flour, sifted
½ teaspoon salt
3 egg yolks, beaten
2 tablespoons margarine
2 teaspoons vanilla extract
1 (9-inch) baked pie shell

Heat 2 cups milk in double boiler. Mix sugar, cocoa, flour and salt in a bowl and stir in ½ cup milk. Then stir into the hot milk. When it begins to thicken, add the beaten egg yolks and margarine while stirring constantly until thick. Add vanilla. Beat with egg beater until nice and smooth. Pour into baked pie shell and top with the following meringue.

Meringue:
3 egg whites
1 tablespoon ice water
¼ teaspoon cream of tartar
¼ cup sugar

Beat until stiff and spread on pie. Bake at 350° until lightly brown.

Yield: 6 to 8 servings

Mary Elizabeth (Bettie) Wilson
Burlington

CHOCOLATE MOUSSE PIE

Mixture:

1 (6-ounce) package semi-sweet chocolate pieces
1 egg
2 egg yolks
2 egg whites
1 cup heavy cream

Melt chocolate pieces over hot water. Remove from heat. Beat in egg and egg yolks one at a time. Beat egg whites until they peak when beater is raised. Whip cream. Fold in with chocolate mixture. Put in baked pie crust. Chill.

Crust:

¼ cup butter or margarine
¼ cup sugar
16 graham crackers

Soften butter and mix with sugar and graham crackers. Press mixture to bottom and sides of a 9-inch pie plate with back of spoon. Bake at 375° for 8 minutes. Cool. Fill with chocolate mixture.

Yield: 6 to 8 servings

Mary E. McClure Phillips
Graham

CHOCOLATE MERINGUE PIE

1 cup sugar
3 squares unsweetened chocolate
3 eggs, separated
2 cups milk
½ stick butter or margarine
½ cup plain flour
2 tablespoons sugar
1 (9-inch) baked pie shell

Preheat oven to 400°. Mix 1 cup sugar, chocolate, egg yolks, milk, butter and flour in top of double boiler. Cook while stirring constantly until very thick. Pour into baked pie shell. Make meringue of the 2 egg whites and 2 tablespoons sugar. Put on top of chocolate. Bake until meringue is lightly brown.

Yield: 6 to 8 servings

This wonderful pie recipe is from the late Carrie Holt, who worked for us for 30 years. She was a beloved person, and almost a member of our family.

Barbara May McNeely (Mrs. C. C., Jr.)
Burlington

MISSISSIPPI MUD PIE

Cake:

2 sticks butter or margarine
½ cup cocoa
2 cups sugar
4 eggs
1½ cups plain flour
Pinch of salt
1½ cups chopped nuts
1 teaspoon vanilla extract
1 large jar marshmallow cream

Melt butter and mix with cocoa. Add the next 6 ingredients. Spoon into a 9x13-inch pan. Bake at 350° for 35 to 45 minutes. While hot, spread marshmallow cream on top.

Frosting:

½ stick butter or margarine
1 (16-ounce) box powdered sugar
½ cup whole milk
⅓ cup cocoa

Combine butter, sugar, milk and cocoa together and smooth on top.

Yield: 18 servings

Dianne Simpson Gerlach (Mrs. John)
Burlington

CHOCOLATE BROWNIE PIE

1 stick margarine
2 squares chocolate (or 6 tablespoons cocoa)
1 teaspoon vanilla extract
1 cup sugar
¼ cup flour
3 eggs
1 cup chopped pecans

Mix margarine, chocolate and vanilla. Add sugar, flour and eggs. Mix well. Add nuts. Pour into buttered pie pan and bake at 350° about 25 minutes. Serve with whipped cream or ice cream.

Yield: 6 to 8 servings

Pamela Anne Morrison
New York, New York

CHOCOLATE PIE

10 large egg yolks
1¼ sticks margarine, melted
1 large can evaporated milk
½ cup water
1 tablespoon vanilla extract
2½ cups sugar
4 level tablespoons cocoa
3 tablespoons cornstarch
1 (9-inch) unbaked deep dish pie shell

Beat egg yolks well. Add margarine, milk, water and vanilla. Mix in sugar, cocoa, and cornstarch until well blended. Pour into unbaked crust. Place pie and its pan in a glass dish for a brown bottom crust. Bake at 300° for 50 minutes.

Meringue:
10 egg whites
1 tablespoon cream of tartar
1¼ cups sugar

Beaters should be clean and dry before starting meringue for best results. Beat whites with cream of tartar until stiff. Gradually add sugar and beat until fluffy. Spread on pie and brown in hot oven.

Yield: 6 to 8 servings

Eunice Evans Carden
Mebane

JAPANESE FRUIT PIE

2 cups sugar
2 sticks margarine, melted
5 eggs
1 teaspoon vanilla extract
1 teaspoon vinegar
1 cup coconut
1 cup white raisins
1 cup pecans
2 (9-inch) unbaked pie shells

Mix sugar and margarine well. Add eggs, one at a time and beat well. Add vanilla and vinegar, mixing well. Add fruits, nuts and mix well. Pour into pie shells and bake at 325° for 35 to 40 minutes or until brown on top.

Yield: 12 to 16 servings

Ila Murray Bryan
Burlington

"MISS DORA'S" COCONUT PIE

5 eggs
1½ cups sugar
¾ cup buttermilk
2 tablespoons vanilla extract
1 cup fresh coconut, firmly packed
1 stick butter or margarine
1 (9-inch) unbaked pie shell

Place all ingredients in mixing bowl and beat at medium speed until well blended. Pour into unbaked pie shell and bake at 350° until brown and shaky in center. Quick, easy, and simple to make, but oh, so good!

Yield: 6 to 8 servings

This recipe is an original of my late sister, Mary Ledora Haith.

Gilberta Jeffries Mitchell (Mrs. R. G.)
Mebane

COCONUT CHESS PIE

4 eggs, separated
2½ cups sugar
3 tablespoons flour
½ cup butter or margarine
1 cup milk
2 teaspoons vanilla extract
1 (6-ounce) package coconut
2 (9-inch) unbaked pie shells

Mix egg yolks with remaining ingredients. Beat egg whites and add to mixture. Pour into pie shells. Bake at 325° about 30 minutes or until firm.

Yield: 12 to 16 servings

Family recipe given to me by Grace Snyder Tate.

Dolly Moore Qualls
Graham

AUNT SARAH'S BROWN SUGAR PIE

1 cup brown sugar
Butter, size of egg
2 eggs, separated
1 cup milk
½ teaspoon vanilla extract
1 (9-inch) unbaked pie shell

Cream butter and sugar. Add egg yolks. Heat milk until scalding and pour into mixture. Beat egg whites and add other ingredients. Pour into a 9-inch pie shell and bake at 350° until firm and brown.

Yield: 6 to 8 servings

Hallie Ragsdale Smith (Mrs. Mack)
Burlington

CHESS PIE

3 eggs
1½ cups sugar
1 stick butter or margarine, melted
1 tablespoon vinegar
1 tablespoon cornmeal
1 teaspoon vanilla extract
1 (9-inch) unbaked pie shell

Beat eggs. Add sugar and butter. Add vinegar, cornmeal and vanilla. Mix well. Pour into pie shell. Bake at 325° for 30 to 40 minutes.

Yield: 6 to 8 servings

Dorothy Mae Brittle
Burlington

EGG CUSTARD PIE

2 eggs
¼ cup sugar, plus 2 tablespoons
1 teaspoon vanilla extract
½ cup milk, scalded
1 (9-inch) unbaked pie shell
Dash of nutmeg

Combine eggs, sugar and vanilla. Beat well. Add scalded milk slowly. Pour into pie shell and sprinkle with nutmeg. Bake at 450° for 20 minutes until slightly shaky in center. Cool.

Yield: 6 to 8 servings

Ruth Ferree Samuels (Mrs. Judson)
Burlington

CHESS CUSTARD PIE

2 eggs
3 egg yolks, reserve whites
1 stick margarine, melted and cooled
1 tablespoon flour
1½ cups sugar
1 tablespoon vanilla extract
2 (8-inch) unbaked pie shells

Beat eggs and yolks, add margarine. Gradually add to the dry ingredients which have been well blended. Mix well, then add vanilla. Pour into pie shells and bake 350° for about 25 minutes or until done.

Topping:
3 egg whites
6 tablespoons sugar
⅛ teaspoon salt

Beat egg whites until they form peaks. Gradually add sugar and continue to beat. Add salt and beat just to dissolve salt. Spread on pies and bake 350° about 10 to 12 minutes.

Yield: 12 servings

Lloyd Lafayette Bramble
Washington, District of Columbia

OLD FASHION EGG CUSTARD PIE

3 eggs, beaten
¾ cup sugar
¼ teaspoon salt
1 teaspoon vanilla extract
½ teaspoon ground nutmeg
2 cups scalded milk
1 (9-inch) unbaked pie shell

Combine eggs and sugar, beating well. Add salt, vanilla and nutmeg. Gradually add scalded milk while stirring constantly. Pour mixture into pie shell. Bake at 400° for 10 minutes; then reduce oven temperature to 325° for an additional 25 minutes, or until a knife inserted in custard comes out clean. The secret is in scalding the milk. Cool before serving.

Yield: 6 to 8 servings

Willis Thompson Durham
Burlington

COTTAGE CHEESE CUSTARD PIE

2 eggs, separated
½ cup sugar
⅛ teaspoon salt
½ cup milk
1½ cups cottage cheese
2 tablespoons flour
1 teaspoon lemon juice
½ teaspoon cinnamon
1 (9-inch) baked pie shell

Beat egg yolks until light. Add sugar gradually and beat well. Add salt, milk, cottage cheese, flour and lemon juice. Mix well. Gently fold in beaten egg whites. Sprinkle cinnamon on top. Bake at 350° for 40 minutes or until knife inserted in center comes out clean. Low calorie if made with skimmed products.

Yield: 6 to 8 servings

Betty Kichline Gerow (Mrs. James A.)
Burlington

BUTTERMILK CUSTARD PIE

2 eggs
2 tablespoons flour
1 cup sugar
1 tablespoon butter or margarine
½ teaspoon baking powder
1 tablespoon vanilla extract
1 cup buttermilk
½ teaspoon baking soda dissolved in milk
1 (8 or 9-inch) unbaked pie shell

Mix all ingredients. Pour into unbaked pie shell and bake at 425° for 15 minutes. Reduce heat to 350° and bake an additional 20 minutes. Cool in oven.

Yield: 6 to 8 servings

This is from the recipes of my mother, Mrs. Elsie Porterfield Cates.

Constance Cates Isley
Burlington

MAMA'S CUSTARD PIE

3 eggs
⅔ cup sugar
Pinch of salt
1 tablespoon cornstarch
2 cups whole milk
1 teaspoon lemon extract
Nutmeg
½ stick butter or margarine
1 (9-inch) unbaked pie shell

Beat eggs. Add sugar and salt. Dissolve cornstarch in milk and add to egg mixture. Add lemon flavoring and pour into pie shell. Sprinkle nutmeg on top. Cut butter into pieces and place on top. Bake at 450° for 20 to 30 minutes.

Yield: 6 to 8 servings

Dianne Simpson Gerlach (Mrs. John)
Burlington

EGG CUSTARD

3 eggs
⅔ cup sugar
½ stick butter or margarine, melted
1 cup sweet milk
½ teaspoon nutmeg
1 teaspoon vanilla or lemon extract
1 (9-inch) unbaked pie shell

Beat eggs well. Add sugar and then butter. Add sweet milk. (If using canned milk, do not dilute). Add nutmeg and vanilla or lemon extract. Bake 400° for 20 to 25 minutes or until set and brown.

Yield: 6 to 8 servings

Mary Catherine Moser
Graham

BUTTERMILK PIE

1½ cups sugar
2 tablespoons cornstarch
2 eggs, beaten
1 cup butter, melted
1 cup buttermilk
1 teaspoon lemon or lemon extract
1 (9-inch) unbaked pie shell

Blend sugar and cornstarch. Beat eggs and add to sugar and cornstarch. Mix well. Add butter and buttermilk. Mix well. Add flavoring and mix well. Pour into a 9-inch pie shell. Bake at 425° for 10 minutes, then reduce to 350° for 35 minutes without opening the oven door.

Yield: 6 to 8 servings

Mary Catherine Moser
Graham

LEMON MERINGUE PIE

1½ cups sugar
½ cup plain flour
2 tablespoons cornstarch
½ teaspoon salt
2¼ cups boiling water
4 egg yolks
6 tablespoons lemon juice
3 tablespoons grated lemon rind
1 (9-inch) baked pie shell or 2 (8-inch) baked pie shells

Combine 1 cup of sugar with the flour, cornstarch and salt in a double boiler. Add the boiling water, stirring constantly. Cook over boiling water until smooth and thickened, stirring constantly. Cover and cook 15 minutes. Beat egg yolks with ½ cup sugar and gradually pour into hot mixture, blending thoroughly. Return to double boiler and cook, covered, an additional 5 minutes. Just before removing from heat, add lemon juice and rind. Mix well. Cool and pour into baked pie shell. Top with meringue.

Meringue:
4 egg whites
6 tablespoons sugar

Beat egg whites until stiff, gradually adding sugar while beating on low speed. Bake at 300° for 30 minutes.

Yield: 6 to 8 servings

Agnes Compton Allen
Mebane

LEMON CHESS PIE

1 cup sugar
1 tablespoon flour
1 teaspoon cornmeal
2 eggs, unbeaten
⅛ cup milk
2 tablespoons grated lemon rind
⅛ cup lemon juice
½ stick butter or margarine, melted
1 (9-inch) unbaked pie shell

Mix sugar, flour and cornmeal in a bowl and toss lightly with a fork. Add eggs, milk, lemon rind, lemon juice and melted butter. Beat until smooth and well blended. Pour into pie shell. Bake at 350° for 35 to 45 minutes or until golden brown.

Yield: 6 to 8 servings

Josephine Graham Umstead
Burlington

FROZEN LEMON PIE

½ cup sugar
3 eggs, separated
Juice of one lemon
1 cup cream, whipped
Vanilla wafers
Vanilla wafer crumbs

Cook sugar, egg yolks and juice over boiling water until slightly thickened. Cool. Beat 3 egg whites until stiff and add 1 cup cream that has been whipped. Combine with above mixture. Line bottom of a 9-inch square baking dish with vanilla wafers. Pour prepared filling over wafers. Sprinkle vanilla wafer crumbs over the top. Freeze. Set out for approximately 15 minutes before serving time. Cut and serve in squares. Delicious and light.

Yield: 6 to 9 servings

Doris Clapp Gilliam (Mrs. Emery)
Elon College

OLD FASHIONED LEMON CHESS PIE

5 tablespoons flour
2 cups sugar
1 stick margarine, softened
6 eggs, separated
Grated rind and juice of 3 lemons
1 (9-inch) unbaked pie shell

Sift flour and sugar together and cream with margarine. Separate yolk and white of each egg, reserving 3 egg whites. Add egg yolks, one at a time to creamed mixture and beat in. Add grated lemon rind. Add lemon juice to suit taste. Fold in 3 well beaten egg whites. Pour into unbaked shell. Begin baking at 400° and lower heat to 325° after pie browns, then bake until firm.

Yield: 6 to 8 servings

Gilberta Jeffries Mitchell (Mrs. R. G.)
Mebane

LEMON SPONGE PIE

2 eggs, separated
1 cup sugar
1 cup milk
3 level tablespoons flour
Juice and grated rind of 1 large lemon
1 tablespoon butter or margarine, melted
Pinch of salt
1 (9-inch) unbaked pie shell

Beat egg whites until stiff. Mix all other ingredients in a bowl. Fold in egg whites and pour into pie shell. Bake at 350° for about 40 minutes.

Yield: 6 to 8 servings

Betty Kichline Gerow (Mrs. James A.)
Burlington

LEMON CHESS TARTS OR PIE

3 eggs
1½ cups sugar
4 tablespoons melted butter or margarine
Juice of 2 lemons
6 tart shells or 1 (9-inch) pie shell, unbaked

Mix all ingredients. Pour into pie shell or 6 tart shells. Bake at 400° for 5 minutes for tarts and 10 minutes for pie. Reduce heat to 250° and continue baking for 15 to 20 minutes.

Yield: 6 tarts or 1 pie

Rose Anne Jordan Gant (Mrs. Roger, Jr.)
Burlington

MAMA'S KEY LIME PIE

1 (13-ounce) can sweetened condensed milk
4 egg yolks
1 egg white, stiffly beaten
½ cup fresh lime juice

Combine milk, egg yolks and lime juice and mix well. Fold egg white into milk mixture and pour into unbaked pie shell.

Meringue:
3 egg whites
6 tablespoons sugar
½ teaspoon cream of tartar

Beat egg whites and gradually add cream of tartar and sugar. Spread meringue over filling, sealing edges, and bake at 350° for 15 to 20 minutes or until meringue is golden brown.

Yield: 6 to 8 servings

A special holiday treat!

Ila Murray Bryan
Burlington

MACAROON PIE

14 saltine crackers, rolled fine
12 dates, cut fine
½ cup pecans, finely chopped
1 cup sugar
¼ teaspoon salt
1 teaspoon almond extract
3 egg whites, beaten
1 (9-inch) unbaked pie shell

Mix first 6 ingredients well and fold in beaten egg whites. Pour into buttered pie shell. Bake at 300° for 45 minutes. Serve with whipped cream, flavored with sherry and powdered sugar, if desired.

Yield: 6 to 8 servings

Lucille Paschal Wofford
Burlington

MOLASSES CRUMB CAKE PIE

3 level cups flour
1 cup sugar
¾ cup shortening
¼ teaspoon salt
½ teaspoon cinnamon
1 teaspoon baking soda
1 teaspoon vinegar
1 cup boiling water
1 cup molasses
2 medium unbaked pie shells

Blend first 5 ingredients with pastry blender into crumbs. Mix soda and vinegar; add water and molasses. Divide liquid into pie shells. Gently add crumbs on top of liquid. Bake at 400° about 30 minutes.

Yield: 12 servings

Betty Kichline Gerow (Mrs. James A.)
Burlington

PEACHES AND CREAM CHEESE PIE

Step 1:

¾ cup plain flour
1 (4¾-ounce) package dry vanilla pudding mix, not instant type
½ teaspoon salt
1 teaspoon baking powder
3 tablespoons butter, softened

Combine all ingredients and beat 2 minutes at medium speed. Pour into greased 10-inch deep dish pie plate.

Step 2:

1 (29-ounce) can drained, sliced peaches, reserving juice

Slice peaches in half and carefully arrange in batter, leaving a ½-inch border.

Step 3:

1 (8-ounce) package cream cheese
½ cup sugar
6 tablespoons reserved peach juice

Combine cheese, sugar and juice and beat 2 minutes. Spoon over peaches, leaving ½-inch of batter as a border.

Step 4:

1 tablespoon sugar
½ teaspoon cinnamon

Combine the 2 ingredients and sprinkle over entire pie. Bake at 350° for 30 to 35 minutes until crust is golden brown. Filling will appear soft. Keep refrigerated.

Yield: 6 to 8 servings

Patricia McHugh Jeffries
Mebane

FRIED PEACH PIES

Filling:

2 (8-ounce) packages dried peaches, cooked according to directions
2 cups sugar
1 teaspoon cinnamon
1 teaspoon salt

Drain peaches, if necessary, and mash. Add sugar, salt and cinnamon. Set aside.

Pastry:

3 cups plain flour
1 teaspoon baking soda
1 teaspoon salt
½ cup solid shortening
¾ cup buttermilk

Combine dry ingredients and cut in shortening until mixture resembles coarse cornmeal. Gradually add buttermilk to make soft dough. Turn onto a well-floured surface and knead. Divide dough into 3 portions for ease in rolling. Cut into 5½ to 6 inch circles and place heaping soup spoon of filling on each half, leaving a ½-inch edge around circle. Fold over half of dough and press edges together with a fork dipped in flour. Prick lightly on top with fork in three places. Fry in ½ to ¾ inch of corn oil until golden brown, turning once.

Yield: 16 to 18 pies

These pies are always a favorite at the annual FIDDLERS' PICNIC sponsored by the museum each spring. People stand in line for these traditional treats!

Gilberta Jeffries Mitchell (Mrs. R. G.)
Mebane

PECAN PIE

1 cup sugar
½ cup light corn syrup
2 large eggs, or 3 small
1 teaspoon vanilla extract
3 tablespoons butter or margarine, softened
1 cup pecans
1 (9-inch) unbaked pie shell

Mix all ingredients and pour into unbaked pie shell. Bake at 375° for about 40 minutes, or until set.

Yield: 6 to 8 servings

Melva Gray Foster
Burlington

PECAN PIE

½ cup sugar
2 tablespoons butter
2 eggs
2 tablespoons flour
¼ teaspoon salt
¼ teaspoon almond extract
¾ teaspoon vanilla extract
1 cup white syrup
¾ cup pecans
1 (9-inch) unbaked pie shell

Preheat oven to 400°. Cream butter and sugar, mixed with flour. Add beaten eggs, salt, extracts and syrup. Stir well, then add nuts. Pour into unbaked shell. Place on cookie sheet in oven. Reduce heat to 325° and cook 40 minutes or until pie no longer shakes in center.

Yield: 6 to 8 servings

Elizabeth (Beth) Gatewood Neal (Mrs. Tom)
Burlington

PECAN PIE

3 eggs, beaten
½ cup sugar
1 cup dark corn syrup
4 teaspoons butter or margarine, melted
1 teaspoon vanilla extract
1 cup pecans, broken
1 (8 or 9-inch) unbaked pie shell

Combine all ingredients. Pour into pie shell. Bake in hot oven at 400° for 10 minutes, then reduce oven to 350° and bake an additional 30 minutes.

Yield: 6 to 8 servings

Lillian Mae Sharpe
Mebane

PINEAPPLE PIE

2 eggs or 4 ounces egg substitute
½ stick margarine, melted
1 (16-ounce) can crushed pineapple, drained
¾ cup sugar
4 tablespoons plain flour
¼ teaspoon salt
1 teaspoon vanilla extract
1 (9-inch) unbaked pie shell

Beat eggs. Add margarine and pineapple. Mix well. Then add sugar, flour, salt and vanilla. Pour into a deep dish pie shell. Bake 350° for 30 to 35 minutes. Browns from outside to shaky center.

Yield: 6 to 8 servings

Hazel Bray Burleson (Mrs. P. K.)
Burlington

WHITE POTATO PIE

1½ cups hot mashed potatoes (¾ pound)
¾ cup sugar
½ stick butter or margarine
¼ teaspoon salt
2 eggs, separated
½ cup milk
1 tablespoon vanilla extract
1 tablespoon lemon extract
1 (9-inch) unbaked pie shell

Preheat oven to 450°. Cook potatoes and put through a ricer and then pack them down slightly in bowl. Add sugar, butter, salt and slightly beaten egg yolks to hot potatoes. Then add milk, vanilla and lemon extracts. Beat egg whites until stiff and fold into potato mixture. The mixture should be fairly thin. Pour into pie shell. Bake for 10 minutes. Reduce heat to 350° and bake an additional 45 minutes or until knife inserted in center comes out clean.

Yield: 6 to 8 servings

Sara Shaw Young
Burlington

PUMPKIN PIE

1½ cups strained pumpkin, cooked
½ cup sugar
3 tablespoons molasses
1 teaspoon cinnamon
½ teaspoon ginger
½ teaspoon cloves
½ teaspoon salt
1 tablespoon margarine, melted
2 eggs
1 large can evaporated milk
1 (9-inch) unbaked pie shell

Mix all ingredients together and pour into pie shell. Bake at 375° about 50 minutes, or until almost set.

Yield: 6 to 8 servings

Annie Patton Young
Mebane

PUMPKIN CUSTARD PIE

1½ cups sugar
3 tablespoons flour
⅛ teaspoon salt
½ teaspoon nutmeg
2 cups pumpkin, cooked
1 cup milk
1 (9-inch) unbaked pie shell

Blend sugar, flour, salt and nutmeg. Add to pumpkin and mix well. Gradually add milk, beating well. Pour into shell and bake at 400° for 25 minutes or until inserted knife comes out clean.

Yield: 6 to 8 servings

Lloyd Lafayette Bramble
Washington, District of Columbia

STRAWBERRY CUSTARD PIE

1 deep-dish pie shell
3 eggs or egg substitute
1 can sweetened condensed milk
1¼ cups hot water
1 teaspoon vanilla extract
¼ teaspoon salt

At 425° bake pie shell for 8 minutes. Beat eggs; add milk, water, vanilla and salt. Pour into pie shell. Bake for 10 minutes. Reduce heat to 350° and bake an additional 25 to 30 minutes or until knife inserted in center comes out clean.

Strawberry Topping:
10 ounces frozen strawberries, thawed; drained and liquid reserved
4 tablespoons grape jelly
5 teaspoons cornstarch

Measure into a saucepan ⅔ cup syrup from the frozen strawberries. Blend with grape jelly and cornstarch. Cook, stirring constantly until jelly melts and thickens. Cool 10 minutes. Stir in drained strawberries and spoon over custard. Refrigerate.

Yield: 6 to 8 servings

Hazel Bray Burleson (Mrs. P. K.)
Burlington

STRAWBERRY PINEAPPLE CHIFFON PIE

3 eggs, beaten
1 cup sugar
1 (8-ounce) can crushed pineapple
1 (3-ounce) package strawberry flavored gelatin
1 large can evaporated milk, chilled
1 (9-inch) baked pie shell

Cook eggs, sugar and pineapple until thick. Add gelatin and mix well. Cool. Whip milk until very stiff. Fold into strawberry mixture and combine thoroughly. Pour into baked pie shell and chill.

Yield: 6 servings

Elizabeth Salmons King
Burlington

ANGEL BERRY PIE

6 egg whites
¼ teaspoon salt
2 cups sugar
1 teaspoon vanilla extract
1 tablespoon vinegar
Non-dairy whipped topping
1½ cups fresh fruit of choice

Beat egg whites and salt. Add 1 cup sugar gradually. Add vanilla. Add second cup sugar gradually—alternating with vinegar. Grease and flour pie pan. Pour mixture in and mold in dome shape. Bake at 375° for 30 minutes, reduce oven to 300° and bake an additional 30 minutes. Spread whipped topping and fruit over meringue. Strawberries or peaches are very good.

Yield: 6 to 8 servings

Jessie Ormond Pyne (Mrs. Minetree)
Burlington

YOGURT PIE

Filling:
2 quarts yogurt, flavor of choice
1 (12-ounce) carton non-dairy whipped topping
1½ cups fresh fruit of choice

Mix together yogurt and topping and pour into crust. Top with fresh fruit. Freeze for 2 hours then refrigerate.

Crust:
2 cups granola cereal
½ cup butter, melted

Mix cereal and butter and press into pie dish.

Yield: 6 to 8 servings

Nancy Matthews Slott (Mrs. Steven D.)
Burlington

YOGURT PIE

1 (12-ounce) carton non-dairy whipped topping
2 cartons strawberry yogurt
3 bananas, mashed in blender
1 ready-made graham cracker shell

Mix together topping, yogurt and bananas. Pour into pie shell and freeze several hours, then store in refrigerator.

Yield: 6 servings

This is a good dessert for diabetics if yogurt is artificially sweetened.

Wilma Howell Suddath
Burlington

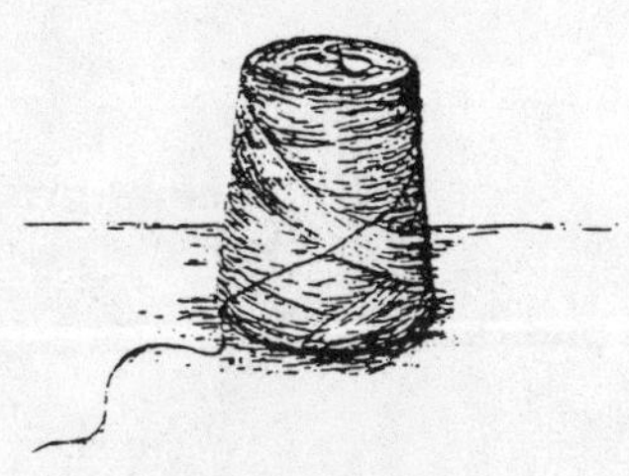

Between the years 1884 to 1887 the number of looms devoted to the production of plaids increased from 2300 to more than 5000. The increased number of looms resulted in over-production of the plaids, however, and the market was soon saturated. In 1888 members of the Plaid Manufacturers' Association agreed to reduce production of the Alamance Plaids by one-third. In the same year, some of the Holt mills began to switch to the production of lighter colored cotton and gingham fabrics.

DENTZEL CAROUSEL

Burlington, N.C.

A popular attraction of Burlington's City Park, the Dentzel Menagerie Carousel was built c. 1906 in Germantown, Pennsylvania. The carousel retains its forty-six original hand-carved animals, each of which was lovingly restored in the early 1980s.

The Burlington City Park remains a favorite spot for picnics, family outings and the celebration of childhood.

ADDIE SPOON'S APPLESAUCE CAKE

1 cup solid shortening
2 cups sugar
2 large eggs
3 cups sifted plain flour
1 teaspoon baking powder
1 teaspoon cinnamon
1 teaspoon allspice
½ teaspoon cloves
½ teaspoon baking soda
¼ teaspoon salt
2 cups unsweetened applesauce
1 cup black walnuts, chopped

Beat shortening to soften. Gradually add sugar and cream until light. Add eggs, one at a time, beating well after each addition. Sift together flour, baking powder, cinnamon, allspice, cloves, soda and salt 3 times. Add to creamed mixture alternately with applesauce. Fold in nuts. Turn into 10-inch tube pan which has been greased, lined with waxed paper, greased again, and lightly floured. Bake at 350° for 1 hour, or until a cake tester comes out clean. Cool in pan 10 minutes, turn out on wire rack and remove paper carefully.

Yield: 16 to 20 servings

Mildred Spoon Alexander (Mrs. Carl B.)
Burlington

FRESH APPLE CRUNCH CAKE

2 cups flour
1½ teaspoons salt
1 teaspoon nutmeg
1 teaspoon cinnamon
1 teaspoon baking soda
1¼ cups vegetable oil
2 eggs
2 cups sugar
2 cups fresh apples, sliced
1 cup chopped nuts
1 tablespoon vanilla extract
½ cup brandy

Stir together flour, salt, nutmeg, cinnamon and soda. Mix oil, eggs and sugar. Add apples, nuts, vanilla and brandy; mixing well. Batter will be very stiff. Spread into lightly greased 13x5x2-inch pan. Bake at 350° for 35 to 45 minutes.

Yield: 15 servings

Elizabeth Hampton Lasley (Mrs. Jim)
Burlington

APPLE-TOP CAKE

2 cups flour
3 teaspoons baking powder
½ teaspoon salt
⅓ cup plus 1 tablespoon sugar
⅓ cup plus 1 tablespoon solid shortening
1 egg, beaten
¾ cup rich milk
¼ teaspoon vanilla extract
1⅓ cups thin apple slices

Sift together flour, baking powder, salt and sugar. Cut in shortening. Beat egg, milk, vanilla; add to batter and blend well. Pour batter into greased 8x8-inch pan. Spread apple slices on batter; push slices down a trifle into the batter.

Topping:
¼ cup butter or margarine
⅓ cup plus 1 tablespoon light brown sugar
¼ teaspoon nutmeg
¼ teaspoon allspice
¼ teaspoon cinnamon
⅛ teaspoon cloves

Mix topping ingredients and sprinkle over apples. Bake at 350° about 1 hour or until done. Serve with whipped cream.

Yield: 12 to 16 servings

In memory of my grandmother, Gladys Minnich.

Sherry Gail Moses
Graham

APPLE SPICE CAKE

1 cup apple pie filling
½ cup raisins
¼ cup pecans
1 (18¼-ounce) package spice cake mix
2 sticks butter

In 8x12-inch ovenproof baking dish, evenly spread apple pie filling. Sprinkle with raisins and nuts. Top with dry cake mix. Slice butter into 3 lengthwise pieces each; top with butter slices. Bake at 350° for 40 to 45 minutes. Serve warm with ice cream.

Yield: 8 to 10 servings

Nancy Norton Holt
Burlington

APPLESAUCE CAKE

½ cup butter, softened
1½ cups sugar
2 eggs, slightly beaten
2½ cups flour
1 teaspoon baking powder
¼ teaspoon salt
1 teaspoon cinnamon
1 teaspoon nutmeg
½ teaspoon baking soda
1 cup applesauce
1 cup chopped pecans or black walnuts
1 cup chopped raisins

Cream butter and sugar. Add eggs. Mix all dry ingredients except soda. Mix soda with applesauce and add to moist mixture. Dredge nuts and raisins in dry ingredients and add to applesauce mixture. Beat thoroughly. Pour into a greased loaf pan and bake at 350° for about 1 hour or until toothpick inserted in center comes out clean.

Yield: 1 loaf

Dorothy Simmons Jordan
Graham

CAKE LAYERS

1 cup butter
2 cups sugar
4 eggs, separated
3 cups sifted cake flour
¼ teaspoon salt
3 teaspoons baking powder
1 cup milk
1 teaspoon vanilla extract

Cream butter and sugar until light and fluffy. Add egg yolks, one at a time, beating well after each addition. Sift dry ingredients together three times and add alternately with milk and vanilla, blending well after each addition. Fold in stiffly beaten egg whites. Pour batter into 3 well greased and lightly floured 9-inch cake pans. Bake at 350° for 25 minutes. Frost as desired.

Yield: 10 to 12 servings

Willis Thompson Durham
Burlington

BANANA CUPCAKES

½ cup flour
1½ cups sugar
2 eggs, beaten
2 cups plain flour
½ teaspoon salt
1 teaspoon baking powder
¾ teaspoon baking soda
¼ cup sour milk
1 cup mashed banana
1 teaspoon vanilla extract

Cream butter and sugar until light; add beaten eggs and blend. Sift flour, salt, baking powder and baking soda into batter alternately with sour milk. Add bananas and vanilla. Fill greased muffin cups ⅔ full; bake at 375° for 20 minutes. Frost with lemon frosting.

Lemon Frosting:
⅓ cup butter
2 cups powdered sugar
3 tablespoons mashed banana
1 tablespoon lemon juice
Pecan halves

Cream butter and sugar. Add banana and lemon juice; mix until smooth. Spread frosting on cupcakes and top with a pecan, if desired.

Yield: 18 to 20 servings

These cupcakes freeze beautifully.

Foy Elder Lane (Mrs. V. Wilton)
Burlington

DUMP CAKE

1 (21-ounce) can cherry or strawberry pie filling
1 (8¼-ounce) can crushed pineapple, undrained
2⅔ cups yellow cake mix
½ cup chopped nuts or coconut
1½ sticks margarine, melted

Place pie filling in 9x13x2-inch greased pan. Pour pineapple over pie filling. Over this sprinkle cake mix then nuts. Pour margarine over all. Bake at 350° for 45 minutes.

Yield: 8 to 10 servings

Frances Tucker Gosnell
Mebane

TIPS ON MAKING BURNT SUGAR

Use a heavy aluminum or cast-iron skillet that will heat evenly and prevent the sugar from scorching.

Add the granulated sugar by itself to the dry skillet. Cook sugar over medium heat. Don't stir until you see it just starting to melt. This will take about 5 minutes for ½ to ¾ cup sugar.

After sugar starts to melt, turn heat down to low. Cook and stir constantly for 1 to 3 minutes for ½ to ¾ cup sugar or until sugar completely melts and turns golden brown (the color of peanut brittle).

Once the sugar has melted, watch syrup closely. The syrup changes color quickly and will taste scorched if it gets too dark.

Remove the skillet from the heat. Working quickly, add at least 2 tablespoons hot water or fruit juice (the amount may vary with the recipe). The syrup will spatter and harden when the liquid is added. To remelt it, return the skillet to low heat. Cook and stir the syrup until smooth.

BURNT SUGAR CAKE

½ cup sugar
¾ cup water
2½ cups flour
1 teaspoon baking powder
1 teaspoon baking soda
2 eggs, separated
¾ cup shortening
1 cup sugar
1 cup milk
1 teaspoon vanilla extract

In a heavy skillet, brown ½ cup sugar to a deep brown. Add water and stir until all sugar is dissolved. Cool. Sift dry ingredients together 3 times. Beat egg whites until stiff and set aside. Beat egg yolks and add to shortening and mix well. Add 1 cup sugar and mix well. Add dry ingredients alternately with milk. Add burnt sugar mixture and vanilla. Fold in egg whites. Pour into 3 greased and floured 8-inch pans. Bake at 350° for 20 minutes or until brown.

Caramel Icing:
1 cup butter or margarine
2 cups dark brown sugar
½ cup milk
Powdered sugar

Melt butter or margarine in saucepan and add brown sugar. Boil over low heat for 2 minutes, stirring constantly. Add milk and continue stirring until mixture returns to a boil. Remove from heat. Cool. Add powdered sugar gradually, beating with electric mixer, until icing is of spreading consistency.

Yield: 16 to 20 servings

Josephine Graham Umstead
Burlington

BURNT SUGAR CAKE

1 cup sugar
½ cup cold water

Heat sugar in heavy skillet over medium heat to melt and brown, stirring as necessary to prevent burning. After browning add cold water; stir and cook until a syrup is formed. A little more water may be needed. Remove from heat; set aside to cool. (This can be stored in refrigerator for days, if not ready to use immediately.)

Cake Layers:
4 eggs, separated
1 cup butter or solid shortening
1½ cups sugar
1 teaspoon baking powder
1 teaspoon baking soda
1 cup milk
3 cups flour
½ teaspoon salt
Burnt sugar syrup
2 teaspoons vanilla extract

Beat egg whites until stiff; set aside. Cream butter and sugar until light; add egg yolks and blend well. Combine baking powder, soda and milk; add to creamed mixture. Sift flour and salt together 3 times and stir into batter. Add syrup and vanilla; beat well. Fold in egg whites slowly to combine with batter. Pour into 3 well greased and lightly floured 9-inch cake pans. Bake in 350° oven for 20 minutes or until layers leave the sides of the pan.

NOTE: Batter can be baked in 4 pans if thinner layers are desired.

Filling/Frosting:
3 cups sugar
1 stick margarine or butter
1 large can undiluted evaporated milk
2 teaspoons vanilla extract

In heavy saucepan, heat sugar and margarine until brown. Stir in milk and continue to stir until mixture becomes thick or forms a ball when dropped in cold water. Add vanilla and stir until of spreading consistency. If mixture becomes too dry, add a few drops of hot water.

Yield: 15 to 20 servings

Sarah Scurlock Rogers
Graham

AUNT E'S CARROT LAYER CAKE
With Pineapple Icing

2 cups plain flour
2 teaspoons baking powder
1½ teaspoons baking soda
1½ teaspoons cinnamon
1 teaspoon salt
1½ cups vegetable oil
2 cups sugar
4 eggs
2 cups grated raw carrots
1 (8½-ounce) can crushed pineapple with juice
½ cup chopped pecans (optional)

Preheat oven to 350°. Sift together flour, baking powder, soda, cinnamon and salt; set aside. Combine oil and sugar in large bowl. Add eggs, one at a time, beating well after each addition. Add sifted dry ingredients; mix well. Stir in carrots, pineapple and pecans. Pour batter into 3 greased and floured 9-inch cake pans; bake for 35 to 40 minutes. Do not overbake. Frost with pineapple icing.

Pineapple Icing:
¼ cup butter, softened
1 (8-ounce) package cream cheese, softened
1 (16-ounce) box powdered sugar, sifted
1 teaspoon vanilla extract
1 (8½-ounce) can crushed pineapple, drained
1 cup pecans, finely chopped

Combine all ingredients and mix well. Makes enough icing to fill and frost the top and sides of a 9-inch, three layer cake.

Yield: 18 to 20 servings

N. Jane Iseley
Burlington

CARROT CAKE

2 cups sugar
3 cups plain flour
1 teaspoon baking soda
¼ teaspoon salt
2 teaspoons ground cinnamon
1½ cups vegetable oil
1 teaspoon vanilla extract
3 eggs, beaten
1 cup crushed pineapple, well drained
1¾ cups grated raw carrots
¼ cup peeled, grated apple
1 cup chopped pecans

Sift together sugar, flour, soda, salt and cinnamon; set aside. Combine oil, vanilla, eggs, pineapple, carrots and apple. Beat well. Stir in dry ingredients and pecans. Spoon batter into 3 greased and floured 8-inch cake pans. Bake at 350° for 25 to 30 minutes. Cool in pans for 10 minutes on wire rack. Remove from pans and cool completely. Spread frosting between layers and on top and sides of cake.

Carrot Cake Frosting:
½ cup margarine, softened
1 (8-ounce) package cream cheese, softened
1 (16-ounce) box powdered sugar, sifted
1 cup chopped pecans

Combine margarine and cream cheese. Cream until light and fluffy. Add sugar, mixing well. Stir in pecans.

Yield: 16 servings

Lou Foster Harper (Mrs. Kenneth)
Elon College

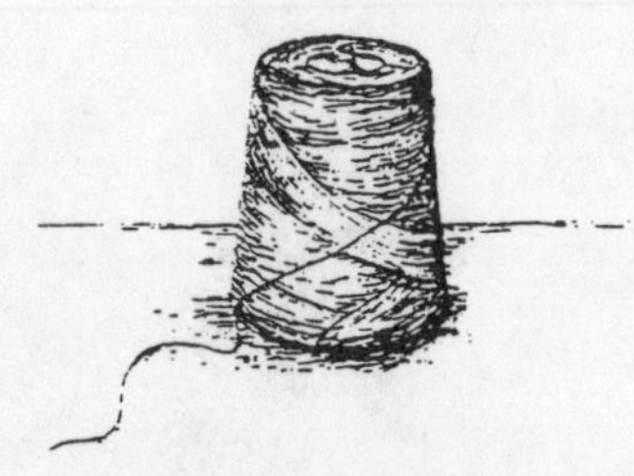

CARROT-PINEAPPLE CAKE

1½ cups plain flour
1 cup sugar
1 teaspoon baking powder
1 teaspoon baking soda
1 teaspoon cinnamon
½ teaspoon salt
⅔ cup vegetable oil
2 eggs
1 cup raw carrots, finely grated
½ cup crushed pineapple with syrup
1 teaspoon vanilla extract

In a large mixer bowl blend flour, sugar, baking powder, baking soda, cinnamon, and salt. Add oil, eggs, carrots, pineapple and vanilla. Mix until moist. Beat with mixer 2 minutes at medium speed. Pour batter into greased and floured 9x9-inch pan. Bake at 350° for 35 minutes. Cool. Frost with Cream Cheese Frosting.

Cream Cheese Frosting:
1 (3-ounce) package cream cheese, softened
4 tablespoons margarine, softened
1 teaspoon vanilla extract
2½ cups sifted powdered sugar
½ cup chopped pecans

Blend together cream cheese, margarine and vanilla. Gradually add sugar. Stir in pecans.

Yield: 9 servings

Hallie Oakley Griswold (Mrs. Ralph)
Burlington

RICH TEXAS CAKE

1 (18¼-ounce) package German chocolate cake mix
2 eggs, beaten
1 stick margarine, melted
½ cup nuts, chopped
2 eggs, beaten
1 (8-ounce) package cream cheese
1 teaspoon vanilla extract
1 (1-pound) box powdered sugar

Blend cake mix, 2 eggs, margarine and nuts. Spread in a well-greased 9x13-inch pan. Mixture will be thick. Mix remaining ingredients and spread on top of cake mix. Bake at 350° for 35 minutes only.

Yield: 6 to 8 servings

Margaret Nelson Patton (Mrs. H. L.)
Kerrville, Texas

CHOCOLATE POUND CAKE

2 sticks margarine
½ cup solid shortening
3 cups sugar
6 eggs, well beaten
3 cups plain flour
5 tablespoons cocoa
½ teaspoon baking powder
¼ teaspoon salt
1 cup milk
1 teaspoon vanilla extract
1 teaspoon black walnut extract
Powdered sugar

Cream margarine and solid shortening with sugar; add well beaten eggs. Sift flour, cocoa, baking powder and salt. Add dry ingredients alternately with milk and extracts. Beat only enough to blend well. Pour batter into a greased and floured 10-inch bundt pan. Bake at 350° for 1 hour, or until done. Let stand in pan 5 minutes to cool before turning out. Before serving, sift powdered sugar on top.

Yield: 18 to 20 servings

Peggy Jones McCuiston (Mrs. John)
Burlington

CHOCOLATE SYRUP POUND CAKE

2 sticks margarine
¼ cup solid shortening
3 cups sugar
6 eggs
3 cups plain flour
½ teaspoon baking powder
½ teaspoon salt
½ cup milk
1 (16-ounce) can chocolate syrup
2 teaspoons vanilla extract

In a large mixing bowl, cream margarine and shortening until light; add eggs, one at a time, beating well after each addition. Sift flour, baking powder and salt together three times; add dry ingredients to batter alternately with milk. Add syrup and vanilla; mix well. Bake in a greased and floured 10-inch tube pan at 325° for 1 hour and 20 minutes, or until cake pulls away from pan. Let cool slightly in pan; remove from pan and cool completely.

Yield: 18 to 20 servings

Martha Ann Shaw
Burlington

CHOCOLATE UPSIDE DOWN CAKE

Cake:

1 cup flour
¼ teaspoon salt
¾ cup sugar
2 teaspoons baking powder
1 to 2 tablespoons cocoa
½ cup milk
2 tablespoons melted butter
1 to 2 teaspoons vanilla extract
½ cup chopped nuts

Custard:

½ cup white sugar
½ cup brown sugar
5 tablespoons cocoa (or 5 teaspoons cocoa plus ¾ teaspoon cornstarch)
1 cup hot water

Sift together flour, salt, sugar, baking powder and cocoa. Add milk, butter and vanilla; beat well. Pour batter into a greased and floured 9-inch square baking pan; sprinkle with nuts. Blend sugar, brown sugar, cocoa, (cornstarch) and water; pour over batter. Bake at 350° for 30 to 40 minutes. This cake is better under baked than over baked. Do not remove from pan until ready to serve, as a chocolate custard forms in bottom of pan. Serve plain, with whipped cream or ice cream.

Yield: 8 to 10 servings

Jean Millikan Frissell (Mrs. Fred, III)
Whitsett, North Carolina

Edith Bowden Huff
Burlington

DARK CHOCOLATE CAKE

2 cups flour
1 cup brown sugar
1 cup white sugar
1 cup sour milk (lemon juice plus milk)
¾ cup oil
¾ cup cocoa
2 teaspoons baking soda
2 eggs
2 teaspoons vanilla extract
¾ cup hot water

Preheat oven to 350°. In cup, measure 1 tablespoon lemon juice and enough milk to make one cup. In large mixing bowl, combine all ingredients. Mix at low speed until thoroughly combined. Beat at medium speed for several minutes, scraping sides occasionally. Pour into greased, floured 9x15 cake pan. Bake for 35 to 40 minutes or until cake tester comes out clean. Cool. Frost, if desired.

Yield: 12 to 15 servings

Sheila Saxman Weckerly
Graham

PICNIC FUDGE CAKE

1 stick margarine
1 cup sugar
4 eggs
1 (16-ounce) can chocolate syrup
1 cup flour
1 tablespoon baking powder
½ teaspoon salt

Cream margarine and sugar until light; add eggs, one at a time, beating well after each addition. Stir chocolate syrup, flour, baking powder and salt into batter. Pour into greased and floured 9x12-inch pan. Bake at 325° for 30 minutes. Pour sauce over hot cake.

Sauce:
1 stick margarine
1 cup sugar
1 teaspoon cocoa
¼ cup milk
Pinch salt
1 cup chopped nuts
1 teaspoon vanilla extract

Combine in saucepan margarine, sugar, cocoa, milk and salt. Cook over low heat until mixture boils, then boil hard for 2 minutes. Add nuts and vanilla. Pour over hot cake.

Yield: 12 to 18 servings

Martha Young Clark (Mrs. T. N.)
Burlington

CHOCOLATE POUND CAKE WITH CARAMEL FROSTING

2 sticks butter
½ cup solid shortening
3 cups sugar
5 eggs
3 cups plain flour
4 tablespoons cocoa
½ teaspoon baking powder
½ teaspoon salt
1 cup milk
1 tablespoon vanilla extract

Cream butter, shortening and sugar until well blended. Add eggs, one at a time, beating well after each addition. Sift flour, measure and sift again with cocoa, baking powder and salt. Add to batter alternately with milk and vanilla. Bake in 10-inch tube pan at 325° for 1 hour and 20 minutes or until done. Cool before frosting.

Caramel Frosting:
1 (16-ounce) box light brown sugar
1 stick butter
5 tablespoons milk
1 teaspoon salt
½ teaspoon baking powder
1 teaspoon vanilla extract

Mix brown sugar, butter, milk and salt in saucepan; bring to a boil. Boil 2 minutes, or until soft ball stage. Remove from heat, and add baking powder and vanilla. Beat until thick enough to spread. If it gets too hard, add 1 tablespoon milk and reheat slightly.

Yield: 18 to 20 servings

Ethel Boone Gant (Mrs. Allen E.)
Burlington

CORNELIA VINCENT BARNWELL'S GERMAN CHOCOLATE CAKE

1 package German sweet chocolate
½ cup boiling water
1 tablespoon vanilla extract
Pinch salt
1 cup solid shortening
2 cups sugar
4 egg yolks, beaten
1 cup buttermilk
2½ cups cake flour, sifted
1 teaspoon baking soda
4 egg whites, beaten

Melt chocolate in boiling water; add vanilla. Add salt after chocolate melts; set aside to cool. Cream shortening and sugar until light; add beaten egg yolks. Add ¾ cup of buttermilk alternately with flour to the creamed mixture, beginning and ending with flour. Dissolve soda in remaining ¼ cup buttermilk and add to batter. Stir in chocolate. Fold in beaten egg whites. Pour into 3 greased and floured 9-inch cake pans. Bake at 350° for 25 to 30 minutes.

Icing:
4 egg yolks
1⅓ tablespoons flour
1⅓ cup sugar
¼ teaspoon salt (rounded)
1 large can evaporated milk
1 small can evaporated milk
1⅓ sticks butter
1 cup chopped walnuts or pecans
1 (7-ounce) can flaked coconut
1 teaspoon vanilla extract

Beat egg yolks; set aside. Sift together flour, sugar and salt into a large saucepan. Add milk gradually, blending well. Cook over low heat; add butter. When butter melts, pour small amount of hot mixture over egg yolks; beat well. Add to above mixture on stove, stirring to blend. Add nuts and coconut; stir constantly until thick. Add vanilla last as icing is removed from stove.

Yield: 16 to 20 servings

Diane Gore Barnwell (Mrs. James A.)
Burlington

CHOCOLATE CAKE

1 cup boiling water
4 squares unsweetened chocolate
1 cup butter
2 cups flour
2 cups sugar
1½ teaspoons baking soda
2 eggs
½ cup buttermilk

Pour boiling water over chocolate and butter. Let stand until cool. Sift flour, sugar and soda together. Add to chocolate mixture. Beat eggs, then add to chocolate mixture and blend well. Add buttermilk and stir. Pour into 2 well greased 9-inch cake pans or 1 12x8-inch pan. Bake at 350° for 30 to 35 minutes.

Yield: 8 to 10 servings

NOTE: A caramel or seven minute frosting can be used.

This recipe was my aunt's, given to me in the late 1930's.

Elsie Pentecost Clapp (Mrs. W. Keith)
Saxapahaw

RED DEVIL'S CAKE

2 cups cake flour
1¼ teaspoons baking soda
6 tablespoons cocoa
¼ teaspoon salt
½ cup butter or solid shortening
1 cup sugar
2 eggs, beaten
¾ cup sour milk or buttermilk
1 teaspoon vanilla extract
⅓ cup boiling water

Sift together flour, soda, cocoa and salt. Cream butter or shortening. Add sugar gradually; beat until light. Add eggs, one at a time, beating well after each addition. Add dry ingredients alternately with milk and vanilla, blending well. Add water and beat until smooth. Bake at 350° for 45 minutes in a well greased and lightly floured 9x13-inch baking pan. Place on wire rack to cool.

Yield: 12 to 15 servings

NOTE: Pan can be lightly dusted with cocoa instead of flour, if desired. Cake turns to a deep red as it cools. No food color is needed.

Jean Turner Anderson (Mrs. Ralph)
Graham

MOTHER'S DEVIL'S FOOD CAKE

½ cup butter
2 cups sugar
2 eggs
2 heaping tablespoons cocoa
½ cup boiling water
2 teaspoons baking soda
Pinch salt
1 cup buttermilk
1 teaspoon vanilla extract
2½ cups flour

Cream butter, add sugar gradually, blending well. Add eggs, one at a time, beating well after each addition. Dissolve cocoa in boiling water; add to batter and blend. Dissolve soda and salt in buttermilk; add vanilla. Stir flour into creamed mixture alternately with buttermilk; mix thoroughly. Pour into 3 greased and floured 8-inch cake pans. Bake at 325° for 20 to 25 minutes. If a wooden toothpick inserted into the cake comes out clean, the cake is done.

Chocolate Frosting:
½ cup cocoa
2 cups sugar
1 cup milk
Pinch salt
1 stick butter
2 teaspoons vanilla extract
Powdered sugar

Sift together cocoa and sugar. Combine in saucepan with milk and salt. Place covered saucepan on medium heat; let mixture come to a boil. Boil to soft ball stage. Remove from heat and add butter and vanilla. Let cool about 10 minutes. Beat well and add sifted powdered sugar until of spreading consistency.

Yield: 12 to 16 servings

Peggy Howe Helms (Mrs. Steve T.)
Burlington

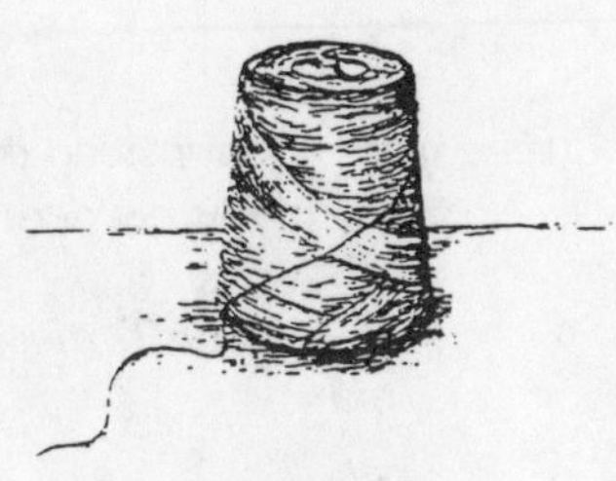

MILKY WAY CAKE

2 tablespoons shortening
¾ cup finely chopped nuts
12 Milky Way Snack Bars
1 cup buttermilk, plain yogurt or sour cream
1 cup butter
1½ cups sugar
½ teaspoon vanilla extract
4 eggs
2½ to 2¾ cups flour
1 teaspoon salt
¾ teaspoon baking soda

Grease a 10-inch tube pan with shortening and coat with nuts. In heavy saucepan over low heat, melt candy with ¼ cup buttermilk until smooth. Beat butter and sugar until fluffy; blend in vanilla. Add eggs, one at a time, beating well after each addition. Add dry ingredients alternately with ¾ cup liquid ingredient of your choice. Blend in candy mixture. Bake 350° for 55 to 60 minutes. Cool 10 minutes. Invert on wire rack and cool.

Yield: 16 to 20 servings

Virginia McPherson Hamby (Mrs. Clayton)
Mebane

BLACKBERRY WINE CAKE

1 (18½-ounce) box white cake mix (any brand)
4 eggs
1 cup blackberry wine
1 cup vegetable oil
1 (6-ounce) package blackberry gelatin

Combine all ingredients for cake; mix well. Pour into greased and floured 10-inch tube pan. Bake at 350° for 45 minutes.

Glaze:
½ cup blackberry wine
2½ cups powdered sugar

Add wine gradually to powdered sugar; blend until smooth. Pour over warm cake.

Yield: 15 to 20 servings

NOTE: This cake is better if made at least a day before serving.

Esther Neely Stadler (Mrs. Charlie W.)
Elon College

COCONUT-TOPPED SHEET CAKE

1 cup butter
1¾ cups sugar
3 cups cake flour, measured before sifting
2½ teaspoons baking powder
½ teaspoon baking soda
3 egg whites

Cream butter and sugar. Sift flour with baking powder and soda. Add to creamed mixture alternately with milk, blending well after each addition. Beat egg whites separately until stiff but not dry. Fold into batter. Turn batter into greased and floured 9x13-inch sheet cake pan. Bake at 350° about 40 minutes or until cake springs back at touch.

Topping:
1 cup brown sugar
4 tablespoons melted butter
4 tablespoons cream or evaporated milk
1 (3½-ounce) can Southern-type coconut

Mix together brown sugar, butter, cream and coconut. While cake is still hot, spread topping evenly over top. Return to oven and broil for a few minutes until topping bubbles. Do not burn! Serve from pan either warm or cold.

Yield: 12 to 18 servings

Good to take to picnics or covered dish suppers.

Lottie Sue Fesperman Arthur (Mrs. Bob)
Burlington

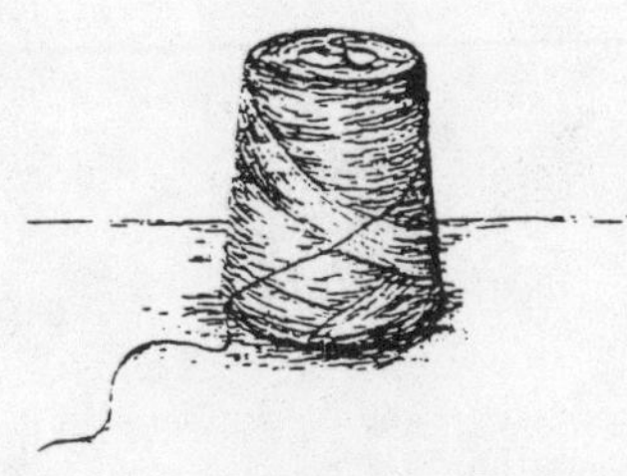

UNCOOKED FRUIT CAKE

1 pound graham crackers, crushed
1 pound miniature marshmallows
1 pound nuts
½ pound red candied cherries
½ pound green candied cherries
1 pound white raisins
1 pound dark raisins
½ pound dates
1 large can crushed pineapple

Mix cracker crumbs with all ingredients well. Pack as firm as possible in a tube pan. Refrigerate for 25 hours. Turn onto plate. Wrap well and keep refrigerated.

Yield: 16 to 20 servings

Virginia McPherson Hamby (Mrs. Clayton)
Mebane

JAPANESE FRUIT CAKE

Cake:
1 cup butter
2 cups sugar
4 eggs, separated
1 teaspoon baking powder
3 cups plain flour
1 cup milk

Cream butter well. Then add sugar and beat until fluffy. Add eggs, one at a time, beating well after each addition. Mix baking powder with flour and add alternately with milk, ending with flour. Divide batter into two parts for making 2 white layers and 2 dark layers. Add the following ingredients and mix well for the dark layers:
1 cup raisins, ground
1 tablespoon cinnamon
1 tablespoon cocoa
1 tablespoon vanilla

Filling:
2 cups sugar
½ cup water
Rind of 1 lemon, grated
Juice of 1 lemon
Meat of 1 coconut, grated
1 cup raisins, ground
Butter, size of an egg

Boil sugar and water until it spins a thread. Add lemon rind and juice, coconut and raisins. Mix well and then add butter. Spread between cake layers.

Yield: 12 to 16 servings

Rena Maude I. Danieley
Burlington

QUICKY FRUIT CAKE

1 pound pecan halves
½ pound candied cherries, uncut
½ pound dates, halved
2 cups coconut
2 cans sweetened condensed milk

Combine all ingredients in a large mixing bowl. Blend carefully. Bake in a 10-inch spring-form pan which has been lightly greased, lined with waxed paper, and greased again. Bake at 275° for 1 hour and 30 minutes or until nicely browned on top. Cool for 10 minutes on wire rack; invert cake on rack and carefully remove waxed paper. Let cool and dry. Refrigerate in cake tin.

Yield: 16 to 20 servings

NOTE: ¼ pound candied pineapple can be substituted for ¼ pound of nuts. Two 4¼x8½-inch loaf pans can be used.

Grace Anderson Thompson (Mrs. A. G., Jr.)
Burlington

LEMON CAKE

1 (18¼-ounce) package lemon cake mix
4 eggs
¾ cup vegetable oil
1 (3-ounce) package lemon gelatin
¾ cup boiling water

Combine cake mix, eggs and vegetable oil in large mixing bowl. Add lemon gelatin which has been dissolved in boiling water; blend well. Pour batter into a well greased and lightly floured 10-inch tube pan. Bake at 325° for 1 hour or until done. If desired, prick small holes in top of cake; pour warm Lemonade Glaze over hot cake.

Lemonade Glaze:
¾ cup sugar
1 (6-ounce) can lemonade concentrate

Dissolve sugar in saucepan with lemonade concentrate. Heat until warm.

Yield: 18 to 20 servings

NOTE: This cake will freeze well.

Karen Gregory Powell (Mrs. Sam C.)
Burlington

LEMON BUNDT CAKE

1 (18¼-ounce) package lemon cake mix
1 (3½-ounce) package lemon instant pudding mix
4 eggs
½ cup vegetable oil
1 cup water

Preheat oven to 350°. Grease and flour a heavy bundt pan. Place all ingredients in large bowl of electric mixer. Beat at medium speed for 2 to 3 minutes, scraping the bowl occasionally with a rubber spatula. Pour into prepared pan and bake for 35 minutes. Cool on wire rack for 5 minutes before removing from pan.

Glaze:
1⅓ cups powdered sugar
5 tablespoons lemon juice
⅓ cup flaked coconut

Blend together sugar and lemon juice until smooth; stir in coconut. Drizzle glaze over top and sides of warm cake, covering as much of the cake as possible. Cake will keep moist for several days.

Sauce:
1 pint sour cream
⅓ cup light brown sugar
½ cup seedless grapes

Fold sour cream and brown sugar together until well blended. Stir in grapes. Serve over slices of Lemon Bundt Cake. Makes 1½ cups sauce.

Yield: 10 servings

Mary Helen Wilson Long (Mrs. Robert)
Burlington

MOM'S JAM CAKE

1 cup butter
2 cups sugar
6 eggs
4 cups flour
1 teaspoon salt
1 teaspoon cloves
1 teaspoon cinnamon
1 teaspoon nutmeg
2 teaspoons baking soda
1½ cups buttermilk
1½ cups blackberry jam

Cream butter and sugar until light; add eggs one at a time, beating well after each addition. Sift together flour, salt, cloves, cinnamon and nutmeg. Dissolve soda in buttermilk; add to batter alternately with sifted dry ingredients. Fold in blackberry jam. Bake at 350° for 20 to 25 minutes.

Cream Filling:
2 cups sugar
1 cup milk
¾ stick margarine
1 teaspoon vanilla extract

Cook sugar, milk and butter 10 to 12 minutes stirring constantly. Cool then spread on cake layers.

Yield: 12 to 15 servings

NOTE: Cake size options: 2 (9-inch) layers; 3 (8-inch) layers or layers can be sliced to double. Let cake ripen at least 4 days.

A favorite of my family for years, especially at Christmas!

Peggy Haywood Smith (Mrs. J. Harold)
Burlington

CHERRY-PINEAPPLE CAKE

1 (20-ounce) can crushed pineapple, undrained
2 (20-ounce) cans cherry pie filling
1 package regular size yellow cake mix
¾ cup chopped pecans
2 sticks margarine, melted

Spread pineapple evenly in 9x13x2-inch greased pan. Spread pie filling evenly over pineapple. Sprinkle cake mix over fruit and the nuts. Pour margarine over all. Do not mix. Bake 350° for 1 hour or until brown. Serve with whipped cream, ice cream or as is.

Yield: 8 to 10 servings

Marian Miller Duff (Mrs. Herbert L.)
Burlington

PINEAPPLE SHEET CAKE

1 box yellow cake mix
1 (16-ounce) can crushed pineapple
¾ cup sugar
2 (3½-ounce) packages instant vanilla pudding
1 medium size carton whipped topping
1 (6-ounce) package frozen coconut

Bake cake in 9x13-inch sheet pan according to directions. Cool. Punch holes in cake with a straw. Combine pineapple and sugar in saucepan and heat to boiling. Set aside. When cool, pour over sheet cake. Mix instant pudding according to directions, adding dash of vanilla if desired. Spread over pineapple on cake and top with whipped topping. Spread coconut on top and refrigerate.

Yield: 15 servings

Nancy Kernodle Sain (Mrs. Tom)
Burlington

SARAH'S HUMMINGBIRD CAKE

3 cups plain flour
2 cups sugar
1 (20-ounce) can crushed pineapple, with juice
2 eggs
1 teaspoon baking soda
1 teaspoon vanilla extract
1 teaspoon ground cinnamon
1 cup oil
1 cup mashed bananas
1 cup chopped nuts

Mix all ingredients together with spoon or mixer. Bake in greased and floured 9x13-inch pan at 350° for 45 minutes.

Icing:
1 (8-ounce) package cream cheese
1 stick margarine
1 box powdered sugar
1 teaspoon vanilla extract

Soften cream cheese and margarine and mix with other ingredients. Spread on top of cake.

Yield: 12 to 15 servings

Sallie Grace Tate
Charlotte, North Carolina

MARY'S PRUNE CAKE

1½ cups sugar
2 cups cake flour
1 teaspoon baking soda
1 teaspoon salt
1 teaspoon cinnamon
1 teaspoon nutmeg
1 teaspoon allspice
1 cup cooking oil
1 cup buttermilk
3 eggs
2 cups cooked prunes
½ cup pecans, chopped
½ cup black walnuts, chopped
1 teaspoon vanilla extract

Put sugar, flour, soda, salt and spices in bowl. Add oil in buttermilk. Beat in eggs, one at a time. Add nuts and prunes. Use mixer or fold in by hand. Add vanilla. Bake at 300° in large broiler (oven) pan for 1 hour. Make topping while cake is cooking.

Topping:
1 tablespoon corn syrup
1 cup sugar
½ cup buttermilk
¼ cup butter
½ teaspoon baking soda
½ teaspoon vanilla extract

Mix all ingredients and bring to a boil. Let simmer for 15 to 20 minutes. Stir so mixture will not boil over until soda dies down. Pour over cake when it comes out of oven. Serve in squares with a dollop of frozen whipped non-dairy topping.

Yield: 16 squares

"A family favorite!"

Mary Johnston Lindley (Mrs. J. Thomas)
Burlington

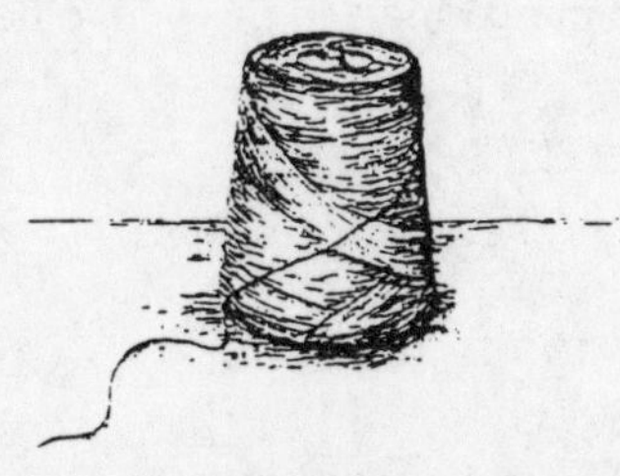

PECAN FRUIT CAKE

¼ pound candied cherries, uncut
¼ pound candied pineapple, cut in ¼-inch slices
1-2 tablespoons flour
2 cups butter
2½ cups sugar
6 eggs
3¾ cups plain flour
1 teaspoon baking powder
1 pound pecan halves
1 teaspoon lemon juice

Dredge fruit in flour; set aside. In a large mixing bowl, cream butter and sugar until light; add eggs, one at a time, beating well after each addition. Add flour which has been sifted with baking powder, blending well. Stir in fruit, nuts and lemon juice. Bake in a 10-inch tube pan which has been greased, lined with waxed paper and greased again. Bake at 300° for 2 hours or until done.

Yield: 15 to 20 servings

Sara Foster Dodson
Burlington

PLUM CAKE

2 cups self-rising flour
2 cups sugar
1 cup vegetable oil
1 teaspoon cinnamon
1 teaspoon cloves
3 eggs
1 cup chopped nuts
2 small jars baby food plums

Mix all ingredients together thoroughly. Bake in well greased and floured 8x8x2-inch pan at 300° for 1 hour.

Glaze:
1 cup powdered sugar
Juice of 1 lemon

Blend sugar gradually into lemon juice. Drizzle over hot cake.

Yield: 9 servings

Edith Bowden Huff
Burlington

MOTHER'S POUND CAKE

2 sticks butter
½ cup solid shortening
3 cups sugar
5-6 large eggs
3¼ cups cake flour or (3 cups all-purpose flour)
½ teaspoon baking powder or (1 teaspoon baking powder)
1 cup milk
2 teaspoons lemon extract or (1 tablespoon lemon extract)
1 teaspoon vanilla extract or (1 tablespoon vanilla extract)

Grease a 10-inch tube pan with shortening. Line the bottom with a circle of waxed paper cut to fit. Grease circle of waxed paper again and dust pan with flour. In a large mixing bowl, cream butter and shortening until light. Add sugar gradually, mixing well. Add eggs, one at a time, beating well after each addition. Sift flour with baking powder and add alternately with milk to the batter, beating well after each addition. Add lemon and vanilla extracts. Pour into prepared tube pan and bake at 350° for 1 hour and 15 minutes. Place on cooling rack for 10 minutes; invert cake on rack and remove the waxed paper carefully; cool completely.

Yield: 18 to 20 servings

Beth Elder Ellington (Mrs. Jeff)
Burlington

Frances Troxler Smith
Burlington

POUND CAKE

2 sticks butter or margarine
½ cup solid shortening
3 cups sugar
6 eggs
3¼ cups flour, sifted
1 cup evaporated milk
¼ teaspoon salt
1 tablespoon vanilla extract

In a large mixing bowl, cream shortening and sugar until light; add eggs, one at a time, beating well after each addition. Sift flour and salt together; add alternately with milk to the batter, blending well after each addition. Add vanilla. Pour batter into a greased and floured 10-inch tube pan. Bake at 325° for 1 hour and 30 minutes or until done. Let cool 10 minutes in pan; invert on cooling rack and cool completely.

Yield: 8 to 10 servings

Nancy Elizabeth (Bettie) Wilson
Burlington

POUND CAKE

1 stick margarine, softened
½ cup solid shortening
½ cup vegetable oil
3 cups sugar
6 eggs, at room temperature
3¼ cups flour, sifted
Dash of salt
1 cup milk
1 teaspoon vanilla extract

In a large mixing bowl, cream margarine, shortening and vegetable oil; add sugar, ½ cup at a time, beating well after each addition. Add eggs, one at a time, beating well after each. Sift flour and salt together; add alternately with milk to the batter, blending well after each addition. Add vanilla. Pour batter into a greased and floured 10-inch tube pan. Bake at 350° for 1 hour and 25 minutes or until done. Let cool slightly in pan; invert on cooling rack and cool completely.

Yield: 18 to 20 servings

Hazel Swanson Roney (Mrs. James A.)
Mebane

MOCK POUND CAKE

2 sticks margarine
½ cup solid shortening
3 cups sugar
6 eggs
3 cups sifted plain flour
1 cup milk
1 teaspoon vanilla extract
1 teaspoon lemon extract
1 teaspoon baking powder, added last

In a large mixing bowl, cream margarine and shortening until light; add sugar gradually, blending well after each addition. Add eggs, one at a time, mixing well after each addition. Stir flour into the batter alternately with milk; add extracts and baking powder. Pour into well greased and lighty floured 10-inch tube pan; bake at 325° for 1 hour and 15 minutes. Place on cooling rack for 10 minutes. Invert on rack and cool completely.

Yield: 18 to 20 servings

Dorothy Sellars Brawley
Burlington

ICE CREAM CAKE AND WHITE FROSTING

2 sticks butter
2½ cups sugar
5 egg yolks
4 cups plain flour, sifted
2 teaspoons baking powder
Pinch of salt
1 cup milk
1 teaspoon vanilla or almond extract

In a large mixing bowl, cream butter and sugar until light; add egg yolks and blend well. Add flour, which has been sifted with baking powder and salt, alternately with milk and extract. Pour batter into a 10-inch tube pan which has been well greased and floured. Bake at 350° for 1 hour or until done.

White Frosting:
2½ cups sugar
5 tablespoons corn syrup
Pinch of salt
½ cup water
2 egg whites
1½ teaspoons vanilla extract

Cook together sugar, corn syrup, salt and water to 240°. In a smooth surfaced utensil, stir only until sugar is dissolved and boiling started. When thermometer registers 238°, quickly beat egg whites until stiff, but not dry. When 242° is reached, pour the syrup into the egg whites in a steady stream, before syrup has time to cool. Add vanilla and beat until of spreading consistency.

Yield: 12 to 15 servings

Mrs. J. Dolph Long
submitted by:
Helen B. Long (Mrs. George A.)
Burlington

VANILLA WAFER CAKE

2 sticks margarine, softened
2 cups sugar
6 eggs
1 (12-ounce) box vanilla wafers, crushed
½ cup milk
1 (7-ounce) package coconut
1 cup pecans, chopped

Mix by hand! Cream margarine and sugar. Add eggs, one at a time. Add wafers and milk alternately. Fold in coconut and nuts carefully. Bake in greased and floured 10-inch tube pan at 300° for 1 hour and 15 minutes. Cool in pan.

Yield: 16 to 20 servings

Martha Ann Shaw
Burlington

FORGOTTEN CAKE

5 egg whites
¼ teaspoon salt
½ teaspoon cream of tartar
1½ cups sugar
1 teaspoon vanilla extract

Preheat oven to 450°. Beat egg whites and salt until foamy. Add cream of tartar; whip until peaks form. Add sugar, 1 tablespoon at a time. Beat 10 to 15 minutes; add vanilla. Pour into greased 9x9-inch square pan and place in oven. TURN OFF HEAT! Leave in oven overnight.

Topping:
1 cup heavy cream
4 tablespoons sugar
¼ teaspoon vanilla extract
1 (10-ounce) box frozen strawberries

Next day, whip cream and add sugar and vanilla. Spread over meringue. Place in refrigerator for several hours. Cut into squares and top with strawberries.

Yield: 8 servings

Claire deHart Lewis (Mrs. Cruse)
Burlington

SEVEN-UP CAKE

2 sticks margarine
½ cup solid shortening
3 cups sugar
5 eggs
1 teaspoon lemon extract
3 cups plain flour
1 (7-ounce) bottle of Seven-Up

(Have all ingredients at room temperature for best results.) In a large mixing bowl, cream margarine and sugar until light; add eggs, one at a time, beating well after each addition. Add lemon extract. Add flour and Seven-Up alternately, beating well after each addition. Bake in a greased and floured 10-inch tube pan at 300° for 1 hour and 30 minutes, or until cake tests done. Let stand in pan 10 minutes; invert on cooling rack and cool completely.

Yield: 18 to 20 servings

NOTE: Layers can be made using 3 (9-inch) cake pans. Use vanilla extract in the batter instead of lemon.

Lillian Mae Sharpe
Mebane

FAMOUS CHEESECAKE

3 (8-ounce) packages cream cheese, softened
3 eggs
1¼ cups sugar
1½ teaspoons vanilla extract
1 teaspoon almond extract
Graham cracker crust for a 10-inch pie plate

In large bowl place cream cheese, eggs, sugar and extracts. Blend, then beat at medium speed for 10 minutes. Pour mixture into crust and bake at 325° for 40 to 50 minutes. Remove from oven and cool at least 1 hour.

Topping:
1 pint sour cream
2 tablespoons sugar
1 teaspoon vanilla extract

In smaller bowl, whip together topping ingredients for 5 minutes. Spread on cooled cake and bake 7 minutes at 450°. Chill overnight.

Glaze:
¾ cup water
1½ cups fresh fruit, 1 (10-ounce) package frozen fruit, or 1 (15¼-ounce) can crushed pineapple
1½ tablespoons cornstarch

To prepare fresh fruit glaze, gradually add water to cornstarch, blending well. Add diced fruit and bring to a boil, stirring constantly. Let boil for 2 minutes; add butter and stir. Cool slightly and spread on cake.

Yield: 8 to 10 servings

NOTE: For frozen fruit or crushed pineapple, reduce water to 1 tablespoon and proceed as above.

Lynn Johnson Moseley (Mrs. W. Phillip)
Graham

ITALIAN CREAM CHEESE CAKE

1 stick margarine
2 cups sugar
½ cup vegetable oil
5 egg yolks, beaten
1 teaspoon vanilla extract
1 cup buttermilk
2 cups plain flour
1 teaspoon baking soda
1 cup chopped pecans
1 (7-ounce) can flaked coconut

Cream together margarine, sugar and vegetable oil. Add beaten egg yolks to mixture. Add vanilla to buttermilk and add alternately with flour, and soda, beginning and ending with dry ingredients. Add nuts and coconut. Fold in stiffly beaten egg whites. Pour into 3 well greased 9-inch cake pans. Bake at 350° for 25 minutes.

Italian Cream Cheese Cake Frosting:

1 (8-ounce) package cream cheese, softened
½ stick margarine
1 (16-ounce) box powdered sugar
1 teaspoon vanilla extract
¼ cup chopped pecans

Blend together cream cheese and margarine. Add sugar, vanilla and nuts; mix well. Spread between layers and on top and sides of completely cooled cake.

Yield: 16 to 20 servings

Elinor Samons Euliss (Mrs. Wade)
Burlington

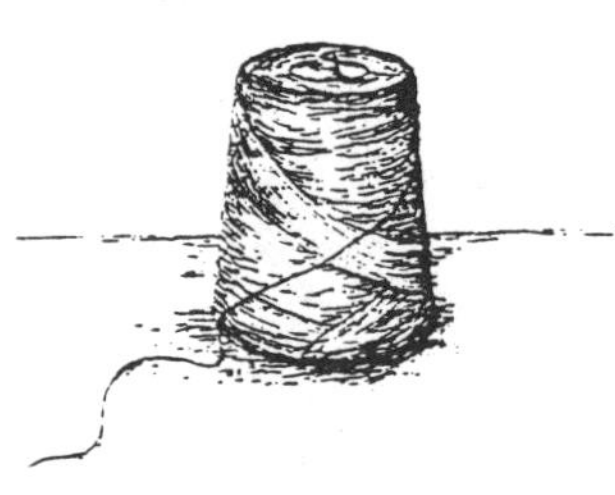

GRANDMOTHER WILLIAMS' COFFEE CAKE

½ cup butter
1 cup sugar
1 egg
2 heaping cups flour
2 teaspoons baking powder
1 cup milk
1 cup chopped dates

Cream butter with sugar; add egg. Sift flour with baking powder and add to creamed mixture alternately with milk; blending well after each addition. Stir in chopped dates. Pour batter into 2 greased 9-inch round pans or 9x13-inch baking dish. Sprinkle with topping. Bake at 350° for 30 minutes.

Topping:
Pecan halves
Butter, size of egg (2 to 3 tablespoons)
¾ cup brown sugar
3 tablespoons flour
1 teaspoon cinnamon

Place pecan halves over batter. Cut butter into sugar, flour and cinnamon.

Glaze:
1 cup powdered sugar
Cream to thin
1 teaspoon vanilla extract

Mix sugar with enough cream to spreading consistency. Spread on cool cake.

Yield: 12 to 15 servings

Hallie Ragsdale Smith (Mrs. Mack)
Burlington

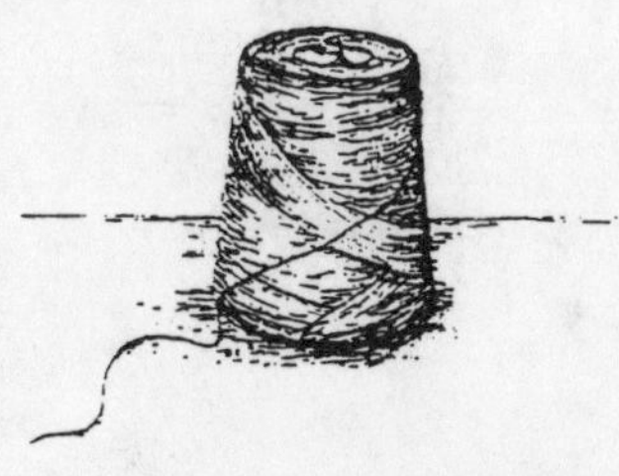

MARIANNE'S CANDY BAR COOKIES

4 cups oatmeal
1 cup brown sugar
¼ cup white corn syrup
¼ cup crunchy peanut butter
1 teaspoon vanilla extract
⅔ cup margarine, melted
1 (6-ounce) package chocolate chips
1 (6-ounce) package butterscotch chips
⅔ cup creamy peanut butter
1 cup salted peanuts

Combine oatmeal, brown sugar, corn syrup, peanut butter and vanilla in a large mixing bowl. Pour melted margarine over all and mix well. Press into a greased 9x13-inch baking dish. Bake at 400° for 12 minutes. While crust bakes, melt chocolate and butterscotch chips together; stir in the creamy peanut butter and salted peanuts. Spread evenly over the crust. Allow to cool. Use a sharp knife to cut into desired squares or strips.

Yield: 20 to 24 servings

NOTE: Can be made ahead and frozen.

Marianne Salogga Roarick (Mrs. Richard C.)
Burlington

CONGO BARS

1¼ sticks butter
1 (16-ounce) box brown sugar
2¼ cups plain flour
2½ teaspoons baking powder
⅛ teaspoon salt
3 eggs
1 teaspoon vanilla extract
1 (6-ounce) package chocolate chips

Melt butter and brown sugar in 3 quart saucepan. Cool to lukewarm. Sift flour, baking powder and salt onto waxed paper. To cooled mixture add dry ingredients, eggs and vanilla; mix well. Stir in chocolate chips. Pour and spread into a well greased 12½x9x2½-inch metal pan. Bake at 350° for 30 minutes... do not overbake.

Yield: 24 to 30 servings

Vicki Burton Vernon (Mrs. John H., III)
Burlington

EDITH'S CHOCOLATE COOKIES

1 stick butter
2 cups sugar
4 tablespoons cocoa
½ cup milk
½ cup crunchy peanut butter
1 teaspoon vanilla extract
3 cups 1 minute oatmeal

Combine butter, sugar, cocoa and milk in a saucepan. Bring to a hard boil. Remove from heat and stir in peanut butter, vanilla and oatmeal. Drop by teaspoonful onto waxed paper.

Yield: 18 to 24 cookies

Mary Maud Sanders Cockman (Mrs. Richard)
Burlington

BROWNIES

½ cup butter or margarine
2 squares (1-ounce) unsweetened baking chocolate
2 large eggs, at room temperature
⅛ teaspoon salt
1 cup sugar
1 teaspoon vanilla extract
½ cup plus 2 tablespoons flour
½ to 1 cup chopped pecans or walnuts

Melt chocolate and butter in top of double boiler over low heat; let cool. Beat eggs and salt until light in color and foamy. Gradually add sugar and vanilla; beat until well blended. Stir in cooled chocolate mixture with a few swift strokes. Fold in flour; gently stir in nuts. Bake in greased 8x8-inch pan at 350° for 25 minutes. Cut into squares when cool.

Yield: 16 servings

NOTE: Chocolate mixture must be cooled or the brownies will be heavy and dry. The quality of the product is improved if mixing is done by hand.

Myrtle Troxler Morgan
Burlington

CHOCOLATE CHIP BLONDE BROWNIES

2 sticks margarine
1 box light brown sugar
2 cups plain flour
1 teaspoon salt
1 teaspoon baking powder
¼ teaspoon baking soda
2 jumbo eggs
2 teaspoons vanilla extract
1 cup nuts, chopped
1 (6-ounce) package semi-sweet chocolate chips

Preheat oven to 350°. Melt margarine in heavy pan. Remove from heat. Add brown sugar and beat until combined. Cool slightly. Sift flour with salt, baking powder and baking soda. Add eggs and vanilla to sugar mixture, beating with a wooden spoon. Add sifted ingredients. Add nuts. Pour into a greased, floured 13x9x2-inch pan. Spread chips on top. Bake 30 to 40 minutes or until sides leave pan. Cool 10 minutes before slicing. Store in tight container.

Yield: 16 to 18 servings

Jacqueline Garrison Powell (Mrs. William C.)
Burlington

BROWNIES

6 eggs
4 cups sugar
2 cups flour
2 cups chopped walnuts
2 cups butter
1 teaspoon vanilla extract
½ pound chocolate, melted

Mix all together except chocolate. Stir in chocolate until well mixed. Pour into a 10x15-inch pan and bake at 325° for 45 minutes.

Yield: 20 to 25 servings

I always thought Mother's were the best until a friend gave me this recipe.

Jan Sellars Scott
Burlington

BROWNIES

Brownie mix
2 cups powdered sugar
½ cup butter
4 tablespoons Creme de Menthe
1 cup chocolate chips
6 tablespoons butter

Prepare brownies per package directions. Cool in pan; do not cut. Mix sugar, butter and Creme de Menthe. Spread evenly over brownies. Melt chips and butter and spread over sugar layer.

Yield: 8 to 10 servings

Edith Bowden Huff
Burlington

RANGER COOKIES

1 cup margarine
1 cup sugar
1 cup brown sugar
1 teaspoon vanilla extract
2 eggs
2 cups plain flour
2 teaspoons baking soda
1 teaspoon baking powder
½ teaspoon salt
2 cups oatmeal
2 cups corn flakes
1 cup chopped nuts
1 (3-ounce) package chocolate chips

Cream margarine, sugar, brown sugar and vanilla until light; add eggs, blending well. Sift together flour, soda, baking powder and salt; add to creamed mixture; mix well. Stir in oatmeal, corn flakes, nuts and chocolate chips; blending well. Drop by ½ teaspoonsful onto greased baking sheets. Bake at 375° for 10 to 12 minutes. Cool.

Yield: 4 dozen

These, and other party fare prepared by Trustees and Docents, are served at the Museum's CHRISTMAS TOUR OF HOMES AND CANDLELIGHT TEA.

Elizabeth Newlin Newlin (Mrs. Harvey R.)
Burlington

DATE BARS

First Mixture:

½ cup light brown sugar
1 cup flour
½ cup butter or margarine

Blend sugar and flour; cut in butter. Press mixture into a greased 6½x10½-inch pan. Bake at 375° for 10 minutes.

Second Mixture:

1 cup light brown sugar
2 eggs, beaten
1 teaspoon vanilla extract
3 teaspoons flour
½ teaspoon baking powder
¼ teaspoon salt
1½ cups shredded coconut
1 cup chopped dates

Mix together sugar, eggs and vanilla. Sift together flour, baking powder and salt. Blend with sugar mixture; add coconut and dates. Pour over baked crust. Return to oven and bake 20 minutes at 375°. Cut into squares or bars when cool.

Yield: 16 to 20 servings

Ann Spoon Cooper (Mrs. Collins)
Windsor, North Carolina

FRUIT PIZZA

1 roll refrigerated sugar cookie dough
1 (8-ounce) package cream cheese
1 (6-ounce) carton non-dairy whipped topping
1 cup powdered sugar
Fruit of choice
1 can any flavor pie filling

Preheat oven as directed on package. Spread dough evenly across rectangular cookie sheet and bake 6 to 8 minutes. Mix next 3 ingredients well and spread evenly over cooled dough. Cover with fruit as desired. Arrange in pattern or at random. Cover with pie filling.

Yield: 16 servings

Elizabeth Pruitt Dunn (Mrs. James)
Baltimore, Maryland

GINGERBREAD MEN OR COOKIES

1 cup butter
1 cup brown sugar
3 eggs
1¼ cups molasses
3 cups plain flour
1 tablespoon baking soda
½ teaspoon salt
1 teaspoon ground ginger
1 teaspoon ground allspice
1 teaspoon ground cinnamon
Raisins
Decorator candies
Decorator icing

Cream butter and sugar. Beat eggs and add to creamed mixture then add molasses. Combine dry ingredients and blend into creamed mixture. Chill dough 1 hour. Work with ½ the dough at a time; refrigerate remainder. Roll dough ¼-⅛-inch thick between two sheets of waxed paper. Remove top sheet and cut with a 4 or 7-inch gingerbread man cutter and remove excess dough. Place greased cookie sheet on top of men, invert and remove waxed paper. Press raisins into dough for eyes and nose. Decorate as desired with decorator candies. Bake at 350° for 10 minutes. Cool about 1 minute. Remove cookies to finish cooling. Trim with decorator icing as desired.

Yield: 2 dozen 4-inch men or 1 dozen 7-inch men

Elizabeth Salmons King
Burlington

GINGERSNAP COOKIES

¾ cup solid shortening
1 cup sugar
1 egg
1 cup molasses
3 cups plain flour
2 teaspoons ginger
1 teaspoon cinnamon
½ teaspoon salt
2 teaspoons baking soda
Granulated sugar

Cream shortening with sugar; add egg and molasses, beating well. Sift flour, ginger, cinnamon, salt and soda together; add to creamed mixture, blending well. Shape into balls using 1 teaspoonful dough for each. Roll in sugar; place 1½ inches apart on ungreased cookie sheet. Bake at 350° until golden brown.

Yield: 4 to 5 dozen

Martha Ann Shaw
Burlington

JUMBO MOLASSES COOKIES

4½ cups sifted plain flour
1 teaspoon baking soda
½ teaspoon salt
1½ teaspoons ginger
¾ teaspoon cloves
¾ teaspoon nutmeg
¼ teaspoon allspice
¾ cup solid shortening
¾ cup sugar
1 cup molasses
1 tablespoon rum extract
⅓ cup water

Sift together first 7 ingredients. Cream shortening and sugar; add molasses and rum extract; beat well. Add dry ingredients alternately with water, blending well after each addition. Wrap dough in foil. Chill overnight in refrigerator. Divide dough in half; roll out on floured surface to ¼-inch thickness. Cut with floured 4-inch round cookie cutter. Bake on lightly greased cookie sheets at 350° for 15 minutes. Cool on wire racks.

Yield: 2 to 3 dozen

Shirley Barbee Fink (Mrs. Howard)
Graham

MOLASSES COOKIES

1 cup molasses
¼ cup solid shortening
1 tablespoon ginger
1 tablespoon baking soda
2 tablespoons warm milk
1 teaspoon salt
2½ cups flour

Heat molasses to boiling and add shortening, ginger, soda dissolved in warm milk, salt and flour; blend well. Chill dough in refrigerator at least 4 hours. Roll out dough to desired thickness and bake at 350° for 5 to 10 minutes, depending on size. Watch as they will burn.

Yield: 4 to 6 dozen

Mary Catherine Moser
Graham

EDENTON TEA PARTY CAKES

3½ cups sifted plain flour
1 teaspoon baking soda
½ teaspoon salt
¾ cup butter
1 teaspoon vanilla extract
2 cups brown sugar, firmly packed
3 eggs

Sift together flour, soda and salt; set aside. Cream butter and vanilla until soft; add sugar a little at a time while continuing to cream. Beat in eggs, one at a time, then stir in flour; mix thoroughly. Divide dough in half; wrap each half in waxed paper and chill several hours until firm enough to handle. Roll out thin on floured board, cut into shapes or use a 2½-inch cookie cutter. Place on greased cookie sheet and bake at 400° for 7to 9 minutes.

Yield: 6 dozen

Essie Cofield Norwood (Mrs. Ralph)
Burlington

OUR CHRISTMAS BELLS

½ cup butter
¾ cup sugar
1 egg
¾ cup molasses
3½ cups flour
1 teaspoon baking soda
1½ teaspoons ginger
1½ teaspoons cinnamon
1 teaspoon cloves
2 teaspoons grated orange rind

Cream butter and sugar. Add egg, molasses and dry ingredients including rind. Mix well. Shape into roll and wrap in waxed paper and chill overnight. Slice circles ¼-inch thick. Place ½ teaspoon filling at top of circle and pinch in bottom to form bell. Use ¼ cherry to make clapper.

Filling:
1 cup brown sugar
1 (8-ounce) box chopped dates
1 cup chopped pecans
1 (8-ounce) jar Maraschino cherries

Combine sugar, dates and juice from cherries and cook slowly until dates melt. Add nuts and cool. Bake on greased cookie sheet at 375° for 8 to 10 minutes.

Yield: 12 to 24 cookies

Sara Foster Dodson
Burlington

GERMAN HONEY CAKES

1 cup honey
¾ cup brown sugar
1 egg
2¾ cups flour
½ teaspoon baking soda
1 teaspoon cinnamon
1 teaspoon cloves
1 teaspoon nutmeg
¼ cup chopped citron
⅓ cup chopped almonds
1 tablespoon lemon juice
Maraschino cherries
Sliced almonds

Boil honey and cool. Add remaining ingredients and mix well. Shape into roll and wrap in waxed paper and chill overnight. Slice into ¼-inch thickness and decorate with ½ cherry and 5 sliced almonds to form a flower. Bake on greased cookie sheet at 400° for 10 minutes. When cool, store in cookie tin.

Yield: 20 to 30 cookies

Sara Foster Dodson
Burlington

SNOWBALLS

1 stick margarine, softened
1 cup sugar
¾ cup pecans, finely chopped
1 (16-ounce) can crushed pineapple, drained
1 cup raisins, optional
2 boxes butter cookies
2 boxes whipped topping mix
14 ounces shredded coconut

Cream butter and sugar; mix in nuts, pineapple and raisins. Use as filling between 3 butter cookies (3 cookies in each snowball). Chill 7 to 8 hours or overnight; frost with whipped topping; sprinkle with coconut. Freeze if desired.

Yield: 25 servings

NOTE: Snowballs can be decorated with 3 jellybeans on top for Easter or cinnamon hearts for Valentine's Day. Decorate after snowballs are thawed, if frozen.

Marian Miller Duff (Mrs. Herbert L.)
Burlington

LECKERLI

1½ cups sugar
½ cup honey
¼ cup each chopped candied orange and lemon peel
2¼ cups sifted flour
1½ teaspoons cloves
1½ teaspoons nutmeg
1 tablespoon cinnamon
Few grains salt
1 teaspoon baking soda
Grated rind of ½ lemon
1 cup almonds with skins, sliced thin
2 tablespoons orange juice glaze

Heat sugar and honey to boiling. Remove from heat, add candied peels, sifted dry ingredients, lemon rind, nuts and orange juice. Knead until well blended. Roll dough to ½-inch thickness, using as little flour as is necessary. Lift carefully onto greased waxed paper on cookie sheet. Bake at 325° about 25 minutes. Turn out on another cookie sheet, peel off waxed paper immediately, turn right side up, spread with glaze.

Glaze:
½ cup sugar
¼ cup water

Combine sugar and water in a saucepan, cook until mixture spins a thread. Spread on while cake is hot. Cool. Cut in small diamonds. Store 1 week before serving.

Yield: 10 to 15 servings

Melva Gray Foster
Burlington

POUND CAKE COOKIES

2½ sticks butter
1 cup sugar
2 egg yolks, beaten
3 cups flour
1 teaspoon vanilla extract
Candied cherries
Pecans

Cream butter and sugar until light. Add egg yolks; mix well. Stir flour and vanilla into batter; blend thoroughly. Drop by teaspoonsful onto ungreased baking sheets. Press cherry or pecan half on each cookie. Bake at 350° for 10 minutes.

Yield: 6 to 8 dozen

Peggy Haywood Smith (Mrs. J. Harold)
Burlington

OATMEAL COOKIES

1 cup shortening
1 cup brown sugar
1 cup white sugar
2 eggs
1½ cups flour
1 teaspoon salt
1 teaspoon baking soda
3 cups quick oats
1 teaspoon vanilla extract
1 (6-ounce) package semi-sweet chocolate chips, optional

Beat together shortening, sugars and eggs. Add dry ingredients and vanilla and mix well. Chocolate chips may be added at this point, if desired. Roll into 1-inch balls—do not flatten. Bake at 350° for 9 to 10 minutes.

Yield: 3 to 4 dozen

Sue McKee Watson (Mrs. Robert A.)
Elon College

OATMEAL COOKIES

½ cup butter
½ cup solid shortening
1 cup light brown sugar
1 cup sugar
2 eggs
2 cups plain flour
2 teaspoons baking soda
1 teaspoon baking powder
½ teaspoon salt
2 cups old-fashioned rolled oatmeal
1 cup nuts or raisins
1 teaspoon vanilla extract

Cream butter and shortening; add sugars and blend well. Add eggs, one at a time, beating well after each addition. Sift flour, soda, baking powder and salt; add to creamed mixture. The batter is stiff at this point, so a wooden spoon may be needed to mix in the oatmeal and nuts. Add vanilla. Drop by teaspoonful onto a lightly greased baking sheet. Bake at 350° for 8 to 10 minutes.

Yield: 3 to 4 dozen

Myrtle Troxler Morgan
Burlington

ORANGE BARS

Crust:

½ cup shortening
1 cup flour, sifted
1 tablespoon sugar

Combine all ingredients and press in the bottom of 9x9-inch pan. Bake at 350° for 10 minutes.

Filling:

1 cup brown sugar
2 tablespoons flour
½ teaspoon baking powder
1 teaspoon vanilla extract
½ cup chopped nuts

Combine all ingredients well and pour over crust. Bake an additional 25 minutes.

Frosting:

1 cup powdered sugar
Orange juice to thin
Orange rind to taste

Combine all ingredients to make a thin frosting. Drizzle over bars while still warm.

Yield: 16 to 20 servings

Catherine Nagel Gilbertson (Mrs. George)
Burlington

PEANUT CRISP BARS

½ cup sugar
½ cup light corn syrup
Dash salt
1 cup crunchy peanut butter
3 cups crisp rice cereal

Cook sugar and corn syrup until sugar is dissolved. Blend in peanut butter and rice cereal. Spread evenly into a 7x11-inch foil lined pan. Set aside.

Topping:
4 tablespoons butter
¼ cup brown sugar
1 tablespoon milk
1 tablespoon vanilla extract
1¼ cups powdered sugar

Melt butter and brown sugar. Remove from heat and add milk and vanilla. Stir in powdered sugar and beat until smooth. Remove cereal mixture from pan and gently peel off foil. Spread topping evenly over all. Chill.

Yield: 16 to 20 servings

Virginia Harvey Sharpe (Mrs. Edwin F.)
Burlington

PUMPKIN SQUARES

4 eggs
1⅔ cups sugar
1 cup vegetable oil
1 (16-ounce) can pumpkin
2 cups flour
2 teaspoons baking powder
2 teaspoons cinnamon
1 teaspoon salt
1 teaspoon baking soda

Mix eggs, sugar, oil and pumpkin until fluffy. Add remaining ingredients and mix well. Bake in a greased 10x15-inch pan at 350° for 25 to 30 minutes.

Icing:
1 (3-ounce) package cream cheese
½ cup margarine, softened
1 teaspoon vanilla extract
2 cups powdered sugar

Mix all ingredients together and ice cake when cooled slightly.

Yield: 15 servings

Eugenia Goley Pruitt (Mrs. Ronald A.)
Burlington

PECAN SANDIES

1 cup sugar
1 cup brown sugar
1 cup margarine
1 cup vegetable oil
1 egg
3½ cups flour
1 teaspoon baking soda
1 teaspoon vanilla extract
1 cup oatmeal
1 cup crispy rice cereal
1 cup chopped nuts

Cream sugars and margarine; add vegetable oil; mix. Beat in egg; add dry ingredients and vanilla. Fold in oatmeal, rice cereal and nuts. Make into 1-inch balls, place on greased cookie sheet and flatten with a glass. Bake at 325° for 10 minutes.

Yield: 8 dozen

NOTE: For a softer cookie, do not flatten!

Marianne Salogga Roarick (Mrs. Richard C.)
Burlington

PECAN TASSIES

Pastry Shells:
1 (3-ounce) package cream cheese, softened
½ cup butter, softened
1 cup flour

Blend cream cheese and butter until smooth; add flour gradually. Chill dough ½ hour. Shape into 2 dozen 1-inch balls. Place in ungreased muffin cups and press dough into tart shapes.

Filling:
1 tablespoon butter
¾ cup brown sugar
1 egg
1 teaspoon vanilla extract
Dash of salt
1 cup chopped pecans (Reserve ⅓ cup for topping)

Combine above ingredients and mix until well blended. Pour into tart shells and top with remaining ⅓ cup pecans. Bake at 325° for 25 minutes or until filling is set.

Yield: 2 dozen

Lyon Miller Fraune (Mrs. Charles)
Washington, North Carolina

CHOCOLATE COVERED COCONUT BALLS

1 (14-ounce) package flaked coconut
1 (14-ounce) can sweetened condensed milk
24 ounces semi-sweet chocolate chips
Paraffin wax

Mix coconut and milk. Chill overnight. Roll into balls about the size of a quarter. Chill. Melt chips in double boiler and add about 1 teaspoon of paraffin shavings. Heat until melted and well blended. Reduce heat. Using a toothpick, dip each coconut ball into chocolate. Spoon additional chocolate over the balls to coat well. Place on waxed paper and chill. After chocolate hardens, candy is ready to eat.

Yield: 60 pieces

Patsy Hand Mobley (Mrs. Wayne)
Burlington

CRISPY PEANUT BUTTER CENTERS

2 cups crunchy peanut butter
½ cup margarine
1 (1-pound) box powdered sugar
3 cups crisp rice cereal
½ cake paraffin wax
1 (6-ounce) package semi-sweet chocolate chips

Combine peanut butter, margarine, and powdered sugar in a large bowl. Blend together well. Add rice cereal and blend into peanut butter mixture. Form into ¾-inch balls. Melt paraffin and chocolate chips in top of double boiler. Dip with toothpick in chocolate to coat. Place on waxed paper to dry.

Yield: 75 pieces

Linda O'Briant Dodson (Mrs. Don)
Gibsonville, North Carolina

ANGEL FOOD CANDY

2 cups brown sugar
1 cup light syrup
4 teaspoons baking powder
½ cake paraffin wax
1 (6-ounce) package semi-sweet chocolate chips

In a large kettle, boil sugar and syrup to 290° on a candy thermometer. Remove from heat and quickly stir in soda. Turn into buttered 9x13-inch pan. Let cool and harden. Remove and break into chunks. Melt paraffin and chocolate bits in top of double boiler. Dip candy into melted chocolate. Place on waxed paper until dry.

Yield: 2 to 4 dozen

Cleo Rumbley Smith (Mrs. Richard H.)
Burlington

TRUFFLES

1 (8-ounce) package semi-sweet chocolate
8 tablespoons heavy cream
2 tablespoons butter
1 to 2 tablespoons any liqueur
Cocoa
Powdered sugar

Mix cream and broken chocolate pieces in 6-inch heavy saucepan. Over low heat, melt chocolate completely. Remove from heat. Stir with spoon while adding butter and liqueur. Place pan in bowl with ice water. While turning pan, scrape mixture from bottom and sides until it forms a smooth mass and "mounts". Remove pan from ice water. Spoon out balls of mixture onto foil lined pan. Let set and become firm. Roll truffles in a mixture of half cocoa and half powdered sugar. Store in tightly covered box in refrigerator.

Yield: 24 servings

Edith Shoffner Hoogenboom
New York, New York

NEVER FAIL CANDY

1 (6-ounce) package chocolate chips
1 (6-ounce) package butterscotch chips
2 tablespoons peanut butter
2 cups Spanish peanuts

Melt first 3 ingredients in double boiler. When completely melted, add peanuts and spoon onto foil in bite sized pieces.

Yield: 50 pieces

Foy Elder Lane (Mrs. V. Wilton)
Burlington

GLAZED PECANS

3 cups sugar
1 cup sour cream
2 teaspoons vanilla extract
3 cups pecan halves

Combine sugar and sour cream in a heavy 2½-quart saucepan. Cook over low heat, stirring constantly, until mixture reaches 240° on candy thermometer. Remove from heat and stir in vanilla. Continue stirring until mixture begins to cool. Add pecans, mixing well, and drop by spoonsful on waxed paper.

Yield: 30 to 40 pieces

Sara Shaw Young
Burlington

ALENE'S FUDGE

2¼ cups sugar
4 tablespoons cocoa
4 tablespoons butter
1¼ cups milk
1 teaspoon vanilla extract
1 cup pecans, broken

Cook sugar, cocoa, butter and milk on medium heat until it forms a firm ball in cool water. (Begin testing after mixture boils). Let cool in pan until you can comfortably hold your hand on bottom. Add vanilla and stir constantly until mixture is of consistency to put into a buttered dish. Add nuts before pouring from pan.

Yield: 25 to 40 pieces

Alene Stonestreet Ventura
Burlington

FLOSSIE'S FUDGE

5 cups sugar
2 sticks margarine
1 large can evaporated milk
1 (12-ounce) package semi-sweet chocolate chips
2 teaspoons vanilla extract
1 cup chopped pecans, optional

Cook sugar, margarine and milk to a rolling boil, then start timing and cook *exactly* 6 minutes, stirring constantly. Remove from heat and add chips and vanilla. Beat until chips are dissolved. Add nuts, if desired. Pour into a buttered 9x13-inch pan and 1 smaller pan. Cool! Cut into 1-inch squares.

Yield: 80 to 100 pieces

Annetta Phillips Hix
Burlington

ALMA'S PEANUT FUDGE

4 cups sugar
2 sticks margarine
3 tablespoons white corn syrup
1 small can evaporated milk
1 (16-ounce) jar smooth peanut butter
2 (8-ounce) jars marshmallow creme
1 teaspoon vanilla extract

Boil sugar, margarine and corn syrup stirring constantly until a hard ball forms in water. Remove from heat and add milk, peanut butter, marshmallow creme and extract and beat until smooth. Pour into a large, greased pan. Chill.

Yield: 20 to 30 pieces

Dorothy Sellars Brawley
Burlington

GRANDMA'S MOLASSES CANDY

2 cups molasses
1 cup sugar
1 tablespoon baking soda
3 cups chopped black walnuts

Cook together molasses and sugar until brittle when small amount is dropped in cold water. Stir in baking soda and walnuts. Pour into greased pan and break into pieces when cold.

Yield: 60 to 80 pieces

Sara Shaw Young
Burlington

AUNT GRACE'S SEA FOAM CANDY

3 cups brown sugar
1 cup water
1 tablespoon vinegar
2 egg whites, beaten
½ teaspoon vanilla extract
¾ cup chopped nuts

Dissolve sugar in water; add vinegar. Cook without stirring to 255° or to the hard-ball stage. Remove from heat and pour gradually over beaten egg whites, beating constantly. Add vanilla extract. Continue beating until candy cools and will hold its shape. Add nuts. Drop by spoonsful on waxed paper, or spread into buttered pan and mark in squares.

Yield: 2 to 4 dozen

Suzanne Thompson Turner (Mrs. Walter L.)
Collinsville, Virginia

CARAMELS

2 cups whole evaporated milk
2 cups sugar
2 cups white corn syrup
1 stick butter
2 teaspoons vanilla extract
Pecans, if desired

Measure evaporated milk into a 2 cup measure; set aside. Mix sugar and corn syrup in saucepan. Place over heat and boil to 246°. Add butter and bring back to a boil. Begin adding milk to boiling mixture slowly. The mixture should not stop boiling during the entire time you are adding milk. Stir constantly and continue cooking until mixture is a deep caramel color and tests a firm ball or a waxy consistency when bitten. It is better to cook this without a thermometer so you should be careful to get just the right texture by the cold water test. Remove from heat. Add vanilla, then nuts if desired. Pour into oiled pan or frame to cool. This recipe will fill a pan 6x14-inches or equivalent, to ¾-inch thick. Cool at least 1 hour before cutting. Cut into ¾-inch squares. Wrap in waxed paper.

Yield: 6 dozen

Rosalia C. Shell
Charlotte, North Carolina

CARAMEL CORN

1 cup margarine
2 cups packed brown sugar
½ cup dark corn syrup
1 teaspoon salt
½ teaspoon baking soda
1 teaspoon vanilla extract
6 quarts popped corn

Melt margarine; stir in sugar, syrup and salt. Bring to a boil stirring constantly; then boil, without stirring, for 5 minutes. Remove from heat and add soda and vanilla. Pour slowly over popped corn, coating well, into 2 greased cookie sheets. Spread out. Bake at 200° for 1 hour, stirring every 15 minutes. Cool completely and break apart. Store in tightly covered container.

Yield: 6 quarts

Norma Campbell Moore (Mrs. Vernon)
Burlington

By the early 1900s the market for Alamance Plaids began to diminish as lighter colored cotton fabrics grew in favor. By 1925, only two mills in the South were still producing these types of plaids, though color was more important than ever in the production of cotton fabrics.

McCRAY SCHOOL **Highway 62 North**

The McCray School is the best-preserved example of an early twentieth century one-room school built for black children in rural Alamance County. Constructed in 1915, and operated until 1951, the school is typical of the educational facilities which served the county's rural black population from c. 1869 to the mid-twentieth century.

The simple building had few amenities and had no indoor plumbing. Students were required to bring their lunches from home. One former student recalls that these lunches typically consisted of "biscuits, 'serves, fried pies and maybe a piece of side meat." Water for student needs was carried in from a nearby farm well.

CRYSTALIZED PICKLES

1 (1 quart, 14-ounce) jar dill pickles, cut into slices
3 cups granulated sugar
5 drops oil of cinnamon, available from drug store
5 drops oil of cloves, available from drug store
1 cup vinegar
1 large piece dried ginger root

Combine sugar, cinnamon, cloves, and vinegar in saucepan. Bring to rolling boil. Drain liquid from pickles. Slice and replace in jar. Add ginger root. Pour hot sugar liquid into jar. Replace top. Store in refrigerator to maintain crispness.

Yield: 1 quart

Trudy Broadwell Rogers (Mrs. Arthur)
Burlington

WATERMELON RIND PICKLES

7 pounds watermelon rind, after peeling
1 (11.5 gram) bottle of slacked lime
9 cups sugar
3 cups vinegar
3 (2-inch) sticks cinnamon, broken
1 tablespoon whole cloves
1 teaspoon whole allspice
1 teaspoon yellow mustard seeds, optional

Trim all green rind from outside of melon and all red and soft meat from inside of rind. Cut rind into 1½-inch squares and place in agate or porcelain vessel. Cover with water. Stir in lime, using hand to thoroughly mix until lime is completely dissolved. Weight down rind with heavy china platter, using extra weight if necessary. Let stand overnight. The next day, drain lime water and rinse with cold water. Place rind in vessel and cover with ice water, adding ice cubes to insure the cold temperature lasts for at least 1 hour. Drain thoroughly before dropping rind into syrup. Make syrup by mixing sugar and vinegar. Tie spices in small cheesecloth bag and add to mixture. Place syrup in large agate vessel; dishpan is suggested. Bring slowly to a boil until transparent, and can be easily stuck with a toothpick. Pack in sterilized jars and pour in syrup to cover rind. Seal. Store in cool, dark place. Chill 6 to 12 hours before serving.

Yield: 4 to 5 quarts

Marion Lea Brown
Burlington

CUCUMBER PICKLES

75 cucumbers, 4-5 inches long or 2 gallons, small
Water
Alum
Salt
Vinegar
Sugar
Pickling spices
Celery seeds

Make a brine of 2 cups salt and 1 gallon water; boil and while hot pour over cucumbers which have been placed in a stone jar. Let stand 1 week. In hot weather it may be necessary to skim top if foam has accumulated. At the end of 1 week remove from brine and cut lengthwise into strips or into chunks. Return to stone jar. For the next 3 mornings make a boiling hot solution of 1 gallon of water and 1 tablespoon of alum. Pour hot over cucumbers. On the 4th morning, drain the alum water. Heat 6 cups vinegar, 5 cups sugar, ½ cup pickling spices and 1 tablespoon celery seeds. While hot pour over pickles. On the 5th day drain solution into container, add 2 cups sugar and heat to boiling point and pour over pickles. On the 6th day drain solution and add 1 cup sugar and heat to boiling point. Pack pickles in jars and pour hot liquid over and seal.

Yield: 6 to 7 quarts

Rena Maude I. Danieley
Burlington

KOSHER DILL PICKLES

Cucumbers, enough to fill 2 to 3 quart jars
1 head fresh dill or 1 tablespoon dill seeds
1 bay leaf, broken
1 garlic clove, cut into 3 or 4 pieces
½ teaspoon mustard seeds
⅓ pod hot green pepper, cut into 3 or 4 pieces
½ cup salt
1 quart water
1 quart vinegar

Place equal amounts of spices and pepper in bottom of each jar. Pack cucumbers in jars. Boil lids. Boil salt, vinegar and water and pour boiling hot mixture over cucumbers. Seal one jar at a time.

Yield: 2 to 3 quarts

Clara Smith May (Mrs. Roy E.)
Burlington

DILL PICKLES

20 to 24 (4-inch) young cucumbers
1/8 teaspoon alum
1 clove garlic
1 or 2 heads of dill
1 small hot pepper
1 quart vinegar
1 cup salt
3 quarts water

Wash cucumbers and let stand in cold water overnight. Pack in quart jars. To each jar add the above amounts of alum, garlic, dill and pepper. Combine vinegar, salt and water. Heat to a boiling point and pour over cucumbers in jars. Seal.

Yield: 6 to 8 quarts

Flossie Kime Shaw
Burlington

MARY RUTLEDGE'S CUCUMBER RINGS

3/4 pound commercial, medium or large sized sour pickles, sliced 1/4 to 1/3 inches thick
1/2 pound sugar
1 tablespoon whole cloves
2 sticks cinnamon, broken

Put pickles in an earthenware, agateware, or glassware container. Sprinkle over sugar and spices and stir well. Put aside for two days, stirring often. The pickles should be ready on the third day. They should be brittle and firm. Do not seal or cover too lightly. Will keep indefinitely.

Yield: 1 quart

Mrs. Rutledge is widely known in the art of cookery. Her friends look forward to having her cucumber pickles at Christmas time. I put my pickles in an earthenware pickle jar which has a cork fitted lid. In this type container, the pickle receives enough breath to keep them firm. Chill pickles before serving.

Marion Lea Brown
Burlington

MUSTARD PICKLES

30 to 40 (4 to 6-inch)
cucumbers, sliced into jars

To each quart jar add:
4 tablespoons sugar
1 tablespoon salt
2 tablespoons dry mustard
Vinegar

Wash cucumbers and pack as many as possible into jars. Add dry ingredients and fill with undiluted cold vinegar. Seal air tight. Shake each jar well. Let stand about 6 weeks before eating.

Flossie Kime Shaw
Burlington

SQUASH PICKLE

1 gallon small squash, sliced
2 medium onions, sliced
½ cup salt
2 quarts ice (or more)

Syrup:
5 cups sugar
5 cups vinegar
1½ teaspoons turmeric
1 tablespoon mustard seeds
1 tablespoon celery seeds

Layer in crock: squash, onions, salt and ice. Cover and let set for 3 hours. (I cover with foil and put plate on top.) Drain very well and wash in cold water. Pack in sterile jars. Combine all ingredients for syrup and heat to just below boiling. Pour over squash while hot. Seal jars and put in hot water bath and simmer for 10 minutes. Water should cover jars by 1 inch.

Yield: 7 quarts

Luzette Callum Brown (Mrs. W. W.)
Burlington

SAUERKRAUT RELISH

1 (16-ounce) can chopped kraut

Empty kraut into colander and rinse with hot water. Drain well.

1 onion, finely chopped
1 cup chopped green pepper
2 cups shredded carrots
1 (2-ounce) jar pimento peppers, chopped
1 cup chopped celery

Mix vegetables thoroughly with kraut and turn into a 2-quart dish.

Marinade:
1 cup sugar
½ cup white vinegar

Bring sugar and vinegar to a boil and pour over vegetables and refrigerate overnight.

Yield: 8 to 12 servings

Annie Lee Thompson
Greensboro, North Carolina

RIPE TOMATO CHOW CHOW

1 gallon ripe tomatoes
1 gallon chopped onions
1 cup salt
1 gallon chopped cabbage
1 dozen or less chopped sweet peppers
9 or less skinny hot peppers, left whole
3 pounds sugar
½ gallon vinegar
½ box pickling spices, tied in cloth bag

Mix vegetables in a large pot that can be used on stove. Let stand 2 hours. Drain well. Add sugar, vinegar and pickling spices to mixture and cook over medium heat all day, stirring occasionally. The longer it cooks, the better it is. Spoon into small jars and seal.

Yield: 4 to 6 quarts

This can be eaten on any kind of beans or peas. More peppers can be added for a hotter chow chow.

Flossie Kime Shaw
Burlington

GRANNY VINCENT'S RELISH

8 green peppers
8 red peppers
8 large carrots
1 medium cabbage
1 bunch celery
8 onions
1 cup plain salt
1½ pints vinegar
1 tablespoon cloves
1 tablespoon pickling spice

Grind vegetables with 1 cup of plain salt. Let stand for 3 hours. Drain. Add 1½ pints of vinegar, a cheese cloth bag containing cloves and pickling spice. Boil 5 to 10 minutes. Seal in pint jars.

Yield: 2 to 3 pints

N. Jane Iseley
Burlington

PEACH DATE CHUTNEY

2 pounds ripe peaches, peeled, pitted and sliced
2 medium onions, chopped
3 cups sugar
½ pound dates, chopped, approximately 1½ cups
½ cup sliced candied ginger
1 cup tarragon vinegar
½ cup white vinegar

Mix all ingredients, except peaches, in a large enameled pan. Cook 30 minutes, stirring frequently. Add peaches and continue cooking 20 minutes or until well blended and thickened. Put in sterile jars and process in hot bath for 10 minutes.

Yield: 3½ pints

Luzette Callum Brown (Mrs. W. W.)
Burlington

SPICED CRANBERRY RELISH

2 cups sugar
½ cup vinegar
¾ teaspoon ground cloves
¾ teaspoon ground cinnamon
4 cups cranberries, fresh, washed and picked
½ orange, unpeeled, seeded, and finely chopped

Combine sugar, vinegar and spices in a saucepan. Place over medium heat and bring slowly to a boil, stirring often. Add the cranberries and finely chopped orange. Cook until the cranberries have "popped." Pour into sterilized 1-quart or 2 (1-pint) jars with tight fitting tops. May be used immediately or stored for future use.

This is an easy way to make a tasty relish.

Marion Lea Brown
Burlington

DELICIOUS FIG PRESERVES

1 pound of figs
1 pound sugar
Juice of ½ lemon

Gather figs when just ripe (not soft or cracked). Peel carefully not to cut too near the seed. Place sugar in a preserving kettle with enough water to keep from sticking. Stir occasionally until it begins to boil. Add lemon juice; this will prevent crystals from forming. Add part of figs, boil until transparent. Remove to platter. Add more figs to boiling syrup until all are used. When all figs are removed, boil syrup down until thick as honey. Return the figs to the syrup and boil 2 more minutes. Set aside until the next morning when they may be packed in jars. Process filled jars for 15 minutes at simmering point. They will keep for several months without processing.

Blanche Stafford Blackwelder (Mrs. Clyde W.)
Burlington

MRS. HOLT'S STRAWBERRY PRESERVES

4 cups strawberries, washed and capped
5 cups sugar
3 tablespoons lemon juice or ½ teaspoon cream of tartar

Place alternate layers of strawberries and sugar in a wide kettle (not aluminum). Bring gently to a boil and boil slowly for 9 minutes. Remove from heat, stir in lemon juice (or cream of tartar). Lightly cover and allow mixture to stand at room temperature overnight. The next day bring again to a slow boil. Allow preserves to cool. Spoon into sterilized glasses then seal with melted paraffin. Place lids on glasses. Cooked this way, the preserves are beautiful and tender; jelly surrounds the plump red berries.

Yield: 1½ pints

This is a perfect strawberry preserves recipe, worked out after many trials and errors.

Marion Lea Brown
Burlington

STRAWBERRY JELLY

¾ cup hot water
4 cups strawberries, capped and washed
4 cups sugar

Dissolve 2 cups of sugar in ¾ cup of hot water in a 6 quart, or larger pot. Bring to a rolling boil. Add 2 cups strawberries and boil hard for 15 minutes. Add another 2 cups sugar to first mixture and bring to a boil. Add another 2 cups strawberries and boil all of this for 15 minutes. Cool overnight. Put into jars and seal with paraffin.

Yield: 5 jelly jars

This was the recipe of my mother, Mrs. Carrie A. Roney.

Nancy Roney Barger (Mrs. James A.)
Haw River

LEMON CURD

½ cup butter
1½ cups sugar
Grated rind of 3 lemons
½ cup fresh lemon juice
6 eggs

Process butter, sugar and lemon rind until rind is pulverized. Add fresh lemon juice and eggs. Pour into heavy saucepan. Cook over low heat until thickened, about 10 minutes. Do not let boil or it will curdle. It will thicken once it is cooled. Refrigerate covered.

Yield: 2 cups

This will keep for a long time. It is a wonderful spread on top of a cheese cake or eaten as a jam with scones or as a filling between two plain sugar cookies.

Sandra Elder Harper
Burlington

COULIS AUX FRAMBOISES
(Raspberry Sauce)

1 pint fresh raspberries
⅓ cup sugar
¼ cup water
2 tablespoons kirschwasser

Rinse the berries and put into blender. Boil the sugar and water until sugar is dissolved and liquid is reduced by about one half. Put this and the kirschwasser (cherry brandy) into the blender and blend about 1 minute. Serve with vanilla ice cream of the best quality.

Robert Burns King
Burlington

HARD SAUCE

¼ cup butter, no substitute
1 cup powdered sugar
2 tablespoons brandy
2 eggs, well beaten
½ cup heavy cream

Cream butter and add sugar gradually, mixing well. Slowly add brandy, then eggs and cream. Cook in double boiler until thick. Cool.

Yield: 2 cups

Edith Ruth Brannock
Elon College

I CAN'T BELIEVE IT'S NOT SOUR CREAM

½ cup lowfat yogurt, plain
1½ cups diet cottage cheese
Low-calorie sweetner to taste
2 teaspoons chives

Mix yogurt, cottage cheese, and sweetner in a blender. Blend well. Remove from blender and add chives. Mix well and chill.

Yield: 2 cups

Holly Jill Smith
Delray Beach, Florida

SAUCE BEARNAISE

1 cup white wine
1 tablespoon minced onion
1 teaspoon chervil, crushed
2 dashes vinegar
1 or 2 teaspoons tarragon
Pepper to taste
3 egg yolks
1 stick butter

Place wine, onion, chervil, vinegar, tarragon and pepper in the top of a double boiler. Put on burner and reduce to 2 tablespoons. Place on bottom of double boiler on low heat. Add egg yolks and butter—a little of each alternately. Cook, stirring constantly, until thickened.

Yield: 2 cups

D. Edward Hudgins
Burlington

HERB BUTTER

1 stick butter, room temperature
1 teaspoon freshly minced garlic
1 teaspoon basil
Pinch of oregano
Pinch of dill weed

Mix herbs with softened butter and refrigerate to harden.

Yield: ½ cup

Holly Jill Smith
Delray Beach, Florida

MEAT MARINADE

½ cup soy sauce
½ cup water
2 tablespoons lemon juice
1 tablespoon brown sugar
2 tablespoons salad oil
¼ teaspoon TABASCO pepper sauce
1 clove garlic, crushed
¼ teaspoon freshly ground pepper

Combine ingredients and use to marinate beef, pork or chicken before grilling or broiling.

Yield: 1¼ cups

Elizabeth Pruitt Dunn (Mrs. James)
Baltimore, Maryland

MUSHROOM, ONION AND RED WINE SAUCE

8 ounces fresh mushrooms, sliced
2 tablespoons olive oil or butter
1 tablespoon beef bouillon granules
½ teaspoon brown bouquet sauce
1 cup water
3 medium onions, sliced
1 cup red wine, Burgundy preferred
1½-2 teaspoons cornstarch
Dash of pepper

Cook mushrooms 3 to 5 minutes on medium-high in olive oil or butter. Dissolve bouillon granules and bouquet sauce in 1 cup hot water. Add to mushrooms and simmer 20 minutes on low. In another pan, cook onions until golden in oil of your choice. Add 1 cup red wine to pan, simmer 20 minutes on low. Dissolve cornstarch in ¼ cup cold water. Combine the 2 sauces in one skillet; add cornstarch to thicken. Add pepper to taste. May be made ahead and reheated and poured over steaks or hamburger patties.

Yield: 2½ to 3 cups

Great on steaks or hamburgers!

Dolores Cheatham James (Mrs. Harry C.)
Burlington

GOLDEN GLOW FRUIT DRESSING

½ cup orange juice
½ cup lemon juice
½ cup pineapple juice
4 eggs
¾ cup sugar

Mix all ingredients. Cook in double boiler until thick. Remove from heat and cool. Add 1 cup whipped cream or non-dairy topping. Store in container. Serve over fresh fruit.

Yield: 1¼ pints

Pattie Fayle Sowder
Burlington

MRS. CORE'S SALAD DRESSING

2 large eggs or 4 small
¾ cup sugar
½ teaspoon salt
1 teaspoon dry mustard
1 cup vinegar, tarragon if preferred

Mix eggs, sugar, salt and mustard well. Carefully add vinegar. Cook until thickened; sometimes a little cornstarch helps to thicken. Store in refrigerator.

Yield: 2 cups

A family favorite since 1945!

Edwina G. Hughes Johnston (Mrs. Bill)
Burlington

BLENDER MAYONNAISE

1 egg
½ teaspoon dry mustard
½ teaspoon salt
2 tablespoons vinegar, or lemon juice
1 cup salad oil (can be a mixture of olive oil and safflower)
Dash of red pepper

Break egg into blender. Add mustard, salt and vinegar. Add ¼ cup of the oil. Cover and turn blender on low speed. Immediately uncover and pour remaining oil in a steady stream until well blended. Add red pepper. Add garlic, or herbs of choice, if desired.

Yield: 1½ cups

Sara Jo Barnett Blair (Mrs. Walker)
Burlington

Through Alamance Plaids color was firmly established as essential to the production of cotton fabrics. Writing in the 1890s, Governor Thomas Holt concluded the account of his participation in the production of the original colored cottons made in the South with the following remarks: "At the present time we are building a new mill. When it is completed we will have in operation at Haw River 940 looms running on colored goods of various kinds. And the whole of it had its origins in the small start made with a copper kettle and washpot."

PROVIDENCE UNITED CHURCH OF CHRIST

Graham, N.C.

Providence United Church of Christ, located in Graham, had its beginnings c. 1763 as a meeting house and school. Discussions concerning the formation of Alamance County from Orange County were held at this site during the period 1848-1849, and the church housed county court sessions until the first courthouse was erected in 1851.

In the nineteenth century the church sponsored Graham College. In 1888 the church was also instrumental in the formation of the successor to Graham College, Elon College. The present church, portions of which were built in the 1870s, is the fourth building on the site.

HEALTHY HISTORIANS

The recipes included in this section were submitted by Friends of the Museum and others were adapted from the Culinary Hearts Cooking Course recipes and Homespun Column (Judith S. Johnson, Home Economics Extension Agent.)

LIGHT EGGNOG

1 cup non-fat dry milk powder
½ cup water
24 packets low-calorie sweetener equivalent to/or 1 cup sugar
1 teaspoon brandy extract
½ teaspoon rum extract
2 eggs
¼ teaspoon nutmeg
2 cups skim milk

Combine dry milk, water and sweetener in blender. Blend on high for 5 to 10 minutes or until smooth and creamy. Add extracts and egg; continue blending. Add nutmeg and milk until well mixed. Refrigerate. Serve with sprinkle of nutmeg.

Yield: 1 quart

A delicious non-alcoholic eggnog!

CREAM OF BROCCOLI AND CAULIFLOWER SOUP

1 (10-ounce) package frozen chopped broccoli
1 (10-ounce) package frozen cauliflower
1 cup shredded potato
1 cup water
2 tablespoons chopped onion
2 teaspoons low-sodium instant chicken bouillon granules
¼ teaspoon pepper
⅛ teaspoon ground nutmeg
3 cups skim milk

Combine all ingredients except milk in a 2-quart casserole. Cover. Microwave on high for 15 to 21 minutes, or until vegetables are tender, stirring 2 or 3 times. Let stand, covered, for about 5 minutes. Process half the vegetables in food processor or blender until smooth. Repeat with remaining vegetables. Return to casserole. Blend in milk. Microwave, uncovered, on high for 7 to 13 minutes, or until heated through, stirring once or twice.

Yield: 9 servings (¾ cup each)

Frances Lee Gillespie (Mrs. James W.)
Burlington

CELERY AND CAULIFLOWER SALAD

1 large head cauliflower
5 stalks celery, sliced
4 radishes, sliced
4 green onions, chopped
1 (8-ounce) carton commercial sour cream
½ cup mayonnaise
Dash of garlic salt
Dash of pepper

Remover outer leaves of cauliflower and break into flowerets. Wash thoroughly. Combine vegetables in a large bowl; toss well. Combine the remaining ingredients, mixing well; pour over vegetables and toss. Chill.

Yield: 10 to 12 servings

CHINESE-STYLE BEEF

2 (1-pound) flank steaks, trimmed
1 tablespoon peanut oil
2 cloves garlic, crushed
¼ teaspoon ground ginger
⅛ teaspoon pepper
3 tablespoons reduced-sodium soy sauce
1 teaspoon sugar
2 cups coarsely chopped green pepper
2 cups fresh bean sprouts
2 medium tomatoes, peeled and quartered
1 tablespoon cornstarch
¼ cup water
4 cups hot cooked rice

Partially freeze steaks; slice diagonally across grain into ½-inch strips. Add oil to wok or heavy skillet, and heat to medium high (325°) for 1 minute. Add steak, garlic, ginger, and pepper; stir-fry 5 minutes or until browned. Add soy sauce and sugar; cook 1 minute. Add green pepper and bean sprouts; stir well. Cover and cook 3 minutes; stir in tomatoes.

Combine cornstarch and water; stir until cornstarch dissolves. Stir into beef mixture; stir-fry 2 minutes. Serve immediately over rice.

Yield: 8 servings

BAKED FISH IN FOIL

4-6 ounces sole filets or fish of your choice
Mayonnaise
1 cup fresh mushrooms, sliced
¾ cup green pepper, diced
¾ cup celery, chopped
¾ cup fresh carrots, sliced
¾ cup onion, diced
4 teaspoons lemon juice
¾ teaspoon paprika
¾ teaspoon dried oregano
1 tablespoon dried parsley

Wash fish filets and brush with mayonnaise. Lightly salt and pepper. Place each filet on a sheet of heavy duty foil. Pour seasonings in a melted margarine base over each filet. Divide mixed vegetables and spread over filets. Seal foil tightly. Bake 450° for 25 minutes. This is a "lean" main course.

Yield: 2 servings

Dr. Bob Ellington
Burlington

CHICKEN PICCATA

4 (8-ounce) chicken breast halves, boned and skinned
3 tablespoons all-purpose flour
2 tablespoons unsalted margarine
1 tablespoon vegetable oil
1 tablespoon unsalted margarine
½ cup chopped onion
1 cup water
1 teaspoon low-sodium chicken-flavored bouillon granules
1 lemon, thinly sliced
2 tablespoons chopped fresh parsley

Place each chicken breast half on a sheet of waxed paper. Flatten chicken to ¼-inch thickness using a meat mallet or rolling pin; dredge with flour. Heat 2 tablespoons margarine and oil in a large skillet over medium-high heat; add chicken and cook 2 to 3 minutes on each side or until golden brown. Remove chicken and set aside. Melt 1 tablespoon margarine in skillet; add onion and sauté until tender. Stir in water, bouillon granules, and lemon; bring to a boil. Return chicken to skillet, reduce heat, and simmer 3 to 4 minutes or until bouillon dissolves and sauce is slightly thickened.

To serve, arrange chicken on a platter. Pour sauce over chicken and garnish with parsley.

Yield: 4 servings

OVEN-FRIED CHICKEN BREASTS

1½ cups bran flakes
½ teaspoon garlic powder
½ teaspoon oregano
½ teaspoon rosemary
¼ teaspoon marjoram
⅛ teaspoon pepper
1 tablespoon oil
¼ cup plain yogurt
4 boned, skinned chicken breast halves or 3 pounds chicken cut in pieces

Place cereal and spices in blender; blend until cereal is finely crushed. Add oil and stir until all crumbs are coated. Dip chicken in yogurt; shake off excess and dip into cereal mixture, coating well on both sides. Place on ungreased shallow baking pan. Bake at 400° for 20 to 25 minutes.

Yield: 4 servings

CHICKEN VERONIQUE

3 chicken breasts, halved and skinned
½ teaspoon salt
¼ teaspoon ground pepper
½ teaspoon dried tarragon
3 tablespoons plus 2 tablespoons margarine
1 cup cracker crumbs
¼ cup chopped onions
½ cup chicken broth (low sodium)
½ cup dry white wine
2 cups fresh sliced mushrooms
2 cups seedless green grapes

Combine crumbs, salt, pepper and tarragon. Coat chicken pieces with this mixture. Brown lightly in 3 tablespoons melted margarine. Remove and place in baking pan. Sauté onions in remaining 2 tablespoons melted margarine, pour in broth and wine. Bring to a boil. Pour around chicken in baking pan. Bake 30 minutes at 350°. Sauté mushrooms and place around the chicken, then place grapes around the chicken. Bake an additional 10 minutes.

Yield: 3 servings

TURKEY A LA KING

3 tablespoons reduced-calorie margarine
½ cup chopped onion
½ cup chopped green pepper
2 tablespoons all-purpose flour
1½ cups skim milk
1 teaspoon chicken-flavored bouillon granules
¼ teaspoon white pepper
2 cups chopped cooked turkey, or chicken
1 (4-ounce) can sliced mushrooms, drained
1 (2-ounce) jar diced pimento, drained
2 cups hot cooked rice

Melt margarine in a medium-sized heavy saucepan over medium heat. Add onion and green pepper and sauté 5 or 6 minutes or until green pepper is tender. Add flour, stirring until vegetables are coated. Cook 1 minute over low heat, stirring constantly. Gradually add milk, bouillon granules and pepper. Cook over medium heat stirring constantly until thickened and bubbly. Stir in mushrooms, pimento and turkey. Cook until thoroughly heated. Serve over rice.

Yield: 4 servings

Frances Lee Gillespie (Mrs. James W.)
Burlington

QUICK SHRIMP SKILLET

1 tablespoon reduced-calorie margarine
½ cup sliced green onions
2 cups diagonally sliced celery
½ cup sliced carrot
1 cup sliced fresh mushrooms
2 cloves garlic, minced
½ teaspoon ground ginger
⅛ teaspoon pepper
2 teaspoons reduced-sodium soy sauce
¾ pound shelled and deveined medium shrimp
2 tablespoons water
1½ cups hot cooked rice

Add margarine to a wok or heavy skillet; heat to medium high (325°) for 1 minute. Add onions, celery, carrot, mushrooms, and garlic, and stir-fry until vegetables are crisp-tender. Add ginger, pepper, soy sauce, shrimp and water; stir-fry until shrimp are pink. Serve over rice.

Yield: 3 servings

SCALLOPS ORIENTAL

2 pounds bay scallops, fresh or frozen
¼ cup honey
¼ cup prepared mustard
1 teaspoon curry powder (or ground cumin)
1 teaspoon lemon juice
Lemon wedges

Preheat broiler for 5 minutes. Rinse fresh scallops in cold water, or thaw frozen scallops. Place in a baking pan. In a saucepan, combine honey, mustard, curry powder and lemon juice. Brush scallops with the sauce. Broil for 5 to 8 minutes, or until browned. Garnish with lemon wedges.

Yield: 8 servings

SAUCY CELERY

4½ cups thinly sliced celery
¼ cup butter or margarine
2 tablespoons flour
¼ teaspoon salt
1 cup milk
1 cup shredded Cheddar cheese, divided
1 (3-ounce) can mushroom stems and pieces, drained
3 tablespoons chopped green pepper

Sauté celery in butter in a large skillet 15 minutes or until tender. Stir in flour and salt; cook 1 minute, stirring constantly. Gradually add milk, cook over medium heat, stirring constantly, until thickened and bubbly. Add ¾ cup cheese, and stir until melted. Stir in mushrooms and green pepper, mixing well. Pour into a greased 1-quart shallow casserole. Bake at 350° for 15 minutes. Sprinkle with remaining ¼ cup cheese, and bake an additional 5 minutes.

Yield: 4 to 6 servings

GREEN BEANS

1 pound fresh green beans, snapped in ½-inch pieces
2 medium Vidalia or sweet purple onions, sliced
3 tablespoons oil
½ teaspoon freshly ground pepper
1 tablespoon lemon juice

Sauté onions in oil. Add beans and stir fry until tender. Add pepper and lemon juice and serve immediately.

Yield: 4 to 6 servings

STIR-FRIED VEGETABLES WITH CURRY

1½ teaspoons vegetable oil
2 cloves garlic, minced
7 cups coarsely shredded cabbage
1 cup sliced celery
⅓ cup chopped green onions
2 cups fresh bean sprouts
1 tablespoon reduced-sodium soy sauce
1 teaspoon curry powder
½ teaspoon sugar
¼ teaspoon vinegar

Add oil to wok or heavy skillet, and heat to medium high (325°) for 1 minute. Add cabbage, celery, and green onions; stir-fry 3 minutes or until crisp-tender. Add remaining ingredients; stir-fry 1 to 2 minutes or until thoroughly heated.

Yield: 5 servings

Stir-frying pointers: Prior to cooking, assemble everything you need. Once you start the cooking process, there's no time to stop and hunt anything or to prepare ingredients without over cooking the ingredients already in the wok. Partially freeze meat, and slice it diagonally across the grain in thin strips so that more surface area is exposed to heat, cooking the meat faster. Slice or chop vegetables in uniform pieces that will cook in the same amount of time. First, add the ingredients that will take the longest time to cook. Then add other ingredients, based on how long they need to cook. Use a lift-and-stir motion to move the food constantly during cooking. Cook vegetables until they are crisp-tender.

OVEN FRIED OKRA

1¾ pounds okra, washed and cut into ½-inch slices
Buttermilk
1¼ cups plain cornmeal

Soak okra in buttermilk for 3 to 5 minutes. Dredge in cornmeal. Place okra in a 15x10x1-inch pan greased with cooking spray. Spread evenly. Bake at 450° for 30 to 40 minutes, stirring occasionally.

Yield: 4 to 6 servings

Peggy Carter Lackey (Mrs. Mack E.)
Burlington

TOMATO SAUCE FOR PASTA

⅓ cup extra virgin olive oil
1 medium onion, diced
1 (28-ounce) can tomatoes
½ teaspoon garlic salt
1 teaspoon marjoram
⅓ cup chopped basil (dried is fine)

Sauté onion in oil. Add contents of whole can of tomatoes, breaking up large pieces by blender or food processor. Add seasonings. Simmer, covered, for at least 20 minutes. Serve over fettucine, linguini, or any favorite pasta.

Yield: 4 to 6 servings

NOTE: Bob and I serve this low cholesterol dish together with a salad of mixed greens and French bread. No dessert!!

Helen Arendell Ellington (Mrs. Bob)
Burlington

POLY WHIPPED TOPPING

This polyunsaturated substitute has a taste and consistency closely resembling whipped cream, but it has no saturated fat.

1 teaspoon gelatin
2 teaspoons cold water
3 tablespoons boiling water
½ cup ice water
½ cup nonfat dry milk
3 tablespoons sugar
3 tablespoons oil

Chill a small mixing bowl. Soften gelatin with 2 teaspoons of cold water. Then add boiling water, stirring until gelatin is completely dissolved. Cool until tepid. Place ice water and non-fat dry milk in chilled mixing bowl. Beat at high speed until mixture forms stiff peaks. Add sugar, still beating, then the oil and the gelatin. Place in freezer for about 15 minutes. Transfer to refrigerator until ready for use. Stir before using to retain a creamy texture.

Yield: 2 cups

DEEP-DISH APPLE PIE

Filling:

3½ pounds red cooking apples, peeled, cored and sliced
⅓ cup sugar
¼ cup all-purpose flour
1 tablespoon lemon juice
1¼ teaspoons granulated sugar substitute
1 teaspoon grated lemon peel
1 teaspoon ground cinnamon
1 teaspoon ground nutmeg
¼ teaspoon salt

Pastry:

1 cup all-purpose flour
¼ teaspoon granulated sugar substitute
⅓ cup margarine
2-3 tablespoons cold water
1-2 teaspoons skim milk

In large bowl, combine apples and remaining ingredients for filling. Spoon into 9-inch square baking dish. Preheat oven to 450°. Prepare pastry: In bowl, place 1 cup flour and ¼ teaspoon sugar substitute. With pastry blender, cut in margarine until mixture resembles coarse crumbs. Add cold water, 1 tablespoon at a time, until mixture just holds together. On lightly floured surface with floured rolling pin, roll out dough into a 10-inch square. Fit pastry over apples. Fold overhang under; make fluted edge. Make several slits in pastry for steam to escape. Brush pastry with skim milk. Bake 10 minutes; reduce oven temperature to 350°. Bake 35 to 40 minutes or until golden brown.

Yield: 10 servings

WHITE MOON CAKE

1¾ cups sugar
1½ sticks margarine
3 cups plain flour, sifted
3 teaspoons baking powder
¼ teaspoon salt
1 cup milk
1 teaspoon vanilla extract
5 egg whites

Preheat oven to 325°. Cream sugar and butter, and add vanilla while creaming. Remove beaters from mixer. Sift flour with baking powder and salt three times. Fold in flour, alternating with milk. Fold in stiffly beaten egg whites. Pour into three greased and floured pans, and bake for 15 minutes then increase heat to 350° and bake 15 minutes longer.

Viola Ringwald Ireland (Mrs. J. R.)
Southern Pines, North Carolina

LOW CHOLESTEROL CHOCOLATE POUND CAKE

½ pound margarine, melted
½ cup butter flavored shortening
3 cups sugar
1 tablespoon vanilla extract
5 egg substitutes
3 cups flour
¼ cup cocoa
½ teaspoon baking powder
1 cup (½% fat) milk

Thaw egg substitutes to room temperature. Cream margarine and shortening. Add sugar and vanilla, creaming until well blended. Add egg substitutes one at a time and beat well. Mix dry ingredients together alternating with milk and mix just enough to blend. Bake in greased and floured tube pan 325° for 1 hour and 20 minutes.

Yield: 16 to 20 servings

Margaret Long Beatty
Burlington

BANANA-DATE COFFEE CAKE

⅓ cup ripe banana, mashed
½ cup margarine, softened
3 large eggs (may substitute egg whites or artificial eggs to lower cholesterol)
1 teaspoon vanilla extract
1¼ cups water
3 cups flour
1 teaspoon baking soda
2 teaspoons baking powder
1½ cups chopped dates

Topping:
⅓ cup chopped dates
⅓ cup chopped pecans

Beat together banana and margarine until creamy. Stir eggs, vanilla and water into batter. Sift flour, soda and baking powder into batter; beat well. Fold in 1½ cups of chopped dates. Spoon batter into a greased and floured 9x13-inch baking pan. Spread batter evenly in pan. Combine topping ingredients; sprinkle over batter. Bake at 350° for 20 to 25 minutes or until a knife inserted comes out clean. Cool on wire rack.

Yield: 12 to 16 servings

"Delicious warm—has no sugar!"

Grace Anderson Thompson (Mrs. A. G., Jr.)
Burlington

REFRIGERATOR PINEAPPLE CHEESE CAKE

1 cup graham cracker crumbs
2 tablespoons margarine, melted
1 tablespoon oil
1 (3-ounce) package pineapple gelatin
1 cup boiling water
1½ pounds low-fat cottage cheese
¼ cup sugar
1 (8½-ounce) can crushed pineapple in juice, undrained
1 tablespoon water
2 teaspoons cornstarch

Combine the first 3 ingredients. Press onto the bottom of an 8-inch springform pan. Chill. Dissolve the gelatin in the boiling water and cool to lukewarm. In a blender, thoroughly mix the cheese and sugar. Slowly add the gelatin and blend well. Pour mixture into the chilled crust, and refrigerate until firm. In a saucepan, bring the crushed pineapple and juice, the water and the cornstarch to a boil, stirring constantly. Cool 15 minutes and spread over the top of the cheese cake. Chill at least 1 hour.

Yield: 16 servings

WINTER FRUIT SALAD

2 firm medium apples, cored and cubed
2 bananas, halved lengthwise, cut into 1-inch pieces
8 dried apricots or 4 dried peach or nectarine halves, coarsely chopped
4 dried pitted prunes, coarsely chopped
½ cup raisins
3 to 5 heaping tablespoons plain yogurt
½ tablespoon honey
Dash of nutmeg
1 to 2 tablespoons orange or apple juice or orange liqueur
2 tablespoons toasted almonds, chopped coarsely

Combine first 8 ingredients in medium bowl and mix well. Stir in juice or liqueur to taste. Cover and chill. When ready to serve, gently mix in almonds.

Yield: Makes 4 servings

POACHED PEARS SERVED CHILLED

¼ cup sugar
2 cups water
4 pears, peeled but left whole
¼ cup apricot preserves
2 tablespoons orange juice
⅓ cup pistachio nuts or almonds, chopped

In a 2-quart saucepan, combine sugar and water. Simmer, stirring frequently until sugar granules are dissolved. Place pears immediately in sugar syrup to prevent pears from discoloring when exposed to air. Turn pears in syrup to coat all sides. Place saucepan over low heat and simmer, gently turning pears from time to time, until soft. Remove saucepan from heat. Cool pears in syrup until they reach room temperature. Remove ¼ cup of syrup and reserve. Refrigerate pears in remaining syrup until thoroughly chilled. To make apricot syrup: Combine preserves with orange juice in a small saucepan. Simmer over low heat until preserves have melted. Remove from heat. Strain apricot preserve mixture and cool. Add 2 to 4 tablespoons reserved sugar syrup, depending upon desired thickness of syrup. When ready to serve, remove pears from refrigerator. Place pears on platter or individual dessert plates. Stir apricot sauce and spoon over pears. Sprinkle with chopped nuts.

Yield: 4 servings

YEAST BISCUITS

1 package dry yeast
1 cup warm water (105°-115°)
7 cups all-purpose flour
2 teaspoons baking powder
¼ teaspoon baking soda
½ teaspoon salt
2 cups nonfat buttermilk
¾ cup vegetable oil
¼ cup sugar
Vegetable cooking spray

Dissolve yeast in warm water; let stand 5 minutes. Combine flour and next 3 ingredients; set aside. Combine buttermilk, oil, and sugar in a large bowl; add yeast mixture and 2 cups flour mixture. Beat at low speed of an electric mixer until smooth. Add remaining 5 cups flour mixture; stir until well blended. Cover and chill 8 hours. Turn dough out onto a lightly floured surface; roll to ½-inch thickness, and cut with a 2-inch cutter. Place on ungreased baking sheets. Bake at 400° for 15 to 18 minutes or until lightly browned. Remove from baking sheets; spray biscuits lightly with cooking spray.

Yield: 4½ dozen

NOTE: Dough may be kept in refrigerator for 7 days.

Of the many mills in North Carolina operated by Holts and related families, including the Williamsons, Whites, Mebanes and Gants, four mills were sold to Burlington Mills in the 1920s and '30s. One of the original directors of Burlington Mills was Eugene Holt, a grandson of Edwin Michael Holt. Over the years, Burlington Mills, headed by J. Spencer Love, grew to become Burlington Industries, a multi-national corporation now recognized throughout the world as a leading textile manufacturer.

ALLEN HOUSE

Alamance Battleground Road

The Allen House, located at the Alamance Battleground site, is a log dwelling characteristic of those occupied by frontier people on the western fringes of Carolina Colony. The house was built by John Allen sometime around 1780. John's sister, Amy, was the wife of Herman Husband, a prominent agitator-pamphleteer active in the Regulator movement.

John Allen's wife, Rachel, was known for her herbal remedies and medicinal recipes, some of which she recorded in booklet form in the 1790s. One recipe, entitled "Diet Drink to be Wrought in Beer", called for an infusion of "water cresses, sassafras roots, nettles, Lignumeity, burdock and sweet bryer root in 3 to 4 gallons of Malt Beer."

Reflections in Plaid

Choice Recipes from CHOICE RECIPES, cookbook compiled for the Ladies' Aid Society of the Christian Church, Burlington, 1907
"It is only when the weaver stops, and the web is loosed and turned,
That he sees his real handiwork—that his marvelous skill is learned."

CHOICE RECIPES

CREAM OF TOMATO SOUP

1 qt. can tomatoes put on the fire, and cook until soft enough to strain through a fine sieve. Put back on stove, add one qt. of water, ¼ teaspoonful of soda, 1 pt. of new milk, heaping tablespoonful of butter, sufficient cornstarch to make as thick as cream. Add salt and a dash of red pepper. Serve with toast.

Mrs. T. S. Faucette

SOUTHERN RICE BREAD

Beat 3 eggs without separating, add 1¼ pt. of milk and 1 cup of cold boiled rice, 1 tablespoon of melted butter, 1 teaspoon of salt and 2 cups of meal or flour. Beat well and add 2 teaspoons of baking powder. Bake in a shallow pan in a quick oven for ½ hour.

Mrs. W. H. Turrentine

CHEESE STRAWS

Two oz. of butter, two oz. of breadcrumbs, two oz. of grated cheese, two oz. of flour and one-half teaspoonful of salt and pepper mixed. Mix, roll the paste thin, cut in strips and bake for ten minutes on buttered paper.

Mrs. D. E. Sellars

GRAHAM GEMS

1 pt. buttermilk, 1 egg, 1 tablespoon of brown sugar, 1 teaspoon of salt, 1 teaspoon of soda. Graham flour enough to make it stiff enough to drop from a spoon. Have gem pans hot.

Mrs. Walter Sellars

SPONGE CAKE

3 eggs, 3 tablespoonsful of water, 1 cup sugar, 1 cup flour, 1 teaspoon baking powder. Put the sugar and water on to boil, when it comes to a boil remove and pour slowly over the beaten eggs. Beat until cold, add flour and baking powder. Flavor to taste.

Mrs. R. M. Morrow

JEFF DAVIS PIE

Take three eggs, one cup sweet milk, one-half cup melted butter, one and one-half cups sugar, three tablespoonsful flour; bake in crusts or as pudding.

Mrs. Thompson

SWEET PICKLE DAMSON

1 lb. sugar to 1 lb. damsons, 3 qts. vinegar to 4 lbs. fruit, cinnamon bark and cloves to taste. Boil the sugar, vinegar and spices and pour over the fruit for five days; the fifth day put the fruit in and simmer a short while. This keeps well.

Mrs. James Bason

BLACKBERRY CORDIAL

Two quarts blackberry juice, two pounds loaf sugar, four grated nutmegs, one quarter ounce ground cloves, one quarter ounce ground allspice, one quarter ounce ground cinnamon; simmer all together in a saucepan tightly closed to prevent evaporation; strain through a cloth when cold and add a pint of the best French brandy. Nothing more efficasious in the summer complaint of children.

Mrs. R. E. L. Holt

CUCUMBER CATSUP

For this, choose large, ripe cucumbers. Pare, remove the seeds and grate. To every pint of this pulp allow: ½ pint of cider vinegar, ¼ teaspoon cayenne, 1 teaspoon of salt, 2 heaping tablespoons grated horseradish. Drain the cucumber in a colander, then mix with all the other ingredients. Bottle and seal.

Mrs. Carroll

JELLY ISLAND CAKE

1 cup butter, 2 cups sugar, 3 cups flour, 4 eggs, ½ cup milk, 3 teaspoons baking powder; bake in jelly tins. For filling, stir together a grated lemon, a large tart apple grated, 1 egg, 1 cup sugar and boil 4 minutes.

Mrs. Stephen Moore

ROAST 'POSSUM

To roast a 'possum, first catch the 'possum. Dress it and soak in salt water for 12 hrs., then wash and parboil in salt water until tender. Have ready some sliced sweet potatoes which have been boiled, until done, in clear water. Lay 'possum out flat in roasting pan, put slices of potatoes all round it, add pepper and sufficient stock. Bake in quick oven until a nice brown. Serve on platter, using potatoes and parsley for garnishing.

Mrs. W. H. Carroll

GRANDMOTHER'S EGG NOG

1 dozen eggs, good
12 slightly rounded tablespoons sugar
Fifth of bourbon
1 quart whipping cream (4 half pints)
Nutmeg (optional)

Separate eggs, putting yolks into bowl large enough to hold finished egg nog. Add sugar, 1 tablespoon at a time, to yolks beaten until pale yellow. Add to this the bourbon, 1 tablespoon at a time, beating constantly.

Add cream beaten until fairly stiff but still smooth, folding in and stirring gently with spoon. Add stiffly beaten egg whites, folding in. This is a thick nog. Reversing the additions of cream and egg whites is less thick mixture. Cover with napkin and chill on back porch. Be sure beaters are clean and dried for beating the separate ingredients. 3 fairly large bowls are needed.

If egg nog is too strong for your taste or not sweet enough, another ½ pint of sweetened whipped cream can be added. Sugar cannot be added to finished product because it will not dissolve in whiskey readily. Stir before serving as whiskey settles. Nutmeg may be sprinkled on top of each cup.

Yield: Fills small to medium punch bowl.

"MERRY CHRISTMAS!"

Olivia Rhodes Woodin (Mrs. Raye)
Burlington

BREAD SOUP

Start with left-over biscuits (the older the better.)
Cut into cubes.
Melt butter in iron skillet on top of stove.
Add the bread cubes to butter, stirring until toasted on all sides.
Add salt and pepper.
Add milk (enough to cover bread cubes).
Heat—DO NOT BOIL.
Serve hot.

Often fed to family of 10 children during the depression years.

Ben F. Bulla
Saxapahaw

CLAM CHOWDER

1 quart raw clams, after taken from shells
1 gallon water
1 large onion, sliced
3 medium potatoes, sliced
2 cans tomato soup
2 strips breakfast bacon (or small piece salt pork)
Salt and pepper to taste
Butter

Cook clams and pork (which have been run through a meat chopper) with water *very* slowly for two to three hours; add onion and potatoes, sliced thin or cut up fine, and salt and pepper. Cook until potatoes and onions are done. Add tomato soup and enough butter to make a rich chowder. This chowder is delicious if allowed to stand overnight, and reheated before serving. Worcestershire sauce may be added if desired.

Captain Arthur Midgett was the captain and chef of a boat kept in Morehead some years ago by an attorney for the Leggett & Meyers Tobacco Company, and he entertained many fishermen and friends from Alamance County during the fishing seasons. This chowder was always a favorite with any group. This recipe came from the files of Mrs. Russell Gant.

Larry A. Alley
Elon College

SOUTHERN RAILWAY BEAN SOUP

1 pound Navy beans, cleaned
1 ham shank
1 (16-ounce) can tomatoes
3 quarts water
¾ cup chopped onions
1 cup chopped celery
1 bay leaf
Salt and pepper to taste
2 cups diced, uncooked potatoes
½ cup cooked, mashed potatoes

Soak beans overnight. Drain and put in large soup kettle with all ingredients except cooked and uncooked potatoes. Cover and simmer 2 hours. Remove ham and bay leaf. Remove meat from bone and cut into small pieces and return to kettle. Add diced potatoes and cook an additional 1 hour. Blend mashed potatoes, in small amounts, into mixture as this helps thicken the soup.

Yield: 12 to 16 servings

This recipe dates to the 1920's. Burlington, formerly known as Company Shops, was established in 1855, as a maintenance facility by North Carolina Railroad Company, a forerunner of Southern Railway.

McSherry Gray Lackey
Burlington

MAYONNAISED CHICKEN

1 box plain gelatin, dissolved in ½ cup cold water
1 cup hot chicken broth, fat removed
1 pint mayonnaise
1 hen, boiled and diced
1 (20-ounce) can green peas, drained
Lemon juice
2 cups diced celery
4 hard-cooked eggs, chopped
2 tablespoons chow-chow (optional)
1 cup almonds or pecans, chopped
Salt and pepper

Add the dissolved gelatin to the hot chicken stock. Cool and add to the mayonnaise. Stir in the remaining ingredients and mold (pound cake mold will do.) More celery, nuts or pimento can be used in place of the green peas. Season to taste with salt, pepper and lemon juice.

Yield: 12 servings

Mrs. Jordan was the wife of B. Everette Jordan, of Saxapahaw, U.S. Senator, 1958-62. Their daughter, Rose Anne Gant, of Burlington, shares this family favorite.

Katherine McLean Jordan (Mrs. B. Everette)

PEPPER HASH

12 red bell peppers
12 green bell peppers
12 onions, peeled
Boiling water
3 pints vinegar
4 cups sugar
2½ tablespoons salt
3 hot peppers, whole

Seed the peppers. Finely chop peppers and onions together and drain. Put into an enamel vessel. Pour over boiling water to cover and let stand 5 minutes. Drain off and discard liquid. Combine vinegar, salt and sugar in a large kettle and heat thoroughly. Add peppers and onions and boil for 10 minutes. Remove from heat. Pack in sterilized jars and seal immediately.

Put sealed jars in kettle, cover with water an inch above tops. Boil for 10 minutes. Let cool and tighten lids.

Yield: 8 pints

This delicious old recipe dates back to 1864.

Luzette Callum Brown (Mrs. W. W.)
Burlington

OLD SOUTHERN BEATEN BISCUITS

"This is a slightly changed old North Carolina Beaten Biscuit recipe. The amount of ingredients may be doubled to make more biscuits."

2 cups sifted flour
½ teaspoon salt
½ teaspoon sugar
⅓ cup vegetable shortening (lard was used in the older recipe)
⅓ cup sweet milk (not skimmed milk)
⅓ cup water (little more if necessary)

Preheat oven to 350 degrees. Thoroughly mix together sifted flour, salt and sugar (sift together if desired). Thoroughly cut shortening into flour mixture. Add the milk and water to form a stiff dough. Hand knead dough until it can be formed into a firm ball.

Roll out the dough on a firm surface (dough board) and beat the dough until it is smooth and satiny. Shape dough back into a smooth ball, and spread it evenly on a floured dough board. Roll out dough with a rolling pin. Cut out biscuits with a tiny cutter (about 1 inch in diameter). Place biscuits on baking sheet. Imprint each with fork prongs. Bake in 350° oven (on middle rack) and cook for 30 minutes, or until biscuits are brown.

Some like the biscuits eaten while hot. If so, as soon as taken out of oven split them and butter them.

To make them "creamy", an old recipe says to keep them warm in a covered pyrex container.

Yield: The number of biscuits vary, according to the size of the cutter.

Versatile and creative, Marion Brown is one of the South's best-selling cookbook authors. She has done textile designing and worked on newspapers as society editor and special staff writer. She is the author of MARION BROWN'S SOUTHERN COOKBOOK and PICKLES AND PRESERVES, beginning her cookbook career with Soup to Nuts, *printed in 1938 for the Episcopal Church of the Holy Comforter. She is presently working on a new book.*

Marion Lea Brown
Burlington

BAKING POWDER "BISQUITS"

2 cups flour
1 teaspoon salt
3 teaspoons baking powder
2 tablespoons butter
2 tablespoons lard
¾ cup milk

Sift together flour, salt and baking powder. Rub into the flour the butter and lard. Mix to a soft dough with milk. Roll out 1-inch thick and cut into biscuits. Place in a greased pan. Do not let biscuits touch. Brush tops with sweet milk and bake 12 to 15 minutes in hot oven.

Yield: Serves 6 to 8

This recipe came from Larkin's Housewives Cookbook, Copyright 1915

Betty Robertson Murray (Mrs. Homer)
Burlington

OATMEAL MUFFINS

1 cup warmed cooked oatmeal
1½ cups milk
3 cups flour
¼ cup sugar
4 teaspoons baking powder
1 teaspoon salt
1 egg, well beaten
1 tablespoon melted butter

To warm oatmeal add milk. Sift together flour, sugar, baking powder and salt. Add to oatmeal. Then add egg and butter and mix well. Fill greased muffin tins. (Do not use paper baking cups.) Bake in 375 degree oven for 30 minutes.

Yield: 18 muffins

"A family favorite from my grandmother's cookbook, dated 1912."

Mary Helms Harden (Mrs. Junius)
Graham

CORN MEAL MUSH

Cornmeal
Water
Salt

Boil quantity of water desired for the finished serving of mush. Salt water and have it boiling when you begin to slowly stir in cornmeal. The water must be boiling to begin the cooking and continue boiling until the mush is the desired thickness. If not stirred constantly and kept boiling, lumps will form. Cook 10 minutes after you stop adding meal. Serve hot with sweet milk and/or butter.

My mother, Mary Ross Iseley, made cornmeal mush, a staple food of Alamance County families.

Rena Maude I. Danieley
Burlington

COMMUNION BREAD

3 cups flour
1 small teaspoon salt
1 level teaspoon sugar
3 tablespoons shortening
1 cup milk, approximately

Sift together the first three ingredients. Cut into this mixture 3 tablespoons shortening. Gradually add the milk, enough to moisten so it can be kneaded. Knead well, roll thinly and cut into narrow strips. Bake in 300-350 degree oven until light brown. Break in small pieces when cool. Store in air-tight container. Can be frozen if made in advance.

This recipe has been used in the Graham Presbyterian Church for over 50 years. It was handed down to me by my mother, Mrs. Allen D. Tate, Sr., who received it from Mrs. J. Harvey White.

Jean Tate Thompson (Mrs. I. H.)
Burlington

CANDIED, BRANDIED CRANBERRIES

4 cups fresh cranberries
2 cups sugar
3 tablespoons brandy

Preheat oven to 325°. Place 4 cups fresh cranberries in shallow baking dish. Sprinkle 2 cups sugar over berries. Cover tightly with foil. Bake for 1 hour. Cool. Stir in 3 tablespoons brandy or to taste. Spoon into a cutglass bowl and send on its bright and merry way to the table.

Yield: 2 cups

Viola Ringwald Ireland (Mrs. John Rich)
Southern Pines, North Carolina

Mrs. Ireland was a resident of Alamance County for many years and well-known for her beautiful food presentations. This recipe was given to her by her sister, Mary, wife of General George Worley, Infantry, WWII.

PERSIMMON PUDDING

2 cups persimmon pulp
2 cups sugar
1½ cups buttermilk
1 teaspoon baking soda
3 eggs, beaten
⅓ cup evaporated milk
1½ cups flour
1 teaspoon baking powder
1 teaspoon salt
½ teaspoon cinnamon
½ teaspoon vanilla
¼ pound butter

Mix pulp with sugar. Add soda to buttermilk and stir until it stops foaming. Add to pulp with eggs. Add evaporated milk. Sift flour with baking powder, salt and cinnamon and stir in. Add vanilla. Melt butter in 10x14-inch baking dish, turning to coat sides. Add to pudding and stir. Pour into baking dish. Preheat oven to 300 degrees and bake 1 hour. Cool in dish. Serve in squares. Top with cream if desired.

Yield: 12 servings

This was my mother, Mrs. C. A. Whittemore's, Sr. recipe and it won first prize at the annual National Persimmon Festival in Indiana.

Elizabeth Ray Whittemore
Graham

AUNT NANNIE'S SWEET POTATO PUDDING

2 cups finely grated raw sweet potatoes
⅛ teaspoon salt
2 eggs, beaten
1½-2 tablespoons brandy
½ cup sugar, rounded

Mix all ingredients. Put into buttered 1-quart baking dish in 350° oven for 40 to 45 minutes. If desired, melted butter or margarine can be added to top after cooking.

Yield: 4 to 6 servings

This is an old Alamance County recipe. It is very simple fare. The grated potato has a shredded texture though done.

Olivia Rhodes Woodin (Mrs. Raye)
Burlington

FARMER'S FRUIT CAKE

3 cups dried apples
2 cups molasses
½ cup butter
1 cup sugar
2 eggs, beaten
2 cups flour
1 tablespoon baking soda
½ teaspoon salt
¼ teaspoon nutmeg
½ teaspoon cinnamon

Wash the dried apples and cut in small pieces. Soak (in just enough water to cover) overnight. Next morning put the molasses in a saucepan on the stove and bring to a boil. Add chopped apples with liquid; let simmer two hours; cook and add to cake made as follows:

Cream butter and sugar; add the beaten eggs and beat thoroughly. Sift dry ingredients and add alternately with the cooled apples and molasses mixture. Bake in a well greased pan at 350°. Serve warm with hard sauce.

"Enjoyed by our family for over 50 years."

Dorothy Simmons Jordan
Graham

ROCKY MOUNT CAKE

8 egg whites
2 cups sugar
1 teaspoon cream of tartar
1 cup butter
3 cups flour
¾ cup milk
½ teaspoon soda dissolved in milk

Bake cake batter in 3 layers.

Filling:
2 cups sugar
½ cup water
3 egg whites
Citron, currants, dates, raisins
Coconut, almonds

Boil 2 cups sugar, ½ cup water until it makes a jelly. Pour over 3 egg whites well beaten. Beat until nearly cold. Stir in 5¢ worth each of citron, currants, dates; 10¢ worth of raisins, 1 grated coconut. Mix well a small quantity of the citron, coconut, raisins with 10¢ worth of almonds and put on the outside of cake.

Family recipe in the early 1900's.

Frances Whitted White (Mrs. Bob)
Burlington

BROWN SUGAR POUND CAKE

1 pound brown sugar
1 cup white sugar
1½ cups shortening—part butter
3 cups plain flour
1 cup milk
1 teaspoon baking powder
½ teaspoon salt
1 teaspoon vanilla
1 cup chopped nuts
5 eggs

Cream butter and brown sugar. Add white sugar and cream again. Add eggs. Sift dry ingredients together and add with milk, vanilla and nuts. Bake for 1 hour at 350° in a 10-inch bundt pan.

This recipe was given to Eda Holt by W. H. May, Jr., member of a family prominent in the textile industry, whose late father, W. H. May, Sr., was an Alamance County native and leader in hosiery and knit goods manufacturing. Eda writes, "This unique recipe from the May family is truly an old gem."

W. H. May, Jr., now resides in Chapel Hill, North Carolina.

WORLD WAR II CAKE

1 cup water
1 cup brown sugar
1/3 cup vegetable shortening
2 cups raisins
1/4 teaspoon nutmeg
1 teaspoon cinnamon
1/2 teaspoon cloves
1 teaspoon baking soda
1 tablespoon water
2 cups flour
1/2 teaspoon baking powder

Mix water, sugar, vegetable shortening, raisins and spices together in a pan and cook 5 minutes. Cool completely. Add soda mixed with 1 tablespoon water. Sift flour with baking powder and add to cooled mixture. Beat 2 minutes. Pour into greased 9x9-inch square pan. Bake at 275 degrees for about 1 hour.

Yield: 9 servings

Jean Turner Anderson (Mrs. Ralph)
Graham

PEACH FRITTERS

"Pare peaches, cut into halves, and remove the stones. Beat two eggs without separating them. Add one cupful of milk and one and a half cupfuls of flour. Beat until smooth. Add a tablespoonful of melted butter or olive oil, a teaspoonful of baking powder. Dip the peaches into this batter and fry in smoking hot fat. Serve with foamy sauce or powdered sugar dusted over."

"From my grandmother's copy of Household News—Mrs. Rorer's Magazine, *September, 1894."*

Anne Patterson Miller (Mrs. Jesse)
Burlington

SNITCHY PIE

Stew dried apples soft in as little water as possible. Sweeten to taste and add a dash of salt. Cool. Roll out pastry to size of saucer, spoon apples over one-half of pastry. Fold other half over and crimp together with tines of fork. Heat grease in skillet and brown pies on both sides. Serve hot or cold.

Watch out for pie snitchers!

Ben F. Bulla
Saxapahaw

CHESS PIE

2 sticks butter, softened
2 cups sugar
6 egg yolks
1 tablespoon vanilla extract
2 unbaked pie crusts

Cream butter and sugar until fluffy. Add egg yolks which have been beaten until lemon colored. Blend mixture well. Add vanilla and blend again. Spread mixture in crusts and bake at 325° for 30-40 minutes or until brown.

Yield: 12 servings

NOTE: This mixture is rather stiff, but is very light and tender when baked. Litsey's son, Luther, submitted this recipe, as it continues to be a Ross family favorite. It was handed down by his great-great-grandmother, who was Pennsylvania Dutch.

Litsey Isley Ross (Mrs. Otis Holt, Sr.)

EGG CUSTARD PIE

4 eggs, well beaten
1½ cups sugar
2 tablespoons flour
Butter, size of walnut (about 2 tablespoons, melted)
1½ cups milk
1 tablespoon vanilla
9-inch unbaked pie shell

Beat eggs. Add sugar blended with flour. Add butter, milk and vanilla. Pour into crust and bake 350 degrees for 30 minutes or until custard is set and crust brown.

Yield: 6 servings

As a young boy, I was always served egg custard pie on my visits to Milton and Maggie Isley, who owned the land near Friendship School that once belonged to my great, great grandfather, Christian Isley. About forty-five years ago Maggie gave me the recipe at my request.

Lloyd Lafayette Bramble
Washington, District of Columbia

MY GRANDMOTHER'S OLD FASHIONED BUTTER COOKIES

½ pound fresh butter
1¼ cup white sugar
1 fresh chicken egg, well beaten
3½ cups regular flour
¼ bottle of cream (now days we use canned milk, 1 small can)

Preheat oven to 350 or 375 degrees. Cream butter and sugar until pale and creamy. (This was done by hand with a wooden spoon and still is the best way, but you can use a mixer.) Add the egg and mix well. Add ⅓ of the flour and 1 tablespoon of cream and mix well. Continue to add the ingredients in ⅓'s and mix well. You will probably add 4 to 6 tablespoons of cream. When all ingredients have been added and mixed well, place in a cookie press using the ribbon disc. Press mixture on cookie sheets and cut into 2 to 3 inch cookies. Watch for doneness.

Yield: Serves 10 to 20

Mrs. Brown is the great granddaughter of Edwin Michael Holt.

Margaret Holt Brown
Burlington

TEA CAKES

4 eggs
¼ cup buttermilk
½ pound butter, creamed
1 tablespoon lemon extract
2 cups sugar
Flour

Beat eggs with buttermilk and add butter, extract and sugar and stir until well blended. Then add enough plain flour to make consistency for spooning onto cookie sheet. Bake at 350° about 5 minutes or until edges begin to brown.

My mother, Mary Ross Iseley, prepared these cookies for her children's school lunch pails. They continue to be a family favorite, and are better 24 hours after baking as they become chewy!

Rena Maude I. Danieley
Burlington

REFLECTIONS IN PLAID

Selections from the MEN ONLY section of the 1938 Soup to Nuts, a cookbook of recipes compiled by the Women's Auxiliary, Church of the Holy Comforter:

GOULASH

"Staley A. Cook, 'Cooker-upper' of the Burlington Daily Times-News, declared that there is 'nothing to' a fresh vegetable stew or goulash which he concocts during the vegetable season. The secret of the flavor, he says, is due to the fact that he keeps his guests waiting so long while the stew simmers that by the time the clarion call is sounded they are in the rawhide-chewing stage. Mr. Cook boils the method down to this:

> The 'ghouloush' concoction develops as one goes along from diced okra, stripped tomatoes, corn, beans, onions, or any other vegetable fresh from the garden; a little salt and pepper, a pinch of butter and any lean meat left over in the icebox such as beef, veal, chicken, etc. Boil all of this down to simmer—simmer—simmer, tasting as you go, then sound the gong!"

SPICED SHRIMP

"W. L. Shoffner, who is as much at home in the kitchen as he is in his law offices, mixes everything (and how!) from a frappe to a spicy shrimp with sauce.

Add 1 box of pickling spices to a saucepan half filled with water. Bring to a boil. Add 2 pounds of raw shrimp. Cook until shrimp are done. Put entire ingredients into icebox and allow to stand 1 day. Remove, peel shrimp and serve with this sauce, or as desired."

SHRIMP COCKTAIL SAUCE

"Place 1 teaspoon of dry horseradish into a cup and cover with cold water. Allow to stand 10 minutes. Add dash of TABASCO pepper sauce and the juice of ½ lemon. Fill out with tomato catsup and stir well."

HOT WAFFLES

"On a Sunday evening when the kitchen is swept clean of the usual staff, Walter M. Brown, likes to whip up a batch of batter, take irons into the living room and before a log fire, brown waffles to a golden turn, heap them with sweet butter and pour on the syrup. He makes them with buttermilk!"

1 cup buttermilk
½ teaspoon soda
½ teaspoon sugar
¼ cup vegetable oil
1 cup flour
½ teaspoon salt
1½ teaspoons baking powder

Beat the above until the batter is smooth. Pour into waffle irons and cook 2 to 4 minutes.

HINTS FROM *CHOICE RECIPES*

FURNITURE POLISH

4 tablespoonsful of turpentine, 4 tablespoonsful of sweet oil, 1 teaspoonful of lemon juice, 10 drops of ammonia. Mix thoroughly and apply with a soft cloth, then rub well with another cloth. Half the virture is in the rubbing.

A GOOD CLEANING SOAP

2 quarts boiling water, with 15¢ worth of Ivory soap dissolved in it. Let stand in a cool place for 20 minutes, then add Sulphurice Ether ½ oz., alcohol 3 oz., ammonia No. 26F, 1½ oz.

To prevent kid gloves from spotting place gum ammonia in the bottom of a box. Put paper over this and shut gloves up in box. This is said to restore gloves that are already spotted from dampness.

Salt sprinkled thickly on a fresh ink spot on carpet will remove stain.

WASHING FLUID

Boil together 5¢ worth of potash and 5¢ worth of borax in half gallon of water. Cool, then add 4 tablespoonsful of benzine and 2 tablespoonsful of kerosine. When cool it is ready for use.

Miss Bessie Holt

RACHEL ALLEN'S 1790 REMEDIES

The following remedies were recorded, c. 1790, in a small handmade notebook kept by Rachel Allen, a pioneer settler of Alamance County. The grammar and spelling appear as originally written:

To make Green Salve take one pound of bores
greese one poind of turpentine and melt it
together then take it of the fire take one ounce
of Verdigreese and pound it and sift it then
put it in and Simmer over the fire but not
to boil to be Sure put Something over thy
face while pounding sifting and stiring and
Stiring in the Verdigreese to make out proud
flesh and dead flesh from old Soars & Clense them

For the consumtion take white turpentine
hunney and fresh Butter mix all
together take the Bigness of a Chestnut
In the Morning

For deafness & busing in ye head peel a
Clove of garlick dip it in honey & peel
it in ye Eare at Lying down
ye Eare Ach from worms drop in warm
Milk Brings them out or Juse of
Wormwood Which kills them
Nurse in the Eare Drop in Juse
of Onions

To clean the teeth Rub them With
ye ashes of Burnt Bread

INDEX

D

E

F

Alamance County Historical Museum, Inc.
Route 1, Box 71
Burlington, N.C. 27215

Please send ______ copy(ies) of TASTES IN PLAID @ $16.95 each ______
Postage and handling in Continental U.S. @ 3.05 each ______
N.C. residents add 5% sales tax @ .85 each ______

Total amount enclosed in U.S. dollars . . . . ______

Checks should be made to: ALAMANCE COUNTY HISTORICAL MUSEUM

Orders of six (6) copies to the same address . . . . $90.00 ______
Postage and handling for 6 copies . . . . 5.00 ______
Sales Tax for 6 copies (N.C. residents only) . . . . 4.50 ______

Total amount enclosed in U.S. dollars . . . . ______

Send to:____

Street Address____

City__________________________State______________Zip____________

Alamance County Historical Museum, Inc.
Route 1, Box 71
Burlington, N.C. 27215

Please send ______ copy(ies) of TASTES IN PLAID @ $16.95 each ______
Postage and handling in Continental U.S. @ 3.05 each ______
N.C. residents add 5% sales tax @ .85 each ______

Total amount enclosed in U.S. dollars . . . . ______

Checks should be made to: ALAMANCE COUNTY HISTORICAL MUSEUM

Orders of six (6) copies to the same address . . . . $90.00 ______
Postage and handling for 6 copies . . . . 5.00 ______
Sales Tax for 6 copies (N.C. residents only) . . . . 4.50 ______

Total amount enclosed in U.S. dollars . . . . ______

Send to:____

Street Address____

City__________________________State______________Zip____________